AN UNDERGROUND FATE

AN UNDERGROUND FATE

The Idiom
of Romance in the
Later Novels
of Graham Greene

BRIAN THOMAS

The University of Georgia Press
Athens and London

© 1988 by the University of Georgia Press
Athens, Georgia 30602

Designed by Sandra Strother Hudson
Set in Linotron 10 on 13 Sabon
The paper in this book meets the guidelines
for permanence and durability of the Committee on
Production Guidelines for Book Longevity of
the Council on Library Resources.

Printed in the United States of America
92 91 90 89 88   5 4 3 2 1

Library of Congress Cataloging in Publication Data

Thomas, Brian, 1939–
An underground fate: the idiom of romance in the later
novels of Graham Greene / Brian Thomas.
p. cm.
Bibliography: p.
Includes index.
ISBN 0-8203-0984-2 (alk. paper)
1. Greene, Graham, 1904–   —Criticism and
interpretation. 2. Romanticism—England. 3. Regeneration
in literature. I. Title.
PR6013.R44Z89 1988
823'.912—dc19   87-12538
                                                      CIP

British Library Cataloging in Publication Data available

To my daughter, Jean

Contents

Acknowledgments

I wish to thank everyone who has aided and supported me in writing this book. A particular sense of gratitude must be expressed to Ms. Karen Orchard for all her patient encouragement; to Professors John Baird, Caesar Blake, John Reibetanz, Roger Sharrock, and David Dooley for their comments on the manuscript and helpful suggestions; and, above all, to Professor Michael Millgate, without whose invaluable advice and assistance it would perhaps never have been written.

Introduction

This book argues that romance constitutes the dominant genre in Graham Greene's later fiction. More precisely, its thesis is that the novels published between 1950 and 1973 constitute a new and distinct phase in the development of Greene's conception of narrative, and that the structural basis of this phase is romance. Such a thesis involves a perception of the novelist himself, a way of regarding him, that seems, to say the least of it, unfamiliar: we are accustomed to think of Greene not as a romancer but as the chronicler of failure and despair, of a modern reality so peculiarly bleak, mean, and squalid as to suggest the very antithesis of romance. This is the Greene usually associated with the central modernist tradition of irony in the first half of our century— although, as the religious context of his vision becomes increasingly clear, his irony is increasingly revealed as being of the kind that modulates to tragedy. But our picture of both the ironist and the tragedian derives primarily from the fiction of the 1930s and 1940s, from texts like *England Made Me* (1935), *Brighton Rock* (1938), *The Power and the Glory* (1940), and *The Heart of the Matter* (1948), and even the most cursory glance at the novels of the fifties and sixties discloses the limitations of this view of Greene. His range of themes seems suddenly to have widened; the characteristic narrative voice has become, if not always more playful, certainly less darkly obsessive; and he has apparently discovered and adapted to his own purposes a radically different type of fictional structure.

To claim that Greene has turned during the latter part of his career from tragedy to romance seems, of course, rather more extravagant than to make the same kind of case about, say,

Shakespeare. But such a dramatic interpretation of this shift in direction starts to look less drastic and more intelligible when we consider that romance has always played a larger part in Greene's work than his critics have noticed. The fact is that his career began, as his first three published novels attest, in just this genre. From one viewpoint, indeed, the trouble with *The Man Within* (1929), *The Name of Action* (1930), and *Rumour at Nightfall* (1931) is that they are, in the broadest sense, altogether *too* "romantic." Greene himself has long been embarrassed by the youthful, dreamy prolixity of these earliest novels, their implausibility and otherworldly remoteness, and he has even gone so far as to try to suppress two of them. Brooding historical fantasies rather than realized fictions, interesting chiefly because they demonstrate so vividly the extent of the influence of Joseph Conrad, they are also romances, however, in exactly the sense in which that term is used in this book. In each, the central character undergoes the paradigmatic process of "descent" and "ascent" outlined by Northrop Frye in *The Secular Scripture:* a sinking into a strange, phantasmagoric world that has the effect of casting the protagonist's very identity into doubt, so that he suffers a form of ritual death, followed by an emergence from it that becomes a form of symbolic rebirth.

Although Greene soon came to better terms with the conventions of narrative realism, he did not entirely abandon the narrative paradigm of romance. To be accurate, one might say first of all that he abandoned half of it. For the next twenty years or so, the movement of descent or fall became the governing rhythm in his fiction. While the railway journey in *Stamboul Train* (1932), for example, seems designed to convey the linear, sequential character of real experience, it is also, figuratively, a downward "progress" into a dreadful limbo: the conspicuous sense of stasis or suspension implicit in the journey becomes a metaphor that not only tends to subvert the idea that Dr. Czinner and Coral Musker are actually getting anywhere, but in fact adumbrates something of the quality of the private hell that appears to be the real destination awaiting each of them. Greene's accommodation with realism, in other words, leads him to the mode of irony. Characters

like Conrad Drover in *It's a Battlefield* (1934) and Pinkie Brown
in *Brighton Rock,* either staggering unwillingly into the lower
depths of a world figured as a Dante-esque inferno or plunging
freely into a moral abyss, find themselves caught up in some process of continuous "fall." Greene explores the implications of the
theme of descent in a variety of more-or-less realistic contexts—
most typically, perhaps, in the framework of the thriller convention of pursuit—but the metaphorical direction in which his protagonists must travel is always downward. The image of "the
basement room" becomes a definitive emblem for Greene's fiction in the 1930s, a domestic icon of ironic downfall.

In the perspective of irony, of course, the inevitable climax of
any rhythm of descent is not the symbolic or ritual extinction of
personal identity but actual death. There are some ambiguous
exceptions to this rule, such as the highly equivocal survival of
the hero in *The Confidential Agent* (1939) and *The Ministry of
Fear* (1943), but, generally speaking, Greene's central characters
end up dead. The genre toward which this type of story always
points is tragedy, and Greene's two great tragic novels, *The Power
and the Glory* and *The Heart of the Matter,* seem to emerge quite
naturally from what might be called the logic of the ironic, rather
than the romantic, view of the motif of fall. Because the theme of
fall has by this time acquired an explicitly theological significance
in Greene's work, the whisky priest and Henry Scobie are tragic
heroes in a distinctly Christian sense. It is not just that the process of fall has to do with the idea of original sin, but that it now
becomes associated with the idea of the Incarnation—the story of
God's descent into the world of human mortality, culminating in
Christ's Passion. The whisky priest and Scobie are "Christ figures" precisely because both are tragic victims or scapegoats;
each functions as a *pharmakos* whose ultimate fate derives its
meaning or intelligibility from the central Christian myth of the
Crucifixion. Their respective lives and deaths become "imita-
tions" of another life and death in a larger, implicit, contextual
narrative.

But this meaning depends as well on the fact that the central
Christian myth is constructed according to an ambiguous princi-

ple of closure: the life of Christ ends, in one sense, with his death, but his death "ends," in another, with his resurrection. The perspective of tragedy offers us a version of the contextual narrative in which the resonance of sacrificial death is dominant and primary. At the same time, though, at least in Graham Greene's tragic novels, the motif of rebirth has a muted but audible secondary resonance of its own, and it points, of course, in the direction of the other half of the romance paradigm—the theme of ascent. We can see in retrospect that it is this secondary resonance which in fact accounts for all those seemingly anomalous elements of romance that have kept turning up even in the most darkly ironic of Greene's previous fictions. In *The Ministry of Fear,* for instance, the whole romantic apparatus of amnesia and the doubling of the protagonist into twinned versions of himself becomes intelligible only in light of the motif of apparent recovery and reintegration near the end of the novel. In *A Gun for Sale* (1936), the curious business of Anne Crowder's entombment in a chimney (with its playfully grotesque evocation of Poe's "Murders in the Rue Morgue") and her subsequent revival makes sense only in terms of an implicit context, however faintly echoed it may be in the novel itself, that has to do with the theme of emergence and of the beginning of a new life.

It is at this stage—after the publication of *The Heart of the Matter*—that Greene returns, in a sense, to the genre in which his career as a novelist was rather shakily launched. With *The Third Man* (1950) and *The End of the Affair* (1951), so the argument of the present study goes, he discovers (or rediscovers, within the conventions of fictional realism) the central structural principle of romance: that upward narrative turn from suspension and death to reanimation and rebirth, the supersession of the motif of falling by its rhythmic counterpart, the motif of rising. This development of the romance pattern in Greene's later fiction is here traced by means of a close analysis of technique and structure in seven novels and one collection of short stories, concluding with a consideration of *The Honorary Consul* (1973).

The fiction published by Greene since 1973 presents a somewhat confused picture, but *The Human Factor* (1978), *Doctor*

Introduction

Fischer of Geneva (1980), *Monsignor Quixote* (1982), and *The Tenth Man* (1985) share a single important feature: each of these works represents a reversion to the earlier mode of irony. In the case of *The Tenth Man,* of course, Greene cannot exactly be said to have "reverted" to that mode, since the story is apparently a reworking of an abandoned and forgotten idea for a film script dating from 1944. *The Tenth Man* is interesting from the point of view of this study chiefly because of the way in which its central plot device—an exchange of legal identities contrived between the protagonist and another character—seems to anticipate the theme of *The Third Man;* but although such an exchange may in itself be viewed as a romance motif, the story as a whole is actually ironic, tracing as it does the course of the hero's decline from a position of social eminence and security to his violent death as an imposter and outcast. *The Human Factor* was also begun by Greene many years before its publication, abandoned, and at last completed in 1977 only because he had by then no other work in view. Although various romance motifs are to be found in this novel, too—most strikingly, the hero's private myth about a dragon that inhabits the world of his childhood—*The Human Factor* has much the same kind of structure as Greene's fiction written in the 1930s and 1940s: a story again primarily about descent or fall, it sustains the possibility of the protagonist's deliverance and emergence until the final pages, only to reveal his hopes at that stage as absurdly illusory. *Doctor Fischer of Geneva* and *Monsignor Quixote,* on the other hand, are not so much novels as allegories: while there are certain conspicuous elements of romance in both (one is a grisly modern "fairy tale," the other a reworking of Cervantes' parody of medieval chivalric romance) these elements are now in the service of the genre of the ironic moral fable. In fact, since each of these four latest fictions is so constructed as to parody the romance patterns that it invokes, it seems fair to say that all the novels published after *The Honorary Consul* must be regarded as fundamentally ironic in form.

Obviously, the theoretical basis of my argument owes a great deal to Northrop Frye and *The Secular Scripture.* Less obviously, perhaps, it also owes something to Patricia A. Parker's *Inescap-*

able Romance, which is itself indebted, historically, to the ideas of the Russian Formalists. There are of course many other views of romance, some of them either implicitly or explicitly at odds with those of Frye or Parker. But the chief object of this book is the exploration of Graham Greene's later fiction rather than of the labyrinthine ways of recent critical theory. As such, it is primarily an exercise in practical criticism, and the real justification for invoking Frye's theory is, quite simply, its utility: his conception of the genre is useful in that it offers a richly promising context, a way of approaching Greene's later novels that seems illuminating and therefore appropriate. For all practical purposes, in fact, this context derives not so much from the strictly theoretical aspect of Frye's conception as from its descriptive basis; not so much from the idea that romance is a "secular scripture" as from the identification of the type of narrative structure on which that idea depends. If we acknowledge that the theme of burial in *The Waste Land* and the consequent blurring of the protagonist's identity in that poem belong to the romance pattern worked out by T. S. Eliot from his reading of Frazer and Jessie L. Weston, then there seems no reason not to recognize, without necessarily subscribing to the entire thesis of *The Secular Scripture,* that the "underground" river in *The Heart of the Matter, The Third Man,* and *A Burnt-Out Case* is a recurrent romance motif probably derived by Greene from his reading of Rider Haggard.

T. S. Eliot and H. Rider Haggard—the incongruous conjunction of names is deliberate, for the real issue here relates to the whole problem of literary sources and technical strategies in twentieth-century writing. Does a novelist like Greene assimilate the materials of romance in the same way as a poet like Eliot? Is there a definable modernist character that distinguishes Greene's accommodations of romance and realism from those of, say, Fielding and Smollett, or even Jane Austen? These are large questions and this is not the place to attempt definitive answers. But perhaps some preliminary clarifications are possible, at least with respect to Greene's own writing.

One difficulty—or at any rate, a potential cause of confusion—lies in the fact that Greene is an author both characteristic and uncharacteristic of his age. He has been considerably influenced, like many other twentieth-century novelists, by the poetry of T. S. Eliot, primarily by *The Waste Land* but also, to a lesser extent, by the structure of the imagery in *Four Quartets*. And this influence would seem to be what links him to the modernist tradition in fiction, to such writers as Joyce and Faulkner, who also happened to be interested in the patterns of romance. At the same time, while he experimented with certain modernist techniques, notably in *It's a Battlefield* and *England Made Me,* Greene has never been a sophisticated innovator of the stamp of Eliot or Joyce or Virginia Woolf. He has always worked a more popular vein, and in this respect it might be argued that the single most important modern influence on Greene's work has been the cinema. If the popular film is the dominant romantic cultural medium in our century, then Greene's appropriation of the idiom of romance is peculiarly cinematic.

His strictly literary sources, however—those which are most genuine and run deepest in his fiction—are to be found, I would suggest, not in the modernist period or even in the modern one, but in certain writers of the later nineteenth century. There has always been an odd blend of the Victorian and the Edwardian about Greene's sense of what a novel ought to be. And this is not due at all to any sort of obtuse conservatism or atavistic yearning for simpler narrative forms. On the contrary, it is a reflection of the sheer intensity of his own response to the books of his childhood and youth. It was from writers like Henty, Haggard, Stevenson, Westerman, Weyman, Wallace, and Marjorie Bowen that Greene first absorbed the formulas of romance, and from them, too, that he learned how to make those formulas seem plausible in the context of the relatively realistic conventions of the adventure story. Greene's lifelong fascination with the form of the thriller and the spy novel can clearly be traced back to his avid early reading of late Victorian and Edwardian popular adventure fiction. A problem for Greene as an aspiring modern novelist, of course, was that the writers who specialized in this kind of fiction had the disadvantage of being not quite respectable as "serious" sources. In this regard, though, there is one towering exception:

the figure who is perhaps the most important romantic novelist in the English language, Joseph Conrad.

Again and again in reading Graham Greene, we are brought back to Conrad, the writer who seems almost as much a living presence in Greene's fiction as a mere influence upon it. Greene begins as a novelist by sedulously imitating Conrad's style and tone. Where he fails in his earliest novels is in not taking sufficient account of Conrad's famous dictum about attempting "to render the highest kind of justice to the visible universe": the universe that Greene tries to map out in his first three novels seems not merely not visible but altogether impalpable. But when he does finally manage to convey the starkly tangible reality of the territory now known as "Greeneland," what he has learned from Conrad about adventurous quests into exotic but also dark and dangerous places becomes an organizing principle which determines the fictive shape of events in that territory. *Heart of Darkness* is perhaps the exemplary fiction for Greene: the story of Marlow's journey of figurative descent into Kurtz's night world, and of his horrified recognition that Kurtz's "darkness" is also his own, echoes and reechoes with both an ironic and a tragic resonance throughout most of Greene's work from *Stamboul Train* to *The Heart of the Matter*. And (even more important as far as the argument of this book is concerned) the story of Marlow's emergence from the night world, which reveals him both scathed and altered by what has happened there, finds another kind of resonance in all Greene's subsequent novels. By the time we reach *A Burnt-Out Case* (1961), we find that *Heart of Darkness* has actually taken on a normative role in the novel's structure, functioning not just as an explicit literary allusion but as one of the sources of narrative meaning—a classic instance of what nowadays tends to be called intertextuality.

This study ultimately argues that allusiveness of that kind becomes in itself an important structural principle in Greene's later fiction, "intertextuality" being a characteristic feature of romance. The later novels are haunted by a whole host of authors from Greene's eclectic personal pantheon: "popular" writers such as Rider Haggard and Marjorie Bowen are invoked in the same contexts as Sir Walter Scott and Tennyson. For the point here is not so much that Greene's literary sources are always romantic as that his reading of them, the way in which he assimilates them to his own fiction, reveals a conception of narrative structure that belongs fundamentally to the tradition of romance. Though his later novels are as allusive in their way as Eliot's *Waste Land,* his affinity with the romance tradition is not deliberately *sought,* as it seems to be for the earlier modernists, but virtually unconsidered, something humbler and more private—a sense of kinship taken at first for granted, which only gradually evolves toward the kind of imaginative self-awareness of which the habit of allusiveness may be a genuine function.

Because of its particular critical emphasis, this book may seem to underestimate Greene's achievement prior to 1950. But no such judgment of comparative value is in fact intended: *The Power and the Glory* and *The Heart of the Matter* remain central texts in the Greene canon, and indeed in the history of modern fiction; my intention is to indicate that they differ in *kind* from *A Burnt-Out Case* and *The Honorary Consul,* certainly not that they are any less important. But given the nature of the argument, perhaps some degree of distortion is inevitable. There has long been a kind of received wisdom about Graham Greene, an "image" based on a popular view of him that had already become a fixed public idea before 1950, and by which even the shrewdest of his critics have tended to be guided. This is at least partly because novels like *The Power and the Glory* and *The Heart of the Matter* presented a formulaic, almost a stereotyped, narrative pattern into which Greene's imagination appeared to be locked. One of the objects of this study is to show how that picture of Greene is itself a distortion, a caricature rather than an accurate portrait. Even in 1950, the truth was that he had never been quite so imprisoned within the method of his earlier fiction as some critics are still inclined to believe. But his way of escape became fully available only with the clear recognition and exploitation of romance as a structural principle.

ONE

The Third Man
and The End of the Affair

It was odd how like the Lime he knew was to the
Lime I knew: it was only that he looked at Lime's
image from a different angle or in a different
light. —*The Third Man*

Hatred seems to operate the same glands as love:
it even produces the same actions. If we had not
been taught how to interpret the story of the
Passion, would we have been able to say from
their actions alone whether it was the jealous
Judas or the cowardly Peter who loved Christ?
—*The End of the Affair*

There is a kind of ill-defined consensus among critics of Graham
Greene that his later novels (roughly speaking, those published
since about 1955) are in some fundamental way different from
his earlier fiction. Although this view has not so far amounted to
much more than a widely held intuition—a tacit assumption of
many commentators to the effect that the conception of narrative
which underlies a novel like, say, *The Comedians* (1966) differs
quite radically from that which underlies *The Power and the
Glory* (1940)—it sometimes finds expression in various rather
imprecise ideas regarding Greene's later work. These are familiar
enough: the sorts of generalization about the latter part of his
career in which it is held that his interest in religion has waned, or
that politics have become the principal theme, or, more simply
and even more vaguely, that he has grown less gloomy and increasingly benevolent over the years. But while there would appear to be some element of truth in all these notions, none stands
up very well, in fact, to close examination.

While Greene's religious vision, for example, certainly seems less intense after the mid-1950s, it is also undeniably true that the obsessions which inform *A Burnt-Out Case* (1961) and *The Honorary Consul* (1973) are not essentially different from those pervading *Brighton Rock* (1938) and *The Heart of the Matter* (1948). In the later novels, his religious concerns tend to be more muted and problematic, but they are still very much there—not much further than ever, arguably, from whatever the heart of the matter in Greene might be. Similarly, although politics become a more explicit and specific preoccupation in the later work than in the earlier, *The Quiet American* (1955) is no more profoundly "political" a novel than *It's a Battlefield* (1934). Again, the developing inclination in Greene's fiction after about 1950 toward certain types of comedy does not seem to mean that the more somber Greene of the 1930s and 1940s has been in any sense supplanted by a humorist. However, none of these particular qualifications is intended to dispel the general impression that Greene has moved in a new direction in his later work. On the contrary, he does indeed seem to have done so, and the impression needs to be accounted for.

Perhaps one way of beginning to account for it is to take notice of a single, concrete fact that pertains more obviously to what we usually think of as technique than to larger questions of theme. In 1950, for the first time in his career, Greene published a novel written in the first person. It could be argued, of course, that *The Third Man* is not so much a novel as a "treatment" for a film, but nevertheless it represents his first novel-length departure from third-person narration. In any case, *The End of the Affair,* published in the following year, is also written in the first person, and this narrative technique is one to which Greene returns again and again in subsequent years. Of itself, the innovation of a new type of narrative voice is not particularly remarkable. Greene himself explains it simply as an attempt to modify a "pattern" in his work: by the time *The Heart of the Matter* had appeared in 1948, he was beginning to share the view held by some of his critics that a certain repetitiveness had crept into his novels.[1] In the context of what this view is actually based on, though, the ramifications of his discovery of the possibilities implicit in first-person narration are considerable. For in Greene's case, the emergence of a new type of narrative voice tends almost inevitably to mean the emergence of a new type of protagonist.

Whatever else he may be, any first-person narrator is, virtually by definition, a survivor. At the very least, he is someone who has survived the telling of his own story. In Greene's earlier novels, the protagonist usually dies, and his death is often tragic; when he does survive, his survival becomes so equivocal as to be deeply ironic. The pattern to which Greene himself refers has to do, at least in part, with the persistence in his fiction of the theme of pursuit, the recurrence of the kind of story in which a central character is hunted down by a pursuer who seeks his death. To the extent that Greene's first-person narrator is the protagonist of his own story, then, he is unlikely, in the framework of this pattern, to be the figure of the victim. He is more likely, in fact, to be the figure of the hunter or the betrayer. Of course, the first-person narrator need not necessarily be the protagonist: he might only be a witness to the events of the story, as Colonel Calloway seems to be in *The Third Man*. At least at the outset of that novel, it is in the role of onlooker that Colonel Calloway chooses to see himself. But he is nevertheless a "hunter" as well, a policeman legitimately obsessed with the pursuit of Harry Lime; and the protagonist of the novel acts in many ways as his agent if not as his surrogate.

It seems clear, at any rate, that a story about pursuit told from the point of view of the pursuer or betrayer will inevitably involve a new thematic emphasis for Greene, a shift in narrative focus that reveals a hitherto familiar arrangement of events in a different light. More tangibly, such a shift in focus inevitably involves a different type of fictional structure too. In novels like *The Power and the Glory* and *The Heart of the Matter,* the basic narrative rhythm is one of continuous descent: the stories of the whisky priest and Henry Scobie are tragedies, and in each case the hero undergoes a process of "fall" which ends only with his death. Beginning in 1950 with *The Third Man*, though, tragedy gradually recedes as the dominant narrative mode in Greene's work.

For *The Third Man* is not just about the death of Harry Lime but also about the rebirth of Rollo Martins: the significance of the survivor's survival, in other words, has to do with the fact that he experiences a recovery from a kind of ritual extinction of his own identity. *The Third Man* does have certain obvious tragic dimensions, but its real structural affinities are with a different genre altogether.

The motif of death and rebirth figures conspicuously as an integral aspect of the plot: Harry Lime stages his own funeral in order to elude the net that has been so carefully drawn around him by Colonel Calloway. The novel's protagonist, however, is not Lime but Martins, and it is Rollo who undertakes the more significant figurative journey into a world of death. Near the beginning of the novel, he goes into a Viennese cemetery in the middle of winter and soon discovers that he has become lost; at the story's conclusion, he walks out of the same cemetery during a springlike thaw. Most of the action in *The Third Man* takes place, that is to say, in a milieu which is perceived symbolically as an underground world. Rollo's entry into and emergence out of this underworld are both linked to the figure of Lime: he is looking, at the outset, for Lime's "funeral," which turns out to have been an illusory or fictive event; and it is only the actual burial of Harry Lime that becomes the occasion of Rollo's ultimate revival, his departure from the graveyard. Lime is his friend, but more important, his personal hero or idol—in the special sense that Rollo has almost literally (and comically) "identified" himself with the man. It quickly becomes clear that Rollo's underground journey in the novel has to do with the fact that his idea of his own identity has always been bound up with his conception of the identity of Harry Lime.

The perspective from which the story is told derives, therefore, from the problem of finding Lime, not just because Rollo follows him, so to speak, or because Harry turns out to be the real "third man," but because the narrator himself sees him as a perplexing enigma. Lime's identity, though, is nothing if not elusive. Even before Rollo's arrival in Vienna, Colonel Calloway has been struck by the aura of legend that has gathered around his quarry.

During their first meeting, Martins boasts, "I don't suppose any-one knows Harry the way I do," and the narrator responds by reflecting on "the thick file of agents' reports in my office, each claiming the same thing."[2] If Harry is Rollo's private mythic hero, he tends to be perceived in similarly quasi-fabulous terms by nearly everyone else in the novel as well. Even Colonel Cal-loway remarks: "It was odd how like the Lime he knew was to the Lime I knew: it was only that he looked at Lime's image from a different angle or in a different light" (22). The question of identity seems inseparable from that of perspective. And the real problem for Rollo in this connection is that his idealization of and romantic identification with Lime have had the effect of ar-resting his personal development: his own boyish identity seems tenuous, and when he first learns of Harry's "death" he finds himself lost almost at once in a shadowy, protean world where nobody is ever quite what he seems. More than anything else, the ethos of *The Third Man* features disguise and duplicity. At every level, the theme of confusion about personal identity be-comes remarkably pervasive. The narrator repeatedly points to the differences between the protagonist's Rollo-self and his Mar-tins-self, both of whom differ from his professional persona, Buck Dexter; and the further confusion between that figure and the celebrated novelist "Benjamin Dexter" forms the basis of the comic subplot. Martins's habit of referring to the narrator as "Callaghan" belongs to the same nexus of ontological uncer-tainty.

This kind of persistent ambiguity—the tendency for roles al-ways to become blurred—is closely related to the peculiar am-bience of postwar Vienna as it is evoked by Greene in the novel. The city is at once a ruined, twilight landscape, a rather frighten-ing and potentially violent place, and yet at the same time a world forever buried peacefully in snow and silence. Images of slumber and forgetfulness are constantly linked with the imagery of ruin, danger, and fear. The world which, in its symbolic aspect, lies underneath the cemetery seems simultaneously realistic and grotesque, and in its grotesquerie simultaneously sinister and risible. In other words, the phantasmagoric quality of Harry

Lime's milieu, as Rollo Martins experiences it, seems to stem from the link between sleep and nightmare: the world of death in the novel is perceived as an environment characterized by a curious fluidity of individual identity because it would appear also to be a world of dreams.

When Rollo Martins drives, at the outset, into "the heart of a forest where the graves lay like wolves under the trees, winking white eyes under the gloom of the evergreens" (17), it is as if he were entering not so much a cemetery as the setting of some northern fairy tale;[3] at the same time, he is beginning a descent into the kind of hallucinatory night world that has always had a certain imaginative primacy in Greene's fiction. From the story of betrayal and pursuit in *The Man Within* (1929), which begins with the sudden plunge of its protagonist into a dark wood containing a fairy-tale cottage, to the story of betrayal and self-immolation in *The Heart of the Matter* (1948), in which a delirious hero is ferried across a dark river into a region that becomes a personal, symbolic underworld, the quintessential narrative terrain for Greene has always been an unmapped, lower region of darkness. This is perhaps clearest in the novels which have as their specific thematic preoccupation the subjects of damnation and salvation: the netherworld is vividly realized in the dark realms inhabited by Pinkie in *Brighton Rock* and the whisky priest in *The Power and the Glory*. But a version of it can be seen as well in the landscapes of amnesiac or hallucinatory perception in *The Ministry of Fear* (1943) and *The Confidential Agent* (1939). This night world appears too in all those earlier novels whose themes are usually regarded as social or political "problems": in *Stamboul Train* (1932) it becomes the peculiar stasis or limbo of the train journey itself; in *It's a Battlefield* (1934) it is imaged in the brutalizing mechanical routines within which all the characters are locked and isolated—figuratively, as if by imprisonment or dense fog; in *England Made Me* (1935) it becomes the compulsive flow of memory and desire just below the level of the characters' consciousness; in *A Gun for Sale* (1936) it is the "Nottwich" where Raven pursues Cholmondely/Davis and Sir

Marcus, a place where anonymous figures in gas masks hunt down everyone who does not look exactly like themselves.

The definitive emblem of this underground world in *The Third Man* is of course the extensive sewer system beneath the city, the "underground river" (134)—explicitly associated by Colonel Calloway with the subterranean voyage to Milosis in Rider Haggard's *Allan Quatermain*—where Harry Lime is finally trapped and killed. But in another sense, Rollo Martins's quest for Harry Lime takes place in a kind of Hadean territory that is perceived more specifically as the underworld of dreams. The importance of dreams has frequently been noted in Greene's work;[4] what has generally been overlooked is the distorting-mirror relationship between the accounts of his characters' dreams and the narrative actuality which forms their context. Rollo Martins has the following dream, for instance, not long after beginning his search for the elusive and illusory "third man":

> He had left Vienna far behind him and was walking through a dense wood, ankle-deep in snow. An owl hooted, and he felt suddenly lonely and scared. He had an appointment to meet Harry under a particular tree, but in a wood so dense how could he recognize any one tree from the rest? Then he saw a figure and ran towards it: it whistled a familiar tune and his heart lifted with relief and joy at not after all being alone. The figure turned and it was not Harry at all—just a stranger who grinned at him in a little circle of wet slushy melted snow, while the owl hooted again and again. (33)

Thematically, this short narrative clearly reflects Martins's situation at the relevant stage in the plot: he feels lost and mocked while the "third man" continues to elude him. But the dream also reflects his own sense of strangeness; it is a dream about a displacement or discontinuity of identity, and as such, it is related structurally to the world in which Rollo finds himself when he is awake. The snow and the dense wood echo the earlier descriptions of the forest where Martins searched for Harry's funeral, and the whistling, grinning stranger, if he is not exactly Harry Lime, anticipates the imaginary featureless man who appears increasingly to haunt Rollo's quest: "After nine o'clock the streets are very empty, and he would turn his head at every padding step coming up the street behind him, as though that third man whom they had protected so ruthlessly were following him like an executioner" (75–76). For Martins, we are told, this "third man had no face: only the top of a head seen from a window" (76). While this is literally true, it is even more significantly true in the figurative sense that the real meaning of Rollo's quest has to do not so much with finding a "third man" or even with Harry Lime as with his terror at meeting a kind of facelessness in himself.

His dream about the grinning stranger in the wintry forest can be characterized, that is to say, as a dream of ontological anxiety. The central question in the novel pertains not to the identity of the "third man" but to the identity of Harry Lime, so that it ultimately becomes a question about the identity of Rollo Martins. At the outset, Lime exists for the narrator as a man who is almost absolutely evil, which means in practice that his fictional reality tends to be largely symbolic. But for Rollo, Harry Lime is an even more intensely symbolic figure: he represents not just someone on whom Martins would stake his life; at a more profound level, Lime is the man on whom he *has* staked his life. As Rollo moves deeper into the underground world of the novel, it becomes increasingly clear that his whole conception of the value of his own existence has always been invested in this "heroic" figure whom he is now obliged to regard as corrupt. So the waking world in which he moves seems more and more to evince the dimension of horror implicit in his dream. He becomes less the hunter and more a hunted stranger himself. The events in which he is involved acquire an increasingly surrealistic character: in one grotesque episode, he is all but identified as the murderer of Herr Koch by a precocious dwarf of a child who bears the conspicuously fabulous name of Hansel. No little boy lost, however, this undersized but exuberant ghoul with his visions of "blood on the coke" (73) takes on a kind of legendary infernal status; running from the scene, Rollo becomes the "foreigner" (73) who flees "the scrutinising cold-blooded gnome-gaze of little Hansel" (74). And later, when—mistaken now for the "real" B. Dexter— he tries to attend to a barrage of literary questions at a meeting organized by the local British Council, what he actually thinks he hears is "the child saying, 'I saw blood on the coke,' and somebody turned towards him a blank face without features, a grey plasticine egg, the third man" (82–83).

Rollo's dream has an extraordinary reverberativeness, then, in the novel's world of actuality. The grotesque aspect of that world is, of course, comic as well as melodramatically sinister—Martins is implicitly perceived as an amiable romantic buffoon who has set out single-handedly to vindicate Harry Lime, perhaps even to avenge Lime's alleged death—and this blend of the frightening and the farcical becomes particularly marked in the episode in which Rollo finds himself trapped in a dark room with a whispering presence that turns out to be a parrot. The revelation of the parrot as the source of the "curious moaning sound" (85) is amusing, but at the same time, as the archetypal echo bird, it may be viewed here as a mocking emblem of narcissistic self-reflection.[5] To the extent that the stranger in the dream who whistles Harry Lime's signature tune is an image of Rollo's own "facelessness," the parrot becomes another version of that image in the novel's world of ordinary consciousness. (The very noises that it makes are to be echoed again by the dying figure of Harry Lime himself.) The distorting-looking-glass reality of the dream suggests a tendency toward a dissolution of individual identity; in the world which it mirrors, we see that it is specifically the identity of Rollo Martins which seems to be in danger of annihilation. Again, even the "little circle of wet slushy melted snow" echoes all the imagery of circularity in the account of the cemetery, and the dream image anticipates "the great black circle of the Prater Wheel, stationary above the ruined houses" (65–66), which becomes the scene of the climactic meeting between Martins and Lime. The fact that the topography of Vienna consists of a concentric series of geometric circles has a relevant iconographic significance here: it might be that the stranger in the dream grins at Rollo from within the center of an illusory magic circle of projected "enchantment," a sort of private and fictive *Innere Stadt,* that constitutes Lime's only genuine identity.

The dominant narrative rhythm throughout most of *The Third*

Man is the one that always characterized the typical structure of Greene's fiction before 1950: a movement of descent. Rollo Martins's search for the mysterious stranger takes place in an environment that amounts, figuratively, to what we have been regarding as a subterranean "world of dream and death." This phrase has been borrowed, because of its peculiar aptness in the present context, from an essay on Dickens by Northrop Frye.[6] In the fiction of Dickens, Frye argues, it is in just such a world that everything which we are inclined to see as Dickensian melodrama originates. He suggests that the mainspring of all the melodramatic action and rhetoric in Dickens is an energy which comes from this "hidden and private"[7] world and which is, as he demonstrates, fundamentally erotic. As the terms of the phrase would in any case tend to indicate, the underworld of dream and death is at once the realm of Eros and Thanatos: a state of existence in which subjective human identity has a way of losing its customary integrity and of merging with the external objects of its perception. It can be argued that Frye's account of this world is as applicable to Greene's fiction as to Dickens's, the most strikingly obvious difference being that the arena of dream and death not only is not "hidden" in Greene but in fact constitutes the essential reality, a world always verging on the realm of the hallucinatory, about which he writes. In the perspective of tragedy, it is primarily a demonic place, as, for example, the fate of the whisky priest in *The Power and the Glory* would clearly suggest. And in *The Third Man* itself, Rollo Martins's disorientation, his sense of somehow having lost himself, pertains just as clearly to a process of "fall" that is at least potentially tragic. Throughout much of the novel, Thanatos rather than Eros seems to be the spirit presiding over the action. But just as the energies of dream and death usually turn out to be redemptive in Dickens, so the rhythm of descent in *The Third Man* reverses itself, so to speak, and becomes a movement of emergence and revival.

Rollo's meeting with Harry Lime on the great revolving Prater Wheel constitutes a crucial movement of discovery: he recognizes Lime for the first time as the "evil" child (123) that he actually is. And as the wheel pauses in its ascent, the possibility of murder also hovers briefly in the air between them: it is as if this perilous brush with death suddenly frees Rollo from his own childish illusions, so that Lime all at once ceases to be a kind of idealized doppelgänger and becomes a narcissistic self-projection that must be repudiated, a personal ghost who must be exorcised. This recognition is the beginning of Rollo's discovery of a real identity of his own, a process that culminates with the real death of Harry Lime. In betraying and killing his friend, Rollo Martins ceases to be a buffoon and becomes a type of Judas; in doing so, however, he gives features to his own "blank face" and exorcises the embodied terror of his dream. But something more is involved here than betrayal and murder. Rollo's love for Anna Schmidt becomes a significant force behind the movement of recovery in the novel. He is impelled, paradoxically, out of his private underworld precisely because the dynamic of that world is creative as well as destructive, for the energy of Rollo's impetuousness and his capacity for love become the basis of his personal rebirth. The chthonic, chiaroscuro region of shifting allegiances and identities which forms the funereal setting of *The Third Man* is also a potential source of new life. The forces of Eros triumph over those of murderousness, and at the end of the novel, as they walk out of the cemetery together, it is as though Anna Schmidt and Rollo Martins have finally emerged from a death process in which both had long been embroiled.

What Northrop Frye characterizes as Dickens's "hidden and private world of dream and death" is closely related, of course, to the more public one that he describes in *The Secular Scripture* as the archetypal "lower world"[8] of romance. In the context of the framework of archetypal reference adduced in Frye's study of the genre, *The Third Man* exhibits all the salient features of romance as a narrative mode: if the novel's theme is the protagonist's loss and recovery of identity, then its structure is based on the narrative rhythms of descent and ascent—a "downward" movement into a world which dramatizes a kind of disintegration of self, followed by an emergence from it which renders intelligible a form of reintegration or rebirth.[9] This type of structure depends, before anything else, on the simple fact of the hero's survival, a narrative shift (in the context of Greene's "pattern") which involves a transformation of the protagonist from the figure of the hunted man to that of the hunter. In this novel, narrator and protagonist are different characters, but the importance of the innovation of the first-person technique depends on the affinity which grows between them: the narrative perspective belongs or at least is available to the survivor rather than to the victim. Greene's adoption of the first-person point of view, then, becomes a process of experimentation with a technical device that offers him "an escape from the pattern" amounting to something considerably more than "a method I had not tried."[10] In effect, it offers him the possibility of a generically different narrative form.

This is not, however, to suggest that Greene proceeded at this stage in his career simply to abandon the narrative forms which had long been congenial to him: his next novel is deeply pervaded by a vision at once tragic and bitterly ironic. *The End of the Affair* (1951) seems, in fact, to have been conceived by Greene in terms more tragic than romantic: it is as if the novelist only reluctantly accepted the logic inherent in a first-person structure which impelled his story to a conclusion (and a principle of closure) other than the one that had perhaps seemed most natural to him: "Sarah, the chief character, was dead, the book should have continued at least as long after her death as before, and yet, like her lover, Bendrix, I found I had no great appetite to continue now she was gone beyond recall and only a philosophic theme was left behind. I began to hurry to the end."[11] What appears questionable, though, in this account of the composition of Book Five is Greene's assumption that Sarah Miles is the novel's "chief character." It is an assumption, of course, that her lover, the novel's narrator, shares. For Maurice Bendrix's capacity for hate is certainly large enough to include not only himself as one of its objects, but even the sound of his own narrating voice: "There it goes again—the I, I, I, as though this were my story, and not the story of Sarah, Henry and, of course, that third, whom I hated without yet knowing him, or even believing in him."[12] But the fact is that *The End of the Affair* remains as much Bendrix's story as Sarah's or anyone else's. Its narrator is also its protagonist. Like Rollo Martins, Bendrix undergoes a process of symbolic or ritual death in which, like Rollo, he discovers that he is "lost in a strange region" (56); and he "come[s] alive" (229) at the story's conclusion despite his own protests about what he sees, analogically, as "the obstinacy" of his own "non-existence" (229) as a character in it. If Sarah Miles is the heroine of the novel in its tragic aspect, Maurice Bendrix becomes, however unwillingly, the hero of the novel viewed, more comprehensively, as a romance.

Bendrix's repeated insistence that his narrative "is a record of hate far more than of love" (1) has much to do with an implicit conception of himself as a kind of isolated and embattled ego, a recording consciousness whose subjectivity can virtually be defined as an acutely agonizing, defensive watchfulness. "Identity" in this context becomes an egocentricity that is validated only by suffering: its integrity depends on a Cartesian awareness of the objective world as an otherness normally perceived as inimical. "The sense of unhappiness," Bendrix notes, "is so much easier to convey than that of happiness": "In misery we seem aware of our own existence, even though it may be in the form of a monstrous egotism: this pain of mine is individual, this nerve that winces belongs to me and to no other. But happiness annihilates us: we lose our identity" (52). It is precisely this conception of personal identity as a kind of jealous selfhood imprisoned by its own isolation that accounts for what is perhaps the most conspicuous structure of imagery in the foreground of Bendrix's narrative— the division of the novel's action into a metaphorical dialectic of interior and exterior worlds. In *The End of the Affair* the imagery of houses, rooms, doors, and windows takes on a prominence that goes beyond the idea of domestic shelter or security in any narrowly literal sense. The world of the domestic interior, and particularly that of the individual room, becomes both an emblematic haven and an emblematic cage or prison cell: in effect, the room tends to be perceived as a figurative ark in a storm, for the exterior world is usually hostile, characterized primarily by bad weather. In the novel's opening scene, Bendrix presents his meeting with Henry Miles on the common as the fortuitous encounter of two storm-tossed ships "slanting across" a "wide river of rain" (1). From the outset, the narrator perceives himself as unaccountably and painfully adrift in an alien marine environment which constantly threatens to engulf him. Once Sarah Miles has absented herself from his life, having fallen in love, as he believes, with some other man, he must live continually with a figurative condition of deluge. So the imagery of bad weather looms significantly in Bendrix's narrative, and all the trivial human objects that are customarily linked with it, like umbrellas and hats, tend to acquire a certain metaphorical weight, becoming emblems of the subjective selfhood's defensiveness. In general, our sense of Bendrix's narrative perspective is of someone watching suspiciously from the window of a room from which he is reluctant to emerge.

His conception of his own identity is also, of course, profoundly narcissistic. Although his narcissism takes the form of self-detestation rather than of self-love, Bendrix's fundamental psychic relation has always been with himself: he is a man who has always suffered from a certain lameness in the spiritual as well as in the physical sense. The novel's definitive image is the mirror. The figure of the looking glass becomes, in fact, the central symbolic device around which the whole structure of the narrative is organized. Virtually our first glimpse of Sarah, for instance, is of her reflection in a mirror, in which she is "separating as though from a kiss" (26) from one of Henry's colleagues. Later, the narrator says of his own relationship with her: "I could feel no trust: in the act of love I could be arrogant, but alone I had only to look in the mirror to see doubt, in the shape of a lined face and a lame leg—why me?" (53). When Sarah has left him, he thinks "with hatred" that "she always has to show up well in her own mirror: she mixes religion with desertion to make it sound noble to herself" (86). Bendrix happens to be wrong about this, but his view of the human talent for self-deception as something based on self-absorption is echoed and generalized in a different context by Richard Smythe, the proselytizing atheist: "Man made God in his own image, so it's natural he should love him. You know those distorting mirrors at fairs. Man's made a beautifying mirror too in which he sees himself lovely and powerful and just and wise. It's his idea of himself. He recognizes himself easier than in the distorting mirror which only makes him laugh, but how he loves himself in the other" (127). The mirror seems to function in the novel, that is to say, as a purely ironic emblem, an image in the light of which all human aspiration is reduced to the terms of a self-involvement which characterizes the outlook not only of the story's narrator but of everyone else in it as well.

However, the figure of the looking glass can also signify something slightly different from what we ordinarily think of as narcissism. In one of his calmer moments, Maurice Bendrix offers the following observation:

> When I began to write I said this was a story of hatred, but I am not convinced. Perhaps my hatred is really as deficient as my love. I looked up just now from writing and caught sight of my own face in a mirror close to my desk, and I thought, does hatred really look like that? For I was reminded of that face we have all of us seen in childhood, looking back at us from the shop window, the features blurred with our breath, as we stare with such longing at the bright unobtainable objects within. (64)

Whatever else he does in the novel, Bendrix is always "looking" or "watching." As narrator, he functions primarily as a kind of spy, not just peering out from the window of his own room but also trying to keep a "vigil" on the "ruined weather-house" in which Sarah still lives with Henry but from which "neither the man nor the woman came out" (17). In this connection, the characters of Parkis and his son act as Bendrix's agents, and Parkis in effect becomes the narrator's comic double, his own distorted image. But what his glance into this mirror near his desk suggests is that the figure of the looking glass might in a sense be metaphorically identical with that of the window. In *The Third Man*, we saw that the world of dreams is essentially a distorted mirror world. So, in effect, is the world inhabited by Bendrix in this novel—the "strange region" of his narrative, the territory for which he has "no map" (56).

In other words, although Bendrix habitually sees himself as someone on the inside looking out, we are also given an odd glimpse of him in which he appears in a rather different light: as someone who is habitually on the outside looking in. And in this perspective, the world that he actually inhabits becomes a reflection or distorted image of an entirely different type of place: the world, in fact, of fulfilled desire, where happiness, as he says, "annihilates" us. Hatred, in Bendix's narrative, is increasingly revealed as the reversed mirror image of love. The point of view from which the story is told turns out to be the angle of vision which might be imagined to obtain on the "other" side, so to speak, of a looking glass: "Hatred seems to operate the same glands as love: it even produces the same actions. If we had not been taught how to interpret the story of the Passion, would we have been able to say from their actions alone whether it was the jealous Judas or the cowardly Peter who loved Christ?" (26–27). The recording "I" of the novel describes a world of dream and death that exists as a distortion or parody of a real world in which identity, as Maurice Bendrix understands it, is *always* annihilated. Richard Smythe, for example, functions in his fanatical atheism as a kind of mock-evangelist whose fervor seems to mirror the very energy that it mocks. For the invisible world reflected and parodied by the novel's love story would seem to be that of the Christian narrative whose central theme is God's readiness to suffer for his love of humanity. So the violence of the explosion which literally does leave Bendrix "annihilated," apparently lying dead beneath the front door of his own house, becomes a manifestation of human hatred that parodies the violence of a divine as opposed to a human longing. The protagonist of this novel undergoes an extinction of identity far more dramatic than that experienced by Rollo Martins. When he regains consciousness, he feels nothing except "a sense of tiredness" as though he "had been on a long journey" (82), but his journey is, in fact, far from over.

The affair between Bendrix and Sarah, with its "little death[s]" (52) as well as all its attendant miseries, mirrors this instant of symbolic extinction. And Bendrix's story is itself a parody— what might be described as a looking-glass account—of yet another narrative. The discontinuity of chronological sequence with

which Greene for the first time experiments here[13] has as one of
its technical functions the effect of locating Sarah's diary within
the novel in such a way that the structure of Bendrix's narrative
can be seen to echo or reflect the structure of Sarah's.

If her diary has a single theme, it would seem to be that of
descent; but by the end of her "story" it is as if this downward
journey of Sarah's had started, at least proleptically, to reverse
itself. As it is presented in the novel as a whole, Sarah's narrative
begins and ends with a dream about what appears to be the imminence of her actual death, a nightmare in which she sinks
slowly into an underwater world. In the sequence of Bendrix's
reading of the diary, the dream becomes both the first and the last
entry. Between this identical beginning and ending, she records
the ongoing process of another kind of personal extinction, one
which is obviously figurative but no less obviously a process of
sinking into a mental state that becomes increasingly recognizable as the condition of death-in-life. She speaks repeatedly, for
example, of finding herself alone in a "desert" (107), and then,
during her inspection with Henry of "the new reinforced shelter
at Bigwell-on-Sea" (117), of finding herself in a world perceived
quite explicitly as subterranean: "Deep shelter problems. The
problem of pretending to be alive. Henry and I sleeping side by
side night after night like figures on tombs" (117). In metaphorical terms, Sarah has actually entered what she specifically
refers to as the "buried" (115) world from which Bendrix is conscious only of having emerged. "It is horrible feeling dead," she
writes. "One wants to feel alive again in any way" (113); and
later she warns the God in whom she does not yet quite believe:
"If I don't come alive again, I'm going to be a slut, just a slut"
(117). Finally, she visits Richard Smythe in the hope that he will
be able to convince her that her original pact with God was in
fact meaningless; but as she tries to follow his "arguments," she
discovers herself "only getting from them a sense of inverted belief" (137): she comes to recognize the presence of God, as it were
in a mirror, in the very vehemence with which Smythe denies his
existence.

Alone in a landscape that is now a desert, now an underworld,

Sarah's love for Bendrix modulates gradually but inexorably to a genuine love of Christ. And this new context gives a new significance to the reiteration of her dream:

> I was walking up a long staircase to meet Maurice at the top. I was still happy because when I reached the top of the staircase we were going to make love. I called to him that I was coming; but it wasn't Maurice's voice that answered; it was a stranger's that boomed like a foghorn warning lost ships, and scared me. I thought, he's let his flat and gone away and I don't know where he is, and going down the stairs again the water rose beyond my waist and the hall was thick with mist. Then I woke up. I'm not at peace any more. . . . I want Maurice. I want ordinary corrupt human love. Dear God, you know I want to want Your pain, but I don't want it now. Take it away for a while and give it me another time. (148–49)

The first fragmentary context in which this passage appears suggests that the dream primarily reflects despair over Sarah's sacrificial renunciation of Bendrix. The ultimate context, however, is her initially reluctant but finally wholehearted conversion to Christianity; here the emphasis falls on the imminence of her actual or literal death as a kind of impending martyrdom. The identity of the "stranger" is by now inescapably clear: in its second recounting, the ultimate fictive form of Sarah Miles's "dying" suggests that an act of erotic self-immolation is about to be translated into the terms of redemptive Christian sacrifice.

As the novel's protagonist, Maurice Bendrix undertakes a figurative journey that corresponds to Sarah's in the sense that the structure of his account of it echoes the structure of the diary account. For Bendrix, however, the emotions which finally inform his own reluctant acceptance of God are not, of course, love and the desire for peace but their distorted looking-glass counterparts, hatred and jealousy. In the novel's opening scene, Maurice was himself envisaged as something of a "lost ship," but after Sarah's death he enters a world, mirroring the "desert" of her narrative, where he feels himself to be even more profoundly abandoned: "It was as though by dying she had robbed me of part of myself. I was losing my individuality. It was the first stage of my own death, the memories dropping off like gangrened limbs" (167). His sense of isolation now ceases to mean an acute awareness of the integrity of his own identity; it becomes, in fact, the awareness of an antithetical process, a form of personal dismemberment that seems almost physical. Bendrix now begins to undergo a new kind of "annihilation." What this seems essentially to involve is his entry into a realm of desolate vacancy, a buried world of forgetfulness:

> The wet of the snow where the passage of many people had melted it, worked through my soles and reminded me of the dew of my dream, but when I tried to remember her voice saying, "Don't worry," I found I had no memory for sounds. I couldn't imitate her voice. I couldn't even caricature it: when I tried to remember it, it was anonymous—just any woman's voice. The process of forgetting her had set in. We should keep gramophone records as we keep photographs. (175)

The details of the dream referred to here have a good deal to do with the way in which the course of Sarah's dying is imaged by Bendrix's sense of self-dispersal, the growing dissolution of his own identity. But *his* dream is not so much about sinking as about rising—a vision, in effect, of personal transformation and even of a form of resurrection. On the evening following Sarah's death, when Henry invites him to take some object by which he might remember her, Bendrix chooses as his keepsake an oddly shaped "pebble" (168). After falling asleep that night, he dreams that he is walking up Oxford Street, anxiously inspecting shops "full of cheap jewellery" (169) and growing increasingly "worried because I had to buy a present" (169). From time to time, he thinks that he has glimpsed "something beautiful and I would approach the glass, but when I saw the jewel close it would be as factitious as all the others" (169). He becomes panicky—"time was short" (169)—and then abruptly Sarah appears. He begs her to help him: "I've got to find something, for to-morrow's the birthday." Sarah's response has a dramatic impact both on Bendrix and on the dream's physical setting: " 'Don't worry,' she said. 'Something always turns up. Don't worry,' and suddenly I didn't worry. Oxford Street extended its boundaries into a great grey misty field, my feet were bare, and I was walking in the dew, alone, and stumbling in a shallow rut I woke, still hearing, 'Don't worry,' like a whisper lodged in the ear, a summer sound belonging to child-hood" (170). The dream's epiphanic conclusion clearly signifies some form of rebirth. The dreamer is translated from a world of "factitious" stones to an environment that seems paradisal, an analogue of some pastoral vision of freedom associated with the innocence of childhood. In this connection, the first part of the dream actually recalls Bendrix's earlier image of the child's face pressed longingly against a shop window. The agent of the trans-formation here is Sarah, but Sarah herself does not appear to be the intended recipient of the birthday present. In fact, the imagery both of the dream and of its narrative context suggests that the Edenic vision might be Sarah's final gift to Bendrix, that what is being adumbrated is not so much Sarah's own resurrection as the rebirth of the dreamer. Bendrix's unconscious fantasy seems to be about the loss of one kind of identity and the recovery of another: the transfiguration of the hard pebble of his own ego into a genu-ine rather than a factitious "jewel." If his narrative can be said to mirror her diary even at the level of their recounted dreams, then Bendrix's dream vision becomes an explicit prophecy of the kind of ascension or emergence from death that is only implicit in Sarah's.

In spite of the return, when he awakens, of Bendrix's sense that he inhabits an empty world, one from which his very memories seem to be vanishing, the theme of ascent is now persistent and pervasive. Paradoxically, Sarah's absence is somehow informed by her presence: "Even vacancy," Bendrix remarks bitterly, "was crowded with her" (197). Henry later tells him that "the house never seems empty" (208) as it sometimes did while she was alive: "I don't know how to express it. Because she's always away, she's never away. You see, she's never anywhere else" (208). So Bendrix leaves his own room and goes to live with Henry—a move, in the context of the imagery having to do with houses and rooms, that becomes a significant journey in its own right. When Richard Smythe calls to pay his respects (and, incidentally, to acquire a lock of Sarah's hair), Bendrix is struck again by the paradox that Sarah is somehow still alive even in her death; even in "vacancy" he is always palpably reminded of her real presence: "[Smythe] was staring round the room: in Cedar Road, coming out of nowhere, she had been as dimensionless, I suppose, as a dream. But this room gave her thickness: it was Sarah too. The snow mounted slowly on the sill like mould from a spade. The room was being buried like Sarah" (171). But if Sarah is always present she is nevertheless palpably absent too. This image of the "buried" room seems to point in two directions at once: it is as if Bendrix had joined her in death and, at the same time, as if Sarah had risen from the coffin, leaving him alone there. The situation verges on a kind of comedy. Indeed, Bendrix suddenly gives way to the urge to laugh: "I wished to shatter the deadness of this buried room with laughter. I sat down on the sofa and began to shake with it. I thought of Sarah dead upstairs and Henry asleep with a silly smile on his face, and the lover with the strawberry mark discussing the funeral with the lover who had employed Mr. Parkis to sprinkle his door-bell with powder. The tears ran down my cheeks as I laughed" (174). In the looking-glass perspective, melodrama tends to become farce. More important for Bendrix, though, the comedy inherent in the situation frees him, at least momentarily, from the obsessiveness of his hatred and jealousy: his laughter represents a kind of mental revolt, a brief, comic recovery of detachment which foreshadows his own eventual emergence from this buried world. And Bendrix's emergence is to be dramatized, as we shall see, in terms that are almost entirely comic.

It should be noted in the meantime that the protagonist has emerged from his own isolation, if from nothing else. He has unwillingly begun, for example, to form a real if limited relationship with Richard Smythe. In a simile presumably intended to echo the violence of an earlier explosive event, Bendrix says of his new affinity with Smythe that "pain was like an inexplicable explosion throwing us together" (174). The source of this affinity, of course, is their mutual love of Sarah. And Sarah's presence now seems to hover over Bendrix's life like that of some attendant spirit, or, to put the matter in religious terms, like that of a patron saint. Quite apart from his growing friendship with Henry,

Bendrix finds himself involved in a whole series of developments that can only be described as miraculous. The most striking of these are the healing of Parkis's son and of Smythe's facial disfigurement. Despite his insistence that these occurrences are natural "coincidences" (232), Bendrix is uncomfortably aware, toward the end of his story, that he has become the chief witness to a kind of ritual pageant of transformation and renewal, a miracle play, in effect, into the plot of which virtually everyone in his own narrative has been appropriated as a character. Again, it is Sarah who seems to be, if not exactly the author, then certainly the presiding genius of this drama. The novel's final phase presents the vision of a general flowering of new life, and in this context, Sarah's "buried room" can be seen as a kind of figurative seed: the force from which her own "resurrection" derives becomes the source of a more extensive process of rebirth.

Not only is Bendrix a witness to this pageant of recovery and revival, he turns out to be one of its principal actors. Unintentionally and even, it appears, unknowingly, the narrator of *The End of the Affair* undergoes a fairly dramatic transformation himself. What Bendrix has thus far regarded as a process of "forgetting" begins to look more like a willed obtuseness, and a spectacular pattern of narrative ambiguity now unfolds: there is a conspicuous disjunction in the last chapters of the novel between what its narrator says and what he actually does, between his proclamations of hate and a sequence of actions which belies his words. For the structure of the story that he tells tends finally to modify if not quite to subvert the sense of hopeless misery that he had intended to convey. Bendrix's new friendship with Henry Miles, based initially on their shared suffering, quickly develops into a relationship based on a genuine tenderness of feeling. This development is specifically comic. In his dealings with Henry, the protagonist who was at first presented as a solitary narcissist unwittingly reveals himself in a role that seems to be, quite simply, wifely: Bendrix is forever fussing and worrying over Henry like the most conventional of anxious spouses in some domestic comedy, untying his shoes for him when he comes home from work and leaving biscuits by his bed while he sleeps. The narrator has entered into a chaste, almost spiritual, union; he has, in effect, taken over one of the roles in Sarah's former life, and his devotion is at once touching and amusing: "I had been one of his worries. He said, 'I don't know what I'd do without you, Bendrix.' I brushed a few grains of scurf off his shoulder. 'Oh well, Henry . . .'" (232). The element of comedy in this springs, of course, from the narrator's own failure to recognize that he has changed almost beyond recognition. Bendrix does not (or does not want to) believe in miracles; but the picture of the novelist/protagonist who has never been anything other than "difficult" now trying to cope with Henry Miles's dandruff problem hints at just how far his journey has, in fact, taken him.

If this is not quite the transfiguration suggested by his dream, it is no less real for that. He tells us that he and Henry "had tried to build a makeshift house together" (235) and he is deeply afraid that their new life will be "broken up" (235). He fears yet another inexplicable explosion. At the same time, though, he has already "come alive" (229)—to invoke his own analogy—as a character in his own story: his phrase echoes one of the key phrases in Sarah's diary, for Bendrix comes alive precisely in the sense that he revives from a condition of figurative extinction. However, it should also be noted that a perceptible undertone of hysteria in-filtrates all the novel's later excursions into comedy, a note of manic desperation that could conceivably be seen as reflecting Greene's own ambivalence about the kind of story that he finds himself writing as he "hurries" to its end. Not unexpectedly, perhaps, the narrator's tone in the last pages veers abruptly toward sadness and pathos, even while the underlying comedy of his new relationship with Henry is still sustained.

For Bendrix continues to live, as it were, in a looking-glass world: the focus of his hatred has shifted to the God in whom he has been forced to believe, who "gave me back," as he bitterly puts it, "this hopeless crippled life" (236). His final "prayer" has a devastatingly bleak quality; the voice which utters it is weary and defeated, that of a man whose survival has been paid for at a very high price indeed: "O God, You've done enough, You've robbed me of enough, I'm too tired and old to learn to love, leave me alone for ever" (237). It is almost as if Greene has been made uneasy by the direction that his novel seems to be taking, as though he has wrenched it, finally, into a realignment with the kind of ironic conclusion that has so often been a characteristic feature of his habitual pattern. But if *The End of the Affair* seems poised uneasily between the modes of tragedy and comedy, in its structure it is clearly a romance: not the type of romance in which the questing hero emerges triumphant from the arduous difficulties of his journey, but the type in which a genuine life that has ultimately been recovered is vividly marked by the scars of deep wounds. Like *Great Expectations,* a text which Greene himself invokes in relation to *The End of the Affair,*[14] it is a somber romance, the survival of its hero qualified by his suffering. Bendrix's bitterness and the fact that he has always been slightly crippled in a physical sense do not diminish the force of what is perhaps the central narrative archetype of his story: the biblical account of Jacob wrestling with the angel, an engagement with a divine energy which inevitably results, for the human antagonist, in lameness as well as in wisdom.

TWO

The Quiet American

One always spoke of her . . . in the third person
as though she were not there. Sometimes she
seemed invisible like peace.

Mr. Chou cleared his throat, but it was only for
an immense expectoration into a tin spittoon
decorated with pink blooms. The baby rolled up
and down among the tea-dregs and the cat leapt
from a cardboard box on to a suitcase.

This was not how the object itself would look:
this was the image in a mirror, reversed.

Greene's novel about the French war in Indochina, published in
England in 1955, in the United States in 1956, had the effect of
appearing to confirm a growing impression that its author's
imaginative attention had begun to shift from a private and idiosyncratic Catholic vision of reality to a more widely familiar public and secular one. The subject of *The Quiet American* is Western colonialism. Writing about the death throes of a traditional
European colonial system and the emergence of a new and sinister American variant, Greene seemed virtually to have abandoned the religious frame of reference which had for so long
formed the essential ideological and mythopoeic context of his
fiction. The narrator of *The Quiet American* suffers from a kind
of despair and a kind of death wish, but he professes atheism;
there is nothing in Thomas Fowler's story that could be regarded
as miraculous, no question of any of the characters being driven
in the direction either of damnation or of sainthood. Yet the reception of this book was marked by at least as much uneasy con-
troversy as had been aroused by any of Greene's "religious" nov-

els; this time, however, the terms of the debate were political rather than theological.

Especially in the United States, *The Quiet American* tended to be viewed as a rather odd and somehow unwarranted polemical exercise, a fictional study of modern geopolitical relations that seemed distinctly lacking in disinterestedness. Greene's long-standing anti-American bias, something which had previously been considered not much more than a marginal aspect of a certain authorial crankiness, now appeared to loom in the very foreground of his narrative and to invite serious critical address. In the United States, some distinguished reviewers were soon engaged in impassioned contention.[1] Their arguments had to do chiefly with the portrayal of Pyle in the novel, his plausibility both as a character and as an American agent, and the larger related question of the burgeoning American presence in Southeast Asia. The debate was much concerned with Fowler's hostility toward Pyle and ultimately with the question whether Fowler's contempt for America was also Greene's—whether the narrator was actually to be taken as a lay figure for the author himself. Given that *The Quiet American* does indeed deal in contentious political issues, these are all, of course, legitimately debatable matters; in the United States, understandably, the novel's reception was largely unfavorable. Even in England, where the figure of Pyle tended to be located in a more specifically literary context (that of the tradition of the American "innocent" abroad), Greene's apparently gratuitous invocation of various unflattering stereotypes met with some disapproval.

If *The Quiet American* is to be read simply as a prophetic thesis about the dangers of American involvement in Indochina, then it could be said, perhaps, that Greene has been retrospectively vindicated by the subsequent drama of historical events. The book is not, however, an argument but a novel. And, of course, within a few years of its publication, critics were attending more appropriately to the text as an imaginative structure of words or, at any rate, discussing it by means of questions pertaining more to philosophy and psychology than to politics. At a distance of thirty years, though, it now seems clear enough that while *The Quiet American* is about colonialism, it is also, more simply, a love story and an adventure story. It has certain obvious affinities, that is to say, with romance. As a tale of love and war, it features as one of its chief characters a highly conventional type of romance hero: Alden Pyle undertakes a lonely and dangerous journey down a river to a place that is perceived as a kind of hell, a figurative underworld where, sure of the rightness of his cause, he first rescues his rival from death and then wins from him the hand of the heroine. Even Pyle's black dog, Duke, seems to function as what Northrop Frye calls the hero's "animal companion" in this lower world.[2] And as one of its central symbols, the story features a highly conventional romance emblem, the image of the tower—usually associated, as it is here, with the kind of perilous epiphany or vision or wisdom granted only to the solitary seeker who keeps a vigil or watch from it.

But the novel, viewed in this way, looks more like a romance that has somehow gone wrong: the "hero," in this perspective, is eventually betrayed and murdered, whereupon the heroine returns to her first lover, the very rival who not only has acted as the betrayer but seems as well to have been given the novel's last word on the subject of romance itself:

> I . . . went into the cinema next door—Errol Flynn, or it may have been Tyrone Power (I don't know how to distinguish them in tights), swung on ropes and leapt from balconies and rode bareback into technicolour dawns. He rescued a girl and killed his enemy and led a charmed life. It was what they call a film for boys, but the sight of Oedipus emerging with his bleeding eyeballs from the palace at Thebes would surely give a better training for life today. No life is charmed. Luck had been with Pyle at Phat Diem and on the road from Tanyin, but luck doesn't last.[3]

Yet despite this intelligently cynical view of a banal and superficial story of adventure, the narrator's own story, although very different in texture, has essentially the same kind of narrative shape as the "film for boys" that he derides. The speaker here is the novel's protagonist; and Thomas Fowler, while he is Pyle's rival, can no more be regarded as the villain of the piece than Pyle can be seen as its hero. But Fowler's own story is informed, as it were contrapuntally, by the structure of the story about Alden

Pyle. *The Quiet American* is not an "ironic" or mock romance— merely a parodic inversion of a familiar pattern—in which the "hero" loses and the "villain" wins, but is in fact a romance of a more sophisticated type than that suggested by the film. What needs to be accounted for, then, before anything else, is the sadness and cynicism of the narrating voice.

We are brought back, in this connection, to the text's conspicuously public and polemical narrative surface. As Greene himself points out, there is "more direct *reportage*" in this novel than in any of his others: "I had determined to employ again the experience I had gained with *The End of the Affair* in the use of the first person and the time-shift, and my choice of a journalist as the 'I' seemed to me to justify the use of *reportage*."[4] During the period in which the novel was written, Greene had actually been working as a journalist himself. In 1951 he had traveled in Malaya, covering the insurrection there as a correspondent for *Life,* and between 1951 and 1955 he had spent four winters in Vietnam, reporting on the Indochina war for the *Sunday Times* and *Figaro.*[5] So he had at least a degree of professional affinity with his narrator. But the sources of the affinity lie even deeper, as Greene, again, discussing this phase of his life in relation to another of his protagonists, seems to suggest:

> In *The End of the Affair* I had described a lover who was so afraid that love would end one day that he tried to hasten the end and get the pain over. Yet there was no unhappy love affair to escape this time: I was happy in love . . . the chief difficulty was my own manic-depressive temperament. So it was that in the fifties I found myself tempting the end to come like Bendrix, but it was the end of life I was seeking, not the end of love. I hadn't the courage for suicide, but it became a habit with me to visit troubled places, not to seek material for novels but to regain the sense of insecurity which I had enjoyed in the three blitzes on London.[6]

This fragment of autobiography tells us much about the genesis of Thomas Fowler. However, the genuinely significant link which it establishes is not that between Fowler and the author but rather that between *The Quiet American* and the novel that preceded it. There is a kind of continuum of imaginative identity between the protagonists of the two stories. Like Bendrix, Fowler is by temperament a solitary and isolated man: his perspective, characterized by a profound and almost self-conscious egocentricity—what he himself refers to as a knowledge of "the depth of my selfishness" (146)—is typically one of detachment and skepticism. These qualities allow him, in his role as journalist, to maintain an appropriate objectivity or "distance." His room above the rue Catinat seems to have much the same sort of symbolic significance as Bendrix's room in south London, the emblem of a withdrawn and defensive selfhood. Like Bendrix, Fowler is an observer and, in a rather different sense, a professional writer. His predilection for opium and even his relationship with Phuong reflect and indeed underline his need for detachment, a preference for the distant and impersonal viewpoint. Phuong is the ideal mistress for Fowler: making no serious demands on him, she prepares his opium pipe and seems otherwise passive and unobtrusive, without any real needs of her own. Fowler has, in fact, elevated his isolated detachment to the status of a sort of faith: " 'You can rule me out,' I said. 'I'm not involved. Not involved,' I repeated. It had been an article of my creed. The human condition being what it was, let them fight, let them love, let them murder, I would not be involved. My fellow journalists called themselves correspondents; I preferred the title of reporter. I wrote what I saw: I took no action—even an opinion is a kind of action" (27).

This self-styled neutrality does not of course mean that he is a man without any affective attachments. He loves Vietnam, for example, in much the way that he loves Phuong. At his first meeting with Pyle, he muses on the beauty of the Vietnamese women: "Up the street came the lovely flat figures—the white silk trousers, the long tight jackets in pink and mauve patterns slit up the thigh: I watched them with the nostalgia I knew I would feel when I had left these regions for ever" (12–13). But even this kind of appreciation has an oddly aesthetic, distanced quality; it is a response to a certain exotic picturesqueness that tends to be conveyed in visually static terms. When he scorns Pyle's merely theoretical knowledge of "these regions," he does so by contrasting it with his own awareness of "the real background"; but his intimacy of understanding is characterized more by visual detachment than by any sense of personal engagement:

> He would have to learn for himself the real background that held you as a smell does: the gold of the rice-fields under a flat late sun: the fishers' fragile cranes hovering over the fields like mosquitoes: the cups of tea on an old abbot's platform, with his bed and his commercial calendars, his buckets and broken cups and the junk of a lifetime washed up around his chair: the mollusc hats of the girls repairing the road where a mine had burst: the gold and the young green and the bright dresses of the south, and in the north the deep browns and the black clothes and the circle of enemy mountains and the drone of planes. (23)

While this kind of reportage is imaginative as well as specific and concrete in its details, it lacks the immediacy of direct, participatory experience. What Fowler offers is essentially a picture, something seen, again, from a certain distance. The repetition of the word "flat" is not perhaps without significance: his Vietnam is often a series of still vignettes which have something of the effect of the picture postcard, even something perhaps of the calendars belonging to the old abbot. And as pictures, they are often curiously silent and remote, suggesting a vision of a reality that somehow seems to lend itself naturally to third-person description. In one sense, Fowler's Vietnam is all "background," an accumulation of physical detail in two dimensions. While his perspective yields a certain loveliness, that is to say, it can sometimes result in an effect as flat in its own way as Pyle's ideological abstractions.

At the same time, however, Fowler's egocentricity manifests itself in quite different terms. Like Bendrix, he is also an abrasive, turbulent figure: if his reporting of the war is neutral, the reportage in his own narrative reflects his sense of the world beyond his room above the rue Catinat as a hostile and violent place, a world fundamentally alien rather than simply exotic. In this sense, his narrative shares the energy of the kind of "hate" that inspires Bendrix's story—and it is from that sort of energy that the much-debated polemicism in the novel derives: Fowler loves Vietnam but hates the war, and if his sympathies are sometimes with the Vietminh, sometimes with the French army, they are never with the Americans, whom, at best, he regards as blundering and foolish idealists. Like Bendrix, too, he has, in spite of his self-centeredness, a desire "to hasten the end and get the pain over": an ambivalent urge toward death that seems at first glance to contrast paradoxically with everything that his room and his opium pipe and Phuong represent to him. Like *The End of the Affair, The Quiet American* presents us with an egocentric first-person voice which gives an account of what might be described as a peculiarly "third-person" reality, a world that seems more than usually "objective," in the sense of being set distinctly apart from the central narrative consciousness, and more than usually unresponsive. So the link between that consciousness and what it reports on becomes at once, paradoxically, a relation of both enmity and attraction for the narrator. More or less alone in the rue Catinat, Fowler is not existentially involved with what he sees from his room, but so long as the external world remains alien and unresponsive, it comes to be increasingly the source and object both of erotic longing and of a hunger for annihilation. For all his celebration of a kind of flat loveliness, Fowler is forever flirting with a murderousness that seems to pervade the world of the novel. His paradoxical relationship with Vietnam is summarized in an account of his relationship with Phuong:

> One never knows another human being; for all I could tell, she was as scared as the rest of us: she didn't have the gift of expression, that was all. And I remembered that first tormenting year when I had tried so passionately to understand her, when I had begged her to tell me what she thought and had scared her with my unreasoning anger at her silences. Even my desire had been a weapon, as though when one plunged one's sword towards the victim's womb, she would lose control and speak. (173)

The paradox about Fowler's perspective—his need for distance combined with an unacknowledged longing for involvement—is rooted in the psychological processes of a romantic nihilism. A world that is silent, however attractive it might seem, is also a world of death. "I came east to be killed" (140), Fowler complains as Pyle noiselessly saves his life. Like many another Greene character, this narrator is fond of nineteenth-century poetry, and his passion for Baudelaire in particular—"*Aimer à loisir, / Aimer et mourir / Au pays qui te ressemble*" (8)—says much not only about his implicit identification of Phuong with her country but also about a profound confusion of erotic and thanatoptic impulses in his own nature. In his fashion (a more "decadent" development of an earlier historical fashion) Fowler is as much a romantic as Pyle. He is the novel's protagonist, too, as well as its narrator: his querulous viewpoint, rather than some unmediated oracular voice, becomes the central technical device of the novel, and as in *The End of the Affair,* one of the things that it signifies is the fact of his ultimate survival. Where Fowler differs crucially from Bendrix as a first-person narrator is in the curious doubleness of his narrative perspective.

This doubleness is perhaps most clearly exemplified in his account of the battle of Phat Diem. Fowler begins by observing the scene from a high and remote vantage point:

> From the bell tower of the Cathedral the battle was only picturesque, fixed like a panorama of the Boer War in an old *Illustrated London News*. An aeroplane was parachuting supplies to an isolated post in the *calcaire,* those strange weather-eroded mountains on the Annam border that look like piles of pumice, and because it always returned to the same place for its glide, it might never have moved, and the parachute was always there in the same spot, halfway to earth. From the plain the mortar-bursts rose unchangingly, the smoke as solid as stone, and in the market the flames burnt palely in the sunlight. The tiny figures of the parachutists moved in single file along the canals, but at this height they appeared stationary. (52)

The cathedral tower is the first of an important sequence of tower images in the novel. What it signifies, clearly, is the type of detachment—the perspective of distance—that we have already seen as one aspect of Fowler's way of looking at Vietnam: the battle of Phat Diem is initially revealed as a silent and static picture, exotic in one sense but oddly flat and "suspended" in another. This view from the bell tower becomes another version,

that is to say, of Fowler's vision of the world from his room above
the rue Catinat, the prospect of an attractive, but somehow essentially alien, objective reality. However, when Fowler leaves the
tower and joins a platoon of paratroopers, the picture of the battle changes radically, suddenly acquiring a dreadful immediacy.
Fowler finds himself, so to speak, *inside* the picture: surrounded
by carnage, he is all at once in the midst of a whole world of
death, translated abruptly and almost literally to a kind of hell:

> The canal was full of bodies: I am reminded now of an Irish stew
> containing too much meat. The bodies overlapped: one head, seal-
> grey, and anonymous as a convict with a shaven scalp, stuck up out
> of the water like a buoy. There was no blood: I suppose it had
> flowed away a long time ago. . . . I . . . took my eyes away; we
> didn't want to be reminded of how little we counted, how quickly,
> simply and anonymously death came. Even though my reason
> wanted the state of death, I was afraid like a virgin of the act. (60)

The obscene picture, it should be noted, is now no longer still, no
longer merely a static or visually suspended "prospect": "Another man had found a punt . . . but we ran on a shoal of bodies
and stuck. He pushed away with his pole, sinking it into this
human clay, and one body was released and floated up all its
length beside the boat like a bather lying in the sun. Then we were
free again, and once on the other side we scrambled out, with no
backward look" (61). The movement from tower to canal is not
just a shift from one mode of reportage to another, but also a
journey of descent: in joining the patrol, Fowler finds himself engaged in a metaphorical as well as an actual quest for an invisible
"enemy" in what amounts to an underworld.

The landscape of this underworld can best be described as figuratively annihilated. The account of the fording of the canal clogged
with gray corpses, horrifying enough simply as an instance of
direct rather than distant reporting, has an unmistakably mythopoeic dimension as well. There is perhaps an unattributed
invocation here of yet another nineteenth-century poet—an echo
of the grisly river-crossing episode in Browning's "Childe Roland
to the Dark Tower Came." At any rate, the canal is certainly a river
in a mythically "lower" world, and Fowler's quest in this realm of

"grey drained cadavers" (61), if it is at all like Childe Roland's, is for a tower of a kind very different from the one atop the cathedral in Phat Diem. But the outcome of the patrol seems strangely inconclusive. There is much "waiting" (62), and no enemy actually appears. The only other victims are a peasant woman and her little boy, "accidentally" shot by a sentry as they lie huddled together in a ditch. However, while Fowler has been half hoping all along for nothing but his own death, this image of the dead mother and child stays with him throughout the remainder of his narrative as a haunting emblematic memory. The symbolic picture of a purely random and gratuitous murder, it seems nevertheless to epitomize the whole significance of the patrol's "progress." Despite the picture's horror, what it seems to hint at, in the immediate context of Fowler's temporary and reluctant involvement, is a type of Pietà vision: a sense that all human death, no matter how grotesque or apparently meaningless, may ultimately be a type of ritual sacrifice, an imitation of the Christian story of the Passion.

The particular hell of this novel, then, becomes a place in which the human body itself is objectified and made hideously anonymous by death. Greene returns again, in other words, to the theme of the annihilation of human identity. And in terms, again, of the perspective of the narrator's involvement, death acquires a figurative as well as a literal meaning. The theme of descent in *The Quiet American* always culminates in a nightmare vision of the reification of personal identity, a process of symbolic extinction anticipated early on in the novel by the nameless "grey heap" (36) of a human figure dragged in by Granger to the bar of the Continental Hotel. The vision is anticipated, too, by the swarming mass of female bodies in the "House of Five Hundred Girls" (38)—a scene which horrifies Alden Pyle, whose reaction to this large-scale sexual objectification of physical beauty becomes the initial source of sympathy between himself and Fowler. Pyle's virginal innocence has a touching and appealing quality for the narrator, but more important, it seems to represent for Fowler a version of his own preference for detachment over involvement—at least in the area of personal relations—which he sees as the basis of a genuine kinship between them. Fowler regards Pyle as someone who shares his own horror at the nullification of human identity. At the same time, however, this shared vision of nullity, the kind of figurative void represented by the canal-crossing episode at Phat Diem, would also seem to have a paradoxical attraction for both of them. What Pyle really shares with Fowler is his love for Phuong, and what this means at the outset of the story is that Phuong represents, for both of them, a kind of anonymous nullity that is conventionally beautiful rather than obscene: both see her in terms of the two-dimensional flatness suggested by the perspective of distance, so that her physical presence ultimately modulates, in effect, into a form of invisibility. For Fowler in particular, Phuong embodies "death" in its most attractive aspect, and it is not for nothing that she is so closely associated in his mind with the sort of escape from reality offered by his opium pipe.

Fowler is both amused and moved by the way Pyle dances with her in the Chalet, holding her formally at arm's length like a nervous schoolboy. When Pyle apologizes "for taking Miss Phuong from you" (50), Fowler responds: "Oh, I'm no dancer but I like watching her dance" (50); and he goes on to reflect on the quality in Phuong that seems to be of the essence of her attraction: "One always spoke of her like that in the third person as though she were not there. Sometimes she seemed invisible like peace" (50). It is as if Phuong were, at once, simply a beautiful woman's body and, simply, a phantom. Later, when he prepares for sleep after the battle at Phat Diem, he thinks about her, "but oddly without jealousy" (65): "The possession of a body tonight seemed a very small thing—perhaps that day I had seen too many bodies which belonged to no one, not even to themselves. We were all expendable" (65). And here the day's vision of gray anonymous corpses modulates suddenly to a vision of a different kind of physical anonymity:

When I fell asleep I dreamed of Pyle. He was dancing all by himself on a stage, stiffly, with his arms held out to an invisible partner, and I sat and watched him from a seat like a music-stool with a gun in my hand in case anyone should interfere with his dance. A programme set up by the stage, like the numbers in an English music-hall, read, "The Dance of Love. 'A' certificate." Somebody moved at the back of the theatre and I held my gun tighter. Then I woke. (65–66)

The "invisible partner" here is certainly Phuong. Pyle in the dream "possesses" a body that is not in fact a body at all but something more like a ghost. Fowler watches. In other words, the dream sums up not only the protagonist's affinity with Pyle but his relationship with Phuong, and, in a broader sense, with Vietnam itself.

As we have seen, there are in effect two Vietnams for Fowler: the exotic but flat picture viewed from a certain distance and the arena of proximate death, characterized as a kind of void or abyss, where the familiar sense of ordinary physical human identity becomes an awareness of the nameless nullity of the body. The dramatic reversal of perspective in the whole Phat Diem episode suggests, in fact, that the dreadful vision of "involvement" is precisely the mirror image of the view from the tower. What Fowler's dream suggests is that the bell tower—associated as it is with his room above the rue Catinat and with the perspective of detachment in general—is in fact a tower of solipsistic vision. Like Tennyson's Lady of Shalott, with whom, oddly enough, he might be said to have a certain spiritual affinity, Fowler not only sees his world from a remote height, he also watches it, so to speak, in a mirror. His dream involves something more than the vision of an invisible nullity: it is also a dream about narcissism. Pyle "represents" him in the dream, but the gun in the dreamer's hand is not there only to protect Pyle: "The Dance of Love" may also be a danse macabre, a dance of death, and the invisible partner a solipsistic projection of Fowler's own death wish.

So his descent from the cathedral bell tower becomes Fowler's descent into his own world of dream and death, a kind of hell where Eros and Thanatos seem to merge and to become indistinguishable from each other. The figuratively annihilated landscape just outside Phat Diem is the terrain of Fowler's own quest, the central metaphorical form of the nether region of his own romance. It is not easy to say just what he seeks there, but it would seem to be some ultimate metaphorical form of nullity, an embodied image of the void in terms of which his senses of both repulsion and attraction are conjoined:[7] in effect, his own "dark tower." At any rate, the intrusive movement "at the back of the theatre" which startles him back into the world of waking consciousness turns out to be the sudden appearance of the real Alden Pyle. It should now be clear, of course, that Pyle's daring night voyage down the river to Phat Diem is really a kind of parody of Fowler's descent from the bell tower, a "boyish" (70) version of a much more significant river journey. For Pyle functions, as he does in the dream, as Fowler's romantic shadow double, becoming increasingly a narrative projection of the protagonist in his role as one who is "afraid like a virgin of the act." Pyle's flatness as a character in the novel is much like Phuong's, an effect produced by the flattening tendency of the perspective of distance. And his eponymous "quietness" as a character is also like Phuong's virtual speechlessness.

The duality of the narrative perspective—our sense that there are two Vietnams—is reflected in the novel in a figurative dialectic of speech and silence, or, more broadly, of human noise on the one hand and an unresponsive emptiness on the other. Pyle's quietness has to do with the fact that he is increasingly revealed, despite the innocence of his boyish romanticism, as a death figure. In the context of the narrator's nihilism, silence means nullity, and Pyle is nothing if not a figurative nil or null, a narrative cipher; in the context of the narrator's solipsism, human noise tends to mean mostly the sound of his own narrating voice. The image of the tower in the novel, besides being the emblem of a self-conscious detachment, has a good deal to do with a figurative view of the human voice as something which asserts a vision of human worth in the face of an all-encompassing, ironic silence: speech, in the broadest sense, becomes a kind of watchtower in the midst of a void. Perhaps the most central emblem of all in this novel is that of a voice crying in pain from a tower set in a flat and empty wilderness. Fowler's "tower," that is to say, is also a tower of words—from one point of view, a metaphorically verbal icon in his creed of noninvolvement; from another, a linguistic construct existentially derived from the need to confront the silence of nullity. In both contexts, the novel's structure of imagery pertaining to speech and silence stems from the two aspects of Fowler's narrative viewpoint, each a reversed mirror image of the other. More important, what this dialectic of speech and silence means is that the protagonist's "tower" is also a form of cage, a place not only of vision but of imprisonment.

In the bizarre Caodaist cathedral in Tanyin, to which he goes for its "coolness" (109), Fowler notices that there is no glass in the windows: "We make a cage for air with holes, I thought, and man makes a cage for his religion in much the same way—with doubts left open to the weather and creeds opening on innumerable interpretations. My wife had found her cage with holes and sometimes I envied her. There is a conflict between sun and air: I lived too much in the sun" (109–10). But despite his atheism, Fowler, of course, has his own peculiar creed. The view from the bell tower at Phat Diem offered a pictorial panorama of the war, a vision of a particular battle seen all at once and as a whole. The perspective of detachment has the virtue of comprehensiveness. At the same time, though, the truth that it provides is partial and limited. For all his brave rhetoric about living "too much in the sun," Fowler really lives, that is to say, in his own particular form of cage. As narrator, he cannot escape the confines of language, which seems on the one hand to manifest only a partial truth and on the other to be inadequate to the experience of nullity; and as protagonist, he cannot, as he has learned at Phat Diem, escape the experience of nullity either. He must live, then, with both speech and silence—in effect, inside "a cage for air with holes." This would seem to be merely a linguistic rather than an "actual" construct, but since Fowler is a writer as well as an atheist, it has no less metaphysical substance for him than the construct represented by his wife's religion—certainly no less than that embodied by the "Walt Disney fantasia" (103) of Caodaism. The second tower symbol in *The Quiet American* is the watchtower on the road from Tanyin to Saigon: here, the tower as an emblem of solitary "verbal" vision actually modulates to the image of a sort of cage on stilts. Fowler's narrative viewpoint becomes, almost literally, a point of demonic epiphany.

As Fowler and Pyle drive back from Tanyin, the exotic picture of Vietnam yields to that of a flat and formless emptiness, a whole world of nothing but "drowned fields" (112): "The last colours of sunset, green and gold like the rice, were dripping over the edge of the flat world: against the grey neutral sky the watchtower looked as black as print" (114). With nightfall, there is a perceptible draining away of color and dimension, a reversal of perspective again, characterized this time by an eerie darkness and silence. We are back in Fowler's private night world, not a world of dead bodies but a figuratively annihilated landscape all the same, in which his own identity once more seems threatened. Climbing the ladder to the tower, he tells us that "I ceased for those seconds, to exist: I was fear taken neat" (115). In the watchtower episode, it is as though the picture of reality as a whole had been turned inside out to become a vision of reality as a hole, the prospect of a void inhabited by figurative phantoms, like the white shadows on a dark photographic negative. The interior of the tower which looks out on this dimensionless reality becomes itself an actual image of the construct suggested by the interior of the Caodaist cathedral. The watchtower seems precisely to be a reversed image of the vantage point represented by the bell tower at Phat Diem: a place for "watching" by day is transformed into a place under the threat of external attack by night. In the context of the night world, even the embrasures in the walls seem to serve only a negative function. Fowler is not, however, alone. Besides the two frightened young Vietnamese sentries, Pyle is with him, and as in the dream of the dance of love, the quiet American functions again in the role of Conradian secret sharer. But this time, silence gives way to speech, so that Fowler has the illusion, after his initial terror, that their conversation together has transformed the tower into a more familiar and comfortable environment: "It is odd how reassuring conversation is, especially on abstract subjects: it seems to normalize the strangest surroundings. I was no longer scared . . . the watchtower was the rue Catinat, the bar of the Majestic, or even a room off Gordon Square" (124). But this illusion is soon dispelled by a disembodied "voice" that "came right into the tower with us," seeming "to speak from the shadows by the trap—a hollow megaphone voice saying something in Vietnamese" (134). Fowler has at last found his invisible enemy, or, at any rate, the enemy has found him. It is as if the exterior nullity had suddenly acquired a ghostly voice and speech of its own, a language that is unintelligible yet menacing, and that seems virtually to displace the very air inside this cage: "Walking to the embrasure was like walking through the voice" (134).

More abruptly than at Phat Diem, Fowler's narrative resumes the theme of descent. He and Pyle have no sooner scrambled down from the tower than a bazooka shell bursts on it. Wounded himself now, and lapsing from time to time into a delirious semi-consciousness, Fowler once again finds himself in a world of death. This time, however, it is a world not of mute corpses but of disembodied voices and sounds. But as at Phat Diem, the descent from the tower leads to a type of hell that seems as well to be a type of limbo—an incomprehensibly horrible place in which there is nothing to be done except to wait. And, waiting, Fowler hears a noise that he cannot help but decipher:

> There was no sound anywhere of Pyle: he must have reached the fields. Then I heard someone weeping. It came from the direction of the tower, or what had been the tower. It wasn't like a man weeping: it was like a child who is frightened of the dark and yet afraid to scream. I supposed it was one of the two boys—perhaps his companion had been killed. I hoped that the Viets wouldn't cut his throat. One shouldn't fight a war with children and a little curled body in a ditch came back to mind. I shut my eyes—that helped to keep the pain away, too, and waited. A voice called something I didn't understand. I almost felt I could sleep in this darkness and loneliness and absence of pain. (138)

Again, the movement of descent seems to involve a reversal of the tower perspective: it is as if Fowler suddenly finds himself inside an almost surreal world, dimensionless and colorless, which was apprehended initially as a kind of dark exterior picture. The wrecked tower itself is now a part of this pictorial negative, and the weeping voice becomes the only thing in it to suggest that the whole landscape might have any meaning: Fowler is reminded of the Pietà scene at Phat Diem—the vision of a brutally sacrificed innocence which, if it does nothing more, locates the dark picture in a mythic context that seems familiar.

Fowler resents Pyle's subsequent heroics, although there is something distinctly comic about his resentment. For the drama now enacted out in the "drowned fields" becomes essentially a comedy of ritual death and revival. Closer than ever to the annihilation that he both courts and fears, what Fowler is waiting for is his own extinction:

> In the very second that my sneeze broke, the Viets opened with stens, drawing a line of fire through the rice—it swallowed my sneeze with its sharp drilling like a machine punching holes through steel. I took a breath and went under—so instinctively one avoids the loved thing, coquetting with death, like a woman who demands to be raped by her lover. The rice was lashed down over our heads and the storm passed. We came up for air at the same moment and heard the footsteps going away back towards the tower. (141–42)

Fowler undergoes a form of symbolic death, but he is not at all pleased to find himself emerging alive from the whole ordeal on the road between Tanyin and Saigon. Pyle insists on saving his life; Fowler is not grateful. The rapport that had been established between them in the watchtower was based on a mutual ambivalence about involvement—chiefly the involvement in erotic experience, but in Fowler's case, a fearful wish "to get death over" (131) as well. As at Phat Diem, the protagonist sees himself as "a virgin" afraid "of the act." Now his sense of an affinity, amounting almost to a shared identity, with Pyle shifts for the time being to the unseen figure of the dying Vietnamese sentry, one of the two youths whom, a few minutes earlier, Pyle was prepared quite casually to murder: "I was responsible for that voice crying in the dark: I had prided myself on detachment, on not belonging to this war, but those wounds had been inflicted by me just as though I had used the sten, as Pyle had wanted to do. . . . I made an effort to get over the bank into the road. I wanted to join him. It was the only thing I could do, to share his pain. But my own personal pain pushed me back. I couldn't hear him any more" (145). It is as if, having emerged from a strange looking-glass world, a world like a photographic negative, Fowler wished to rejoin his own image there. He is unable to do so. If his quest is for a Browningesque dark tower, then he has found it, but at virtually the moment of discovery, it becomes a literal and ironic *tour abolie*. The epiphany yielded by the watchtower is of nothing other than apparently meaningless suffering and death, yet the object of the quest is not entirely ironic, nor does it disappear altogether: the "voice crying in the dark" stays with Fowler, like the memory of the murdered child and his mother at Phat Diem.

What redeems Fowler in the novel is the capacity for imaginative sympathy that Pyle seems at first to share with him. The rhythm of the narrative increasingly suggests that his brushes with death bring him closer and closer to the kind of involvement that he both fears and longs for. "Afraid of the act," Fowler nevertheless undergoes a process of constant subjection to death— what amounts to a gradual but increasingly radical violation of his detachment. Pyle, on the other hand, remains the boyish adventurer. The quiet American begins to be perceived as the kind of romantic "hero" whose spiritual virginity will always remain intact precisely because he does not recognize that the country of romance is not just an exciting place but one which always tends to swallow up anyone who wanders into it. Pyle cannot extend his imaginative horror at the vision of the reification of female beauty to an awareness that the world he inhabits is also the House of Five Hundred Girls writ large, an enshrouding, figuratively subterranean place in which the urge toward nullity is at least as strong as the urge toward life and freedom. Pyle does not see that he *belongs* to this world, that he is inevitably an agent as well as an observer of nullification. In a way, the relationship between Fowler and Pyle is like a reversed looking-glass image of that between Harry Lime and Rollo Martins: Pyle is like a Rollo who learns nothing from his underground journey. He remains innocent in the sense that he lacks the capacity for guilt, invulnerable in the sense that he lacks the capacity for vulnerability.

Still, he remains Fowler's private symbolic doppelgänger, too, a secret sharer whom the novel's protagonist never seems quite able to shake off or cast adrift. At this stage, Pyle disappears from the story for a while, but at the same time his presence persists as a kind of narrative phantom. "I had not seen Pyle while I was in the Legion Hospital," Fowler remarks: "His absence and silence, easily accountable (for he was more sensitive to embarrassment than I), sometimes worried me unreasonably, so that at night before my sleeping drug had soothed me I would imagine him going up my stairs, knocking at my door, sleeping in my bed" (168). Fowler's sense of having been displaced from his own life by Pyle is in fact part of a larger experience of displacement and bemusement. The pattern of events which now unfolds in his story becomes strange and mysterious to him, as though it were he and not Pyle who had suddenly become the naive outsider, the character for whom the real significance of things had to be deciphered and explained. In spite of his symbolic return to life on the road from Tanyin, it is as if Fowler—continually haunted by a voice crying from a tower—had not actually emerged from the incomprehensible horror of his experience there. We have noticed that the two Vietnams in the novel are perceived as reflections of each other: Fowler still seems in some way to inhabit the mirror world of dream and death, the world of the photographic negative. He is, in short, lost, still spiritually immersed in the drowned fields. The character of the protagonist's experience in the latter part of his narrative corresponds to that of the romance hero who finds that he has wandered into a labyrinth.

In one sense, Fowler abets the process of his own growing bemusement. Trying to recover something of the character of his life before the appearance in it of Alden Pyle, he returns with a kind of vengeance to his opium pipe and to Phuong. But his perception that he has somehow lost his old life is only heightened; even Phuong, whom he correctly suspects of preparing to leave him for Pyle, now becomes an embodied loneliness:

> I made love to her in those days savagely as though I hated her, but what I hated was the future. Loneliness lay in my bed and I took loneliness into my arms at night. She didn't change: she cooked for

43

me, she made my pipes, she gently and sweetly laid out her body
for my pleasure (but it was no longer a pleasure), and just as in
those early days I wanted her mind, now I wanted to read her
thoughts, but they were hidden away in a language I couldn't
speak. (181)

In a broader sense, the whole of the reality with which Fowler
must deal at this stage in his story is also "hidden away in a
language I couldn't speak": the Vietnam that he has assumed he
knows so well becomes increasingly mystifying, even unintelligible, to him. Now, fortunately, the curious figure of Mr. Dominguez comes to his aid, directing him to Mr. Chou's house in Cholon. The ascetic Dominguez seems to function here as the kind of
enigmatic magus figure who often turns up in romance, the her-
metic, oracular wise man or priest who helps the hero out by
offering him a clue to the design of the labyrinth. But Mr. Chou
and his domestic retinue seem at first to be the very embodiment
of the sort of sheer unintelligibility with which Fowler is now
everywhere confronted. Mr. Chou is an emaciated opium addict
whose memory has been virtually destroyed and who lives with a
bewildering ménage of relatives, domestic pets, and assorted
"junk" in a "jackdaw's nest of a house" (161) perched above a
Cholon warehouse. Quite apart from Chou's addiction to
opium, the effect for Fowler is that of having stepped into a distorted looking-glass reality, a grotesque private "tower" in a
night world set in a district that is itself like "a pantomime set"
(161)—an experiential context held up to the main setting of the
novel like a mirror. The old addict himself is unhelpful: "Mr.
Chou cleared his throat, but it was only for an immense expectoration into a tin spittoon decorated with pink blooms. The
baby rolled up and down among the tea-dregs and the cat leapt
from a cardboard box on to a suitcase" (165).

Fowler is led away from this impenetrably surrealistic scene by
Chou's assistant, Mr. Heng, a character almost as omniscient-
seeming and enigmatic as Dominguez. Heng shows him the
empty "Diolacton" drum and indicates that it is connected in
some way with Pyle's unofficial activities on behalf of the U.S.
government. The drum, however, "means nothing" (165) to

Fowler. Heng then shows him a "mould" whose significance the protagonist also tries in vain to interpret: "This was not how the object itself would look: this was the image in a mirror, reversed" (167). However, Heng gives Fowler an additional clue, directing him to Mr. Muoi's garage. And yet again, the protagonist finds himself at a "level of life" that seems superficially accessible but at the same time peculiarly and profoundly indecipherable:

> In the Boulevard de la Somme you lived in the open: everybody here knew all about Mr. Muoi, but the police had no key which would unlock their confidence. This was the level of life where everything was known, but you couldn't step down to that level as you could step into the street. I remembered the old women gossiping on our landing beside the communal lavatory: they heard everything too, but I didn't know what they knew. (186–87)

At last, though, in the shed behind Mr. Muoi's garage, Fowler discovers the press, the purpose of which explains not only the Diolacton and the mold but Pyle's connection with them and with the renegade General Thé. It is not, however, in its literal or utilitarian capacity that this press initially manifests itself. The shed contains "one piece of machinery that at first sight seemed like a cage of rods and wires furnished with innumerable perches to hold some wingless adult bird. . . . I switched on the current and the old machine came alive: the rods had a purpose—the contraption was like an old man gathering his last vital force, pounding down his fist, pounding down . . ." (187). Before realizing that he is looking at a device for making plastic bombs, in other words, Fowler again stares briefly into a kind of mirror. In the light of his own involvement with the war on the road from Tanyin, Fowler is of course himself a "wingless adult bird" in a cage—the image precisely reflects both the ineffectuality and the sense of confined remoteness inherent in the perspective of detachment—and he is himself the "old man" who pounds down with his fist, for he cannot help but recognize that his own impotence in the matter of preventing the young sentry's death did not diminish the extent of his own responsibility for it.

Having at last recognized an image of himself, however unwelcome, Fowler begins to recognize as well that another image, that of the quiet American, has come to inform the world of his narrative and to give it its meaning. No longer entirely mystified now, he returns to the rue Catinat only to learn that he has lost Phuong to Pyle. His first impulse is to find a different world, and so he travels to the war zone in the north. The final tower emblem in the novel becomes the cockpit of a French dive bomber poised above a northern village captured by the Vietminh. And this last "tower" is also, again, a cage: "there was no way to get out: you were trapped with your experience" (194). But the image of a distanced, solitary vision suddenly acquires a new dimension: the aircraft which offers such splendid panoramas of the sheer physical beauty of Vietnam is also an instrument of death. The repeated attacks on the village are followed, almost like an afterthought, by an attack of a rather different kind:

> Down we went again, away from the gnarled and fissured forest towards the river, flattening out over the neglected rice fields, aimed like a bullet at one small sampan on the yellow stream. The cannon gave a single burst of tracer, and the sampan blew apart in a shower of sparks: we didn't even wait to see our victims struggling to survive, but climbed and made for home. I thought again as I had thought when I saw the dead child at Phat Diem, "I hate war." There had been something so shocking in our sudden fortuitous choice of a prey—we had just happened to be passing, one burst only was required, there was no one to return our fire, we were gone again, adding our little quota to the world's dead. (195)

All at once, the two aspects of Fowler's narrative perspective have converged. For the B-26 bomber in fact represents what might be described as a "killing tower," and Fowler's sense of his own complicity in the general ethos of murderousness is heightened. At Phat Diem, his involvement with "the world's dead" was indirect, his role more that of observer than participant; on the road from Tanyin, he became aware of an element of personal responsibility, an involvement in a wider death process that, in existential as well as in ethical terms, was much more direct; now it is almost as if he had actually committed murder himself. The only thing he is left with, again, besides a hatred of war, is the memory of the Pietà vision at Phat Diem, a sense of the ritual inevitability of the sacrifice of innocents. But he begins at the same time to see that he has no choice but to identify himself with the killers as well as with the victims. This position is, of course, logically impossible, and in the terms of the novel's moral (as opposed to its figurative) dialectic, Fowler must soon choose sides.

Following the explosion in the Place Garnier, that is exactly what he does. And in the process, like Rollo Martins and Maurice Bendrix, he becomes a type of Judas. Metaphorically, the effect of Pyle's plastic explosives is to shatter the looking-glass reality, the solipsistic world, in which Fowler, obsessively but confusedly, has so long wandered. The "world that I inhabited," he tells us, "suddenly inexplicably broke in pieces":

> Two of the mirrors on the wall flew at me and collapsed half-way.
> . . . A curious garden-sound filled the café: the regular drip of a fountain, and looking at the bar I saw rows of smashed bottles which let out their contents in a multi-coloured stream—the red of porto, the orange of cointreau, the green of chartreuse, the cloudy yellow of pastis, across the floor of the café. The Frenchwoman sat up and calmly looked around for her compact. I gave it to her and she thanked me formally, sitting on the floor. (209)

The surrealistic quality of this scene suggests, oddly enough, that the collapse of the mirror reality has somehow returned the protagonist to a more innocent world. In one sense, it has: since Pyle caused the explosion, then to the extent that Pyle's innocence remains intact, Fowler finds himself once again in a world of the quiet American's devising. But the initial sensation of having suddenly woken up in a garden is quickly revealed as an illusion. By the time Fowler arrives in the square, he discovers a scene that is in many ways more horrifying than that of the canal-crossing episode at Phat Diem:

> The doctors were too busy to attend to the dead, and so the dead were left to their owners, for one can own the dead as one owns a chair. A woman sat on the ground with what was left of her baby in her lap; with a kind of modesty she had covered it with her straw peasant hat. She was still and silent, and what struck me most in

the square was the silence. It was like a church I had once visited during Mass—the only sounds came from those who served, except where here and there the Europeans wept and implored and fell silent again as though shamed by the modesty, patience and propriety of the East. The legless torso at the edge of the garden still twitched, like a chicken which had lost its head. (212)

Fowler has been returned not to a garden world but to the deathly silence at Phat Diem and in the rice fields adjacent to the watchtower: at the center of the picture what he sees is yet another dead child in its mother's arms.

So, as Fowler's shadow double or secret sharer, Pyle ceases to be the phantom embodiment of the protagonist's sense of his own lost innocence and becomes instead the embodiment of his sense of guilt. Fowler exorcises Pyle's ghost by betraying him, at last becoming, in effect, a murderer himself. This is not to say that Pyle, as a character in the novel in his own right, ever ceases to be anything but innocent: "He looked white and beaten and ready to faint, and I thought, 'What's the good? he'll always be innocent, you can't blame the innocent, they are always guiltless. All you can do is control them or eliminate them. Innocence is a kind of insanity'" (213). Pyle's innocence, like Harry Lime's, is that of a child who has never grown up. He is a man with all the right ideas and attitudes but with no real passion and no real moral center. He begins as a conventional romance hero but is increasingly revealed as a kind of villain. The trouble with Pyle seems to be that he is not quite human: he resembles his dog more closely than he knows—"They ought to have called him Fido," Fowler muses at an earlier stage in the story, "not Alden" (128). Or, to put the character of Pyle in a different context, he may be said to resemble what is known in the parlance of science fiction as a humanoid. His affinity with Fowler has to do with the protagonist's initial detachment: what they share is a mutual horror at the brutal "mess of life" (243). But Fowler becomes increasingly humanized in the course of his story, increasingly involved in the mess of love and war, while Pyle looks more and more like an amiable zombie, a mindless death figure capable of any sort of destructiveness in the name of an abstract idealism.

He is not a romance hero, in fact, because he never becomes involved at all: unlike Fowler, he never really enters into the underworld of romance itself.

Fowler, on the other hand, sinks deeper and deeper into a kind of phantasmagoric night world; but following the betrayal and murder of Pyle, he emerges from it at the conclusion of his narrative as a different man from the detached and querulous cynic he appeared to be at the outset. There is, in other words, an ascent theme in *The Quiet American* as well as one of descent. By the time Phuong returns to him at the end of the novel, he has begun to see her as an actual and ordinary (if exceptionally beautiful) woman, rather than as merely an exotic phantom: her name means "Phoenix" (3), and her almost literal return to physical life coincides with a spiritual rebirth for the narrator, too. In this context, even Fowler's anti-Americanism is suddenly cast in doubt. After having delivered Pyle into the hands of the Vietminh, he describes a meeting with the long-despised Granger: Fowler begins to see that his contempt for his American colleague, whose son turns out (rather conveniently for Greene's purposes) to be dangerously ill, has always been based on not much more than the limitations inherent in his former detachment. Whereas Granger was once "like an emblematic statue of all I thought I hated in America—as ill-designed as the Statue of Liberty and as meaningless" (240), he now looms suddenly before Fowler, "bulky and shapeless in the half-light, an unexplored continent" (241). In one sense, the narrator of *The Quiet American* ends by sounding like a romantic protagonist almost as much in the F. Scott Fitzgerald as in the Graham Greene manner. And like the actor-hero of the "film for boys" alluded to earlier, Fowler rescues a girl, kills his enemy, and goes on to lead a charmed life.

Yet this is not quite the whole story of the novel's ending. At the very last, the narrating voice still conveys a certain sadness and skepticism, as well as an additional undertone of guilt. "Everything had gone right with me since he had died," Fowler says about Pyle in his final sentence, "but how I wished there existed someone to whom I could say that I was sorry" (247). Like the story of Maurice Bendrix, *The Quiet American* concludes with a distinctly pointed ambivalence of narrative mood. Fowler remains suspicious of what might be described as the most obvious conventional principle of closure in romance, that of the happy ending. His own sense of guilt works against his sense that a new world has ultimately been opened up to him. As he broods silently about Pyle, Phuong describes a film that she has recently seen: a story of ill-starred love set during the French Revolution, which she herself chooses to see as a romance gone wrong. She objects to its apparently tragic climax and wishes that the lovers in it had been allowed to escape—" 'to America—or England,' she added with what she thought was cunning" (246). Fowler then opens the telegram from his wife, in which she unexpectedly agrees to the divorce he has so long been seeking. "Here's your happy ending" (246), he tells Phuong. But for the protagonist, the ending is more mixed: his guilt about his betrayal and his urge to "confess"—if not to Vigot, then to the reader of his story—continue to qualify his bewildered realization that he has indeed gone on to lead "a charmed life."

As in the conclusion to *The End of the Affair,* it is as if Greene felt almost instinctively impelled to revert to one of the elements of a former pattern: a virtually reflexive need to move back toward the familiar ground of the mood of tragedy: "Was I so different from Pyle, I wondered? Must I too have my foot thrust in the mess of life before I saw the pain?" (243). The recurrence in the novel of what has been referred to here as the "Pietà vision" confirms the fact, in any case, that irony and "religious" tragedy—an inclination to keep returning to the figure of the innocent sacrificial victim—have always been significant threads in the design of Fowler's narrative. But his bleak urge to confess does seem to coexist uneasily with the Columbus-like glimpse of "an unexplored continent" in the improbable person of Granger. Fowler's consciousness of himself as a Judas tends to shift the emphasis of his story away from the "happy ending," and again, as in *The End of the Affair,* to realign it with Greene's earlier taste for endings of a more ironic kind. *The Quiet American* shares with *The End of the Affair* the sense of its protagonist's discovery of a new life as something equivocal and even flawed. Both these novels, that is to say, may be regarded to some extent as representing a kind of transitional narrative phase between tragedy and romance.

THREE

A Burnt-Out Case

Wherever he went he always came to the same
place where the same things happened.

I wish you'd told me a romantic story.

Graham Greene's life has not yet been subjected to biographical
scrutiny, but his own memoirs reveal certain clearly discernible
patterns. Perhaps the most striking of these is a dialectical tension
between the need for what he often calls "peace" and a craving
for danger. During the 1930s, for instance, one picture that
emerges is of a rather retiring young man who cherishes the domestic virtues and the secure discipline of religious orthodoxy;
on the other hand, there is the figure of the compulsive wanderer,
the Greene who treks perilously through Liberia and Mexico as if
he were some Victorian explorer with an eccentric interest in
primitivism and repression. "Peace," for Greene, would seem to
be a kind of meditational cell in which his contemplations are
always transmuted into an irresistible urge for escape and excitement. It is a cyclical business: mania turns out to have its own
monotonies and yields again to depressiveness. By the beginning
of the 1950s, this cycle had apparently entered a critical stage.
He tells us that "the fifties were for me a period of great unrest,"[1]
and there can be little doubt that his manic phase was in the
ascendant for most of that decade. More acutely afflicted than
ever by boredom and depression, he sought the relief of insecu-
rity, embarking on an extended globe-trotting quest for danger
that included nearly all the more exotic trouble spots on the geopolitical map.[2] Whatever the exact nature of his personal difficulties during this time, he gives us no reason to suppose that the
idea of an adventurous escapism might be misleading as a way of
accounting for his divagations: on the contrary, he himself sees

"escape" as the organizing principle of his career at a time when that career had evidently reached a watershed. During the 1950s, in other words, Greene seems to have spent his time looking—almost like the heroes of his boyhood reading in Henty and Haggard, Westerman, Weyman, and Stevenson—for nothing less than active adventure and realized romance.

The restlessness of his life during this period is reflected in his work. It translates into the note of agitation and uncertainty that marks *The End of the Affair* and *The Quiet American,* an inclination to see things from the viewpoint of the betrayer rather than that of the victim. More particularly, his exploration of the first-person technique, especially the possibilities implicit in a discontinuous time scheme, may be viewed as Greene's response to a growing uneasiness with the characteristic forms and structures of his own imagination. He was haunted by the sense that he had begun to repeat himself: "The slow discovery by a novelist of his individual method can be exciting, but a moment comes in middle age when he feels that he no longer controls his method; he has become its prisoner. Then a long period of ennui sets in: it seems to him he has done everything before. He is more afraid to read his favourable critics than his unfavourable, for with terrible patience they unroll before his eyes the unchanging pattern of the carpet."[3] His way of escape from the tyranny of his own method seems to have been to immerse himself in a process of technical experimentation. In the years immediately following the publication of *The Quiet American* there is not much evidence of fresh conceptual inspiration: *The Potting Shed* is an adaptation of an idea for a novel begun in 1945[4] and *Our Man in Havana* the reworking of another story that Greene sketched out before the war and abandoned by 1946.[5] The evidence—and the real focus—of his creativity around this time is in a restless search for new ways of proceeding, the exploration of less familiar fictional modes.

We have already noticed a developing tendency toward various kinds of comedy, particularly the embryonic farce that seems to lie just beneath the surface of melodrama. Closely related to this tendency is an interest in fantasy and the conventions of the fairy tale: the structure of *Loser Takes All* is based almost entirely on those conventions, and Greene explicitly refers to *Our Man in Havana* (1958) as "a fairy-story."[6] Of course, the most startling development of all is the fact that he began to write for the theater. While Greene's plays can hardly be said to constitute his best or most important work, it is significant that his subsidiary career as a dramatist began in the fifties. The period is altogether transitional. But this phase is characterized by such an extensive experimentation with such a variety of literary kinds that what it suggests is a search not so much for new themes as for an imaginative base that might be broader in a purely formal sense.

Some new themes do inevitably enter the picture: there is a general, though not notably discrete, shift in focus from religion to politics. One persuasive interpretation of Greene's career in the fifties sees him moving from religious tragedy toward a type of fiction conceived in terms of absurdist secular comedy, leaving behind the God-haunted world of *The Power and the Glory* and *The Heart of the Matter* in favor of the bizarre political arena of the third world, as it is exemplified in novels like *The Comedians* (1966) and *The Honorary Consul* (1973).[7] There is obviously something to be said for this view, especially as Greene himself seems almost to vouch for it: in *Ways of Escape* he speaks of having "discovered Comedy"[8] during the latter part of the decade. Yet the perspective remains partial and incomplete: it is obliged to overlook the evidence of a continuing preoccupation with religion and tragedy—to ignore *The Living Room* (1953) and *The Potting Shed* (1958)—and to regard *A Burnt-Out Case* (1961) not only as "comic" but also as a kind of endorsement of agnosticism. The fact is that the uncertainties of this transitional phase do not quite support the notion that Greene was interested in radically changing his subject. What they do tend to support is the idea that he was looking for a more inclusive generic context. But the genre that he eventually "discovered" does not seem to be comedy, exactly; Greene's later work has close affinities with comedy and yet it appears at the same time to be capable of assimilating tragic modes as well.

The terms of the problem bring us to his interest in drama. The attractions of the theater for Greene seem clear enough; as much as anything else, it would appear to accommodate his taste for both melodrama and farce. The five plays add up, in fact, to a surprisingly mixed bag, ranging from tragedy to sophisticated domestic comedy and even including an attempt in the direction of the theater of the absurd. More important, each of the plays exhibits some degree of what looks like internal generic confusion, an authorial inclination to veer with disquieting abruptness from one set of literary conventions to another. To a certain extent, the apparent confusion can be attributed to Greene's new apprentice status. Yet the charge of mixing genres had long been laid against him,[9] and it so regularly recurs in the commentary on his later work that it becomes almost a critical motif. On the face of it, Greene often seems uncertain about just what *kind* of story he wants to tell. In his "period of great unrest," this uncertainty at times acquires a distinctly manic character. *The Potting Shed*, for instance, presents us with a mysterious and potentially tragic hero who tends to be displaced in his heroic role by the offstage figure of a dog named Spot. Incongruities and disjunctions of this type are entirely characteristic of the metaphysical world of the plays.

The Potting Shed is perhaps the most considerable of Greene's flights into drama; structurally, it is certainly the most interesting. First produced in New York in 1957, it was received with a certain wary respect—the novice dramatist was a well-established novelist—and also with muted bafflement. Theatergoers were being asked to take seriously a realistic play that required them to accept the notion of a literal resurrection from death. *The End of the Affair* had covered similar territory and presented similar difficulties, but the exigencies of realism are more rigorous in drama than in narrative fiction. Reviewers of *The Potting Shed*, mindful of Greene's reputation as a kind of Catholic celebrity, were inclined to skirt nervously around the issue of plausibility, which is in fact the central problem of the play. The London production in 1958 met with much the same response. The third act is slightly different in the English version, and Greene notes somewhat cryptically that he has "reverted to the last Act as it was originally written,"[10] but the changes in some of the details of the plot are superficial and do not amount to anything like a radical reconception of the whole.[11] The element of the miraculous is still, in any case, a delicate subject. Greene himself has always felt uneasy about that dimension of *The Potting Shed*,[12] but his dissatisfaction apparently stems from a sense of his own technical ineptitude rather than from any doubts about the plausibility, as such, of the play's central event. His view seems roughly to be that it is Graham Greene rather than God who has failed to breathe new life into James Callifer.

This assessment is probably accurate enough, but the play remains oddly impressive. The source of its power is the idea of the miracle at its center—the notion, however awkwardly executed, that a human being might die and then be reborn. To the extent that the idea is identifiably "religious," however, it also becomes the play's principal liability: Greene's Christianity tends to work against him whenever it can be perceived as ideologically exclusive, a matter only of belief or disbelief. The paradox dissolves, of course, if the story of the play is regarded as "merely" fabulous. But mereness is beside the point; there is no imaginative way to respond to it except as a fable: the miraculous resurrection in *The Potting Shed* becomes genuinely intelligible only when it is identified as mythic. In other words, the play itself is not so much a supernaturalistic melodrama as a speculative fairy tale, a story about the loss and recovery of human identity. The ultimate issue of James's new relationship with God is his new relationship with his wife.

Again, this is a story that posits a fairly bizarre looking-glass world. The curtain goes up to reveal Dr. Frederick Baston gesturing before a mirror. This dumb show pertains, as it turns out, to a rehearsal of his funeral oration for his dying friend, H. C. Callifer; but the mirror is there because it is in fact the play's threshold symbol. It suggests a liminal point of convergence between two different but related dramatic perspectives. One of these belongs to the household at Wild Grove, a place wholly informed by the patriarchal spirit of H. C. Callifer. Wild Grove regards itself, so to speak, as eminently realistic and sane, a liberated island of enlightenment in a sea of superstition. As the play proceeds, though, another perspective emerges, in which the Callifers' earnest atheism looks increasingly absurd. This absurdity has to do not just with its total single-mindedness but with the fact that it appears increasingly to be a thoroughgoing parody of something else. The most striking thing about the Callifer household is the way in which its outlook tends to simulate that of a familiar, traditional, and sometimes fanatical piety. The sheer enthusiasm of the Callifer disbelief echoes the devoutness of the kind of religiosity which it deplores. While H. C. Callifer, for instance, is presented as a sort of rationalist prophet, what this offstage figure suggests in the parody perspective is nothing so much as an effigy of the Victorian paterfamilias, some modestly famous scholar and divine who is surrounded on his deathbed by a group of hushed disciples. In other words, Wild Grove amounts, as its name implies, to a type of fallen Eden that is entirely conventional: a place that really exists through a looking glass, yet another kingdom of dream and death. The doubleness of the perspective here is reflected in the binary character of the play's construction; everybody comes, as it were, in twos. There are two pairs of brothers and two fathers with errant or prodigal sons. The element of parody is formal and mythic, bearing not only upon an outlook but on a structure. Absurdity in this context acquires a profoundly sinister resonance when the sons begin to look like the sacrificial victims of the fathers; for the story that is ultimately being parodied is the Christian one about the family of God. The figure of the mirror leads us, in fact, into a world of reversed images, parody gestures that point obliquely to the genuine reality which they mimic.

The pervasiveness of the device of the symbolic counterpart or double gives a peculiarly literary quality to *The Potting Shed*, the sense of an insistent artifice by means of which the story is always calling attention to itself as a story. The structural patterning in the play is based, of course, on the schizoid condition of its hero: there are in effect two "real" James Callifers, the one who hanged himself at the age of fourteen and the one who is ultimately reborn. These twin identities are joined in the zombielike character who inhabits the central limbo of the play's action, and they are at the same time separated by the amnesia which afflicts him there. The "doubling" perspective which derives from this view of self-division seems to extend through every relationship in the story. And while James's situation is conceived as desperate, it is also perceived as comical: he is "represented" at one figurative level by his absurd legendary dog, but even that sad creature turns out eventually to have its own wandering doppelgänger or "impostor" (70). The principle of symbolic parody is self-consciously frivolous as well as serious, a conjuring trick involving an indefinite series of mirrors. This kind of artistic exuberance brings us close to the playfulness which is at the heart of all imaginative experience. It is a relatively superficial reflection of the great dream of desire in literature, the endless erotic energy that is forever making apocalyptic identities out of all conceivable correspondences. Wandering in his private limbo, James is a pathetic, hangdog figure; but Greene has also made him into a type of the Zoroaster mentioned in Shelley's *Prometheus Unbound,* the "Magus" who "Met his own image walking in the garden":

> That apparition, sole of men, he saw.
> For know there are two worlds of life and death:
> One that which thou beholdest; but the other
> Is underneath the grave, where do inhabit
> The shadows of all forms that think and live
> Till death unite them and they part no more.[13]

James Callifer's predicament is fundamentally romantic, not because it has anything much to do with Shelley's brand of neoplatonism but in the sense that the governing archetype of his situation is that of romance. The dark underworld where James wanders so blindly is also a garden where he "meets" himself, and both places belong specifically to a particular kind of story.

The direction in which Greene is moving in the 1950s begins to be clearer; the fertile comic sense that he now displays and his interest in happy endings both pertain generically to something other than comedy. With its motifs of amnesia and self-division,[14] *The Potting Shed* invokes the world of romance in a remarkably conspicuous, even ostentatious, way. The Callifers deplore what are repeatedly referred to as "fairy stories"—what Mrs. Callifer calls "those sentimental myths, virgin births, crucified Gods" (7)—and yet they find themselves caught up in a situation that seems absurdly fictive. Waking up as it were in a garden, James Callifer is released from his nightmare of spiritual numbness when he learns that he was driven to suicide by his father and then reborn through the efficacy of his uncle's prayer. His own story could hardly be more "sentimental," echoing as it does not only the myth of Lazarus but also that of the crucified Christ. Sentimentality in this context appears to mean wishful thinking, the tendency of desire to try to impose its own will on reality. From the Callifer perspective, the story of James's resurrection is absurd because the success of such an imposition seems inconceivable. But there is another perspective as well, and the play's structure suggests that there is more than one kind of absurdity.

The principle of symbolic parody extends to the central mystery surrounding the hero, for there are two versions of it. In mythic or romantic terms, this mystery is a story about a son sacrificed to appease the wrath of his father and his redemption from death through the power of love. The official Callifer version is more realistic and skeptical. But the plausibility of the Callifers' version is subverted by the fact of what it really appears to mean to them: that James must be sent into a dreadful exile in which his familial identity and indeed his very existence are denied him. In this version, the son has been ontologically murdered on the altar of the father's legalistic disbelief. The official family account functions, that is to say, as a cruel, sentimental parody of the romantic story; and its parody status renders it absurd in a different sense: the effect is to make the mythic version the genuinely credible one. Romance is of course creatively absurd: it always deals in miracles, insisting, so to speak, on its own fictiveness; hence, from the viewpoint of realism, is derived the convention of romantic implausibility. But when realism is perceived and presented as a kind of mimicry of romance then it is revealed in an absurd light of its own, tending as it inevitably does to confirm the fictive validity of the conventions which it mocks. Greene has found a dramatic equivalent here of the familiar narrative technique of "displacement": the linear shape of a realistic sequence of events parodies a more vertical mythic structure that hovers behind it. But this technique also inverts the kind of displacement peculiar to realistic narrative: instead of assimilating romance to realism, Greene reverses the process in *The Potting Shed* and exploits the sheer implausible artifice of romance conventions.

From one point of view, the infamous Spot signifies merely an ordinary helpless dogginess; he is James Callifer's wretched alter ego or wandering shadow. From another, Spot is a conspicuous romance symbol,[15] also James's shadow double but in a wider literary context. This dog recalls Pyle's Duke in *The Quiet American* and, in terms of *The Potting Shed*'s detective-story affinities, plays much the same role. As a romance symbol—the hero's animal companion in a lower world—Spot is directly descended from the dog in the "Burial of the Dead" section of T. S. Eliot's *Waste Land*: the "friend to men" that is always liable to dig up the "corpse" planted in last year's garden.[16] In this case, of course, the corpse is James Callifer himself. Underlying the irony of Mrs. Callifer's dislike of dogs because they are "parodies" (8) of human beings is her implicit fear of James's dog as a potential agent of resurrection. Last year's garden is also this year's, the garden of Wild Grove itself where the "real" James lies buried. The motif of burial is closely related to the symbolic function of the dog as a digging creature; both belong to the complex of figurative associations surrounding the play's eponymous symbol. The potting shed is literally the place where seeds are buried in earth. Metaphorically, it is the central *topos* in the allusive framework of the play's romance structure; it is the figure in terms of which the death and rebirth of James Callifer are rendered intelligible because his metaphorical "corpse" doubles as a metaphysical "seed."

The potting shed amounts to a kind of room at the bottom of the garden. Its counterparts in the realistic or parody perspective are the cell-like rooms of despair in which James and his alcoholic uncle have "buried" themselves, the domestic prisons that signify figurative death because they are "room[s] without faith," or, worse, "room[s] from which faith has gone" (69). The 1958 version of *The Potting Shed* has the reborn James locked in an upstairs room by his family as they try to decide, just prior to the final scene, whether he should be more permanently incarcerated. The ordinary domestic room tends to function in this play again as an emblem of the isolated self, as the interior of what T. S. Eliot might call an "upside down tower" in an underworld.[17] The dismal domestic cages in the play constitute ironic parodies of the potting shed because the potting shed is itself a room in which a more intelligible or imaginative vision of "burial" becomes possible. Readers of Greene have already encountered this garden room with its packets of seed and its smell of mold. In his first published novel, *The Man Within,* there is a potting shed which figures both as a place of refuge and as a symbolic limbo between life and death, an annex attached to the heroine's house into which the hunted hero retreats to plot a getaway that adumbrates his more radical escape at the end of the story. In *Brighton Rock,* there is the garage that "had become a kind of potting shed"[18] and becomes in turn a sanctuary for Pinkie as he runs from the razors of Colleoni's racetrack gang. In the perspective of romance, the potting shed is an archetypal place of refuge because it is the place in which all buried life is symbolically stored; and since its ultimate significance has to do, at least proleptically, with the idea of rebirth, it would seem to belong more to the realm of what Mrs. Callifer dismisses as fairy tales than to the kind of world that we normally have in mind when we think about "serious" fiction. And yet there is a sense in which every seedy room in Greene's whole seedy universe is a kind of potting shed.

Whatever else Greene's critics disagree with each other about, they display a remarkable unanimity of consensus about the definitiveness of the adjective "seedy." The word fits both characters and settings. Greeneland is a place very much in the self-consciously drab tradition of ironic modernism, its topography too familiar to require further descriptive rehearsal here: putting the matter at its simplest, it is always a figurative underworld. But one of the most suggestive extrapolations that can legitimately be made from the symbolic structure of *The Potting Shed* is that the "seedy" world is also, however paradoxically, the landscape of romance. Greene himself noted a version of the paradox at a relatively early stage in his career. His Liberian expedition in *Journey without Maps* begins as a rather routinely romantic quest into a very literary sort of African interior, but it ends with the rediscovery of sheer ordinariness. "One was back," he remarks in the penultimate chapter, "or, if you will, one had advanced again, to the seedy level."[19] What this remark seems to mean in the light of *The Potting Shed* is that the most ordinary, down-at-heel places may be revealed as exotic and miraculous: the end of the quest turns out to be a genuine discovery of its beginnings or roots, a matter of arriving unexpectedly at the starting place and knowing it for the first time. The subterranean imagery of *The Potting Shed* clarifies much that might otherwise seem obscure or confusing in Greene. He is obsessed by the seediness of underground life precisely because buried seeds hold the promise of astonishing renewals.

From the Callifer perspective, all promises of that kind are of course sentimental fables. But the play itself is a fairy tale about the Callifer family, and its total structure evinces what is perhaps the most elemental or "unsentimental" of all forms of romance, the story about an ailing and impotent king. If we stand back, as it were, from this play—to adopt Northrop Frye's analogy about looking at a picture from a distance[20]—we see a kind of communal lamentation over a dying patriarch, a prophet once honored but now neglected by his people, an accidental "scattering" of his body like seed over the garden of his native land, and the gradual emergence from beneath that garden of his son and heir. In this "undisplaced" perspective, H. C. Callifer has a shadow double of his own, one who, after fulfilling what would seem to be a hopeless quest in a lower world of shadows, returns to the surface of the earth to redeem his name. And if we move closer again to the play, we see that James's redemption is the recovery of his Callifer identity, so that the father is simultaneously redeemed by the son's story, by what is sometimes referred to in Christian terminology as his word. *The Potting Shed* is ironic in texture (perhaps the most intriguing character from any realistic viewpoint is the shadowy Corner) but romantic in structure. As a romance, it is both "heroic," in the sense that an arduous quest is involved, and "pastoral," in the sense that the potting shed in the garden is emblematic of escape and recovery; and it includes among its phases both melodramatic tragedy and farcical comedy.

We have already glanced at the romantic tendencies which manifest themselves in *The End of the Affair* and *The Quiet American*. The figure of the Narcissus mirror and that of the imprisoning tower of solipsistic vision are probably the most important romance archetypes in those novels, but there are others as well. Many of them, it should be noted, would seem to be echoes from Greene's earlier fiction. For the argument here is not that romance is a new development for Greene, that it somehow sprang fully blown from his imagination during the 1950s. The fact is that it has always been a crucial, if not the single most persistent, generic element in his work. *The Ministry of Fear* (1943), for instance, with its themes of identical twins and amnesia, seems in one sense to be almost a rehearsal for *The Potting Shed*. In *A Gun for Sale* (1936) we have the entombment in a chimney of Anne Crowder and her miraculous revival through the surprising heroic agency of Raven. There are the echoes of Dante's *Inferno* in *It's a Battlefield* (1934) and the echoes of Shakespeare's *Pericles* in *England Made Me* (1935). The motifs of romance have never been hard to find in Greene; but up to 1950, all the novels are either ironic or tragic in their primary generic focus. The conclusion of *The Ministry of Fear* presents a quite different and much darker vision of the renewal of marriage from that in *The Potting Shed*, and Anne Crowder is obliged to consign her experience with Raven to oblivion at the end of *A Gun for Sale*. Romance is a structural phase rather than a governing archetype in the earlier novels. Roughly speaking, the thrillers and entertainments, though full of marvels, deal ultimately in a kind of bitter, socially focused irony, and the religious novels, though full of miracles, in outright tragedy. Greene did not "discover" romance after 1950, but he certainly rediscovered it, so to speak, as a structural principle. In *The Third Man, The End of the Affair*, and *The Quiet*

American romance does become the governing archetype, and the generic form of every subsequent novel is essentially the form of the "fairy story."

We have noted a kind of continuum of identity between Maurice Bendrix and Thomas Fowler. It should now be clear that this extends to include James Callifer as well: by undergoing a process of entombment and rebirth, James manages to "find" himself as a genuine human individual. The process suggests the notion that the basic narrative rhythm in Greene's mind by this time is ontological in design, having to do with the type of story that is actually about the identity of a central character: characterization as fictive discovery or revelation. His next important novel, together with the journal that he published almost simultaneously as a sort of companion piece, tends to corroborate the inference. For the hero of *A Burnt-Out Case*, the Querry who began life as X in *In Search of a Character,* is sought and discovered in the course of *his* story much as James was in *The Potting Shed*. Regarding his own sense of failure over the play, Greene remarks: "I was to make a better attempt . . . to draw a 'hollow man' in *A Burnt-Out Case*";[21] but the important point in the present context is that Querry belongs to the same continuum as the protagonist who preceded him.

It might well appear, of course, that no novel of Greene's could be further from the world of the fairy tale than *A Burnt-Out Case*. This is his most bleakly austere fiction, the "blackest book,"[22] to use his own phrase, that he has written. And yet it is also in a curious way one of the most grotesquely comic and fantastic. Moreover, he himself regards it as marking "a turning point" in his work—the novel in which he "succeeded," as he says, "in breaking the pattern in the carpet."[23] First published in Sweden in 1960, it appeared in England and America in 1961 and had a very mixed reception. It seems to have been in many ways an unexpected book: the blackness of Querry's story surprised those critics who had been celebrating Greene's recent inclination toward a certain lightheartedness; on the other hand, those who approved of what they regarded as its definitively Greenean darkness were disturbed by a strain of mysticism that seemed extravagant. Some non-Catholic critics saw in the story a disappointing reversion to the earlier religious obsessions, while many Catholic commentators read it as the appalling record of Greene's own loss of faith. Others, like Frank Kermode, viewed the novel both as a kind of unwarranted repetition of *The Power and the Glory* and *The Heart of the Matter* and, more significant, as a structural failure.[24] Kermode argues that Querry exists merely as a cipher; that he is a protagonist who amounts to not much more than a heraldic device signifying a "rigidly self-conscious despair"[25] which Greene has failed to dramatize in realistic terms—as, say, Scobie's conflict with God is dramatized in *The Heart of the Matter*. In one sense, Kermode hits the nail squarely on the head, but his reading is otherwise based on a misunderstanding of the novel's generic intentions. The protagonist does indeed exist as a cipher because that is how he was deliberately conceived.

The novel began in the author's mind as a story about nothing more than a man who mysteriously "turns up"[26] in a leper colony in the Belgian Congo. When Greene traveled to Africa in 1959 in order to go up the river beyond Yonda himself, he knew no more about it than that,[27] and his *Congo Journal* never in fact gets any further with X: the search for the character was not completed until his story was written. Querry's fictive reality consists largely in his being, precisely, an enigma, a man with a murkily troubled past who has turned his back on that past and wishes to take no more interest in it. He is a cipher not simply because he "represents" religious despair but because he is the embodiment of the kind of ontological reification which proceeds from that despair. Like James Callifer, Querry is a petrified man, a character whose identity has become virtually allegorical: finding himself transformed into "*the* Querry," he has been almost literally translated to the third person. The public aggrandizement involves a personal diminution. It is a reduction of him which ultimately turns out to mean that he becomes the figurative victim or "quarry" of his own figurative quest or "query." Yet his story is not simply a reworking of the tragedy of Scobie, for it is not a tragedy at all. Though Querry's passivity irritates

Kermode, it is a quality that follows logically from his attempt to escape, not just from Europe but from the whole pattern of his life. And while escapism may be a form of ontological nihilism, it may also be more than that. Querry's explorations are an allegorical quest which, although "dark" both as a process and in its fulfillment, belongs conventionally to the world of romance. The labyrinthine forest that constitutes the setting of *A Burnt-Out Case* is a traditional and familiar locus, not in this case an exact replica of Ariosto's *selva oscura* but a dark and confusing wood nevertheless, and one which has the same symbolic function. Among its features it even includes a man who has become a paralyzed tree, rather like Spenser's Fradubio.

But of course Querry would seem to be only an ironic parody or shadow of the type of chivalric hero who might wander into a romantic forest. He is a narrative phantom in the sense that he is an almost totally displaced person, and the African jungle constitutes a woody maze for him chiefly in the sense that it is baffling or unintelligible. Kermode's reservations about the novel appear to derive, at least in part, from the way in which it presents a hero who seems unconcerned not only with his own past but with the very story in which he is the central figure. Querry has traveled to Africa in order, precisely, to lose himself; his despair seems to be a kind of formality. It is interesting to notice in this connection that Kermode's dislike of the whole idea of the ghostly protagonist conforms remarkably closely to Querry's peculiar sense of repugnance about himself. For much of the narrative he has little to say for himself because he finds little worth saying; this is another novel in which silence tends to signify as much as speech. However, the basic technique here reverses the procedure of the three previous novels: *A Burnt-Out Case* is not a first-person story. Greene has chosen an authorial narrative voice that seems conventionally omniscient and neutral, but it is also one which has a way of sounding remarkably similar to Querry's own rather wearily inexpressive tones. The most important effect of this similarity is that it tends to reflect the schizoid character of his self-alienation, our sense that he exists at once in both the first and the third persons.

The narrative in *A Burnt-Out Case* appears to be not the romantic revelation of self but its opposite: a fictional treatment of an attempt at a kind of self-annihilation. Querry is a new type of protagonist for Greene, someone whose story would seem inevitably to be the antithesis of what we normally think of as romance. Yet Querry does become gradually more loquacious as the story proceeds; near the climax, we find him telling an elaborate fairy tale that is revealed as an allegorical and autobiographical prologue to the action of the novel itself. In its structure, this fairy tale is also a formal microcosm of the novel: *A Burnt-Out Case* is a third-person rather than a first-person narrative, but the protagonist also tells a story in the third person about a character who "is," again, himself. The fairy tale functions, in other words, as the structural model of the larger story. This is not just an instance of technical ingenuity. For although Querry is a shadow lost in a maze, the real point is that the story in which he ultimately finds himself turns out to have a design which is no less intelligible than that of his fairy tale and which in fact echoes it. As a character, he represents a kind of fictive premise which seems to reverse the perspective represented by characters like Bendrix and Fowler, yet he arrives eventually at much the same place.

He starts out, however, as a deliberately stylized parody of a familiar type of romance hero, traveling down a river, like Conrad's Marlow, into what is clearly meant to suggest a heart of darkness. The echoes of Conrad in the opening chapter are numerous and insistent. The forest that surrounds the bishop's boat has the same sort of vastness and unknowable strangeness as the jungle which fascinates and horrifies Marlow in *his* boat; even the priest-captain's passion for shooting at virtually every form of wild life that comes within his range inevitably recalls the trigger-happy "pilgrims" of Conrad's story or the French warship that lies off the coast in *Heart of Darkness*, absurdly lobbing shell after shell into an unresponsive continent. The literary parallels here are intended to invoke the ethos of a certain type of quest: like Marlow, it is suggested, this "cabin-passenger"[28] is on a symbolic journey into an interior underworld that is at once fictively "foreign" and fictively familiar. Marlow tends, of course, to be as much an ironist by nature as he is a romantic, but the object of his quest—the mysterious, legendary Kurtz—draws him almost against his will into the realm of dark romance, the figure of Kurtz becoming the projected image of a secret self, Marlow's own Hadean shadow or double. But while Greene starts out by evoking the same figurative quest pattern, he also inverts it; for the protagonist of *A Burnt-Out Case* is himself a shadow from the outset. The cabin passenger is not only, like Marlow, a knight-errant finally reduced to ascetic, spectral proportions; he is a man whose very existence seems to be in doubt. This protagonist broods not so much about looking for or finding anything in particular as on the problematic question of his real identity. Nameless on his river voyage, he writes in his diary "a parody of Descartes: 'I feel discomfort, therefore I am alive' " (3). Whether such "life" is desirable or not remains ambiguous. The literary context of Querry's journey is Conradian, but it has a more explicitly ontological dimension. The cabin passenger's "descent" to the leper colony is an attempt both to bury and to recover himself, to identify himself, in fact, in the very act of self-interment.

So the central metaphorical dialectic of *The Potting Shed* recurs again, but it is now translated into the figurative terms of a symbolic construct more appropriate to narrative than drama: the archetypal image of the labyrinth. In the first place, the African forest in *A Burnt-Out Case* is perceived topographically as a maze. There is the labyrinthine jungle itself, the river and the paths and the precarious roads that wind through it, and there are the little colonial enclaves within it: the Chantins', the Perrins', the Rykers', the provincial capital of Luc, and, of course, the leper colony itself. Each of these forest clearings regards itself as a kind of human center, but the story always manages to suggest that the real center is somewhere else—that it is somewhere deeper or farther in, an elusive African and narrative "heart" that Querry is forever trying to reach. However, the novel's setting is labyrinthine in another, less literal, sense too. Querry's world is a maze simply because it leads nowhere. It embodies a vision of reality in which all places become the same place. The reason for the protagonist's sense of his inability to penetrate any further than the self who feels discomfort is that it is as if he were always looking into a mirror. The downward direction of his journey is actually presented in terms of a threshold image that is by now familiar: "The colour of the water in this wider reach was pewter, except where the wheel churned the wake to chocolate, and the green reflection of the woods was not mirrored on the surface but seemed to shine up from underneath the paper-thin transparent pewter" (8). The novel's "underworld" is a deep looking-glass world, and it is labyrinthine because Querry's elliptical Cartesian perspective makes it so: a mysterious, shadowy phantom himself, he finds nothing beyond himself but mysterious, shadowy phantoms.

The epistemology of *A Burnt-Out Case* takes us back to Fowler's Vietnam, to the white-on-black phantasmagoria of the photographic negative. Querry is another solipsist, and he travels into an Africa that seems to be an infernal maze because that is precisely what he wants to make of it. During his early weeks in the leper colony he resents the priests of the mission to the extent that they tend to lose their original anonymity: "As the faces began to develop features as negatives do in a hypo bath, Querry separated himself all the more from their company" (26). In fact, he resists "development" of every kind, even as he longs for it. He is in a literal limbo, a labyrinth organized on the principle of a demonic identity or sameness.

Since this is a world of reversed mirror images, all the shadows in it seem to be white rather than black. White is the central figurative color in the story, the definitive shade of Querry's perceived reality. It is symbolically connected to the idea of death, partly because it is the color of the *colons* rather than of the colonized, but principally because of its associations with an enshrouding oblivion. In the cabin of the bishop's white boat there is a "nostalgic photograph of some church in Europe covered in a soutane of heavy snow" (4). The icon that is intended to represent a cool and distant peace functions here as an ironic image of burial. And we find a tropical version of the same irony, for the white cabin is itself like a coffin: Querry's escape into Africa becomes a process of getting lost in a maze which also figures as a kind of sepulcher. The imagery of whiteness or paleness in *A Burnt-Out Case* invariably signifies a form of entombment, some manifestation of life in a state of ghostly suspension. Africa is conventionally a Conradian darkness, but we are in a realm of visual "negatives" now; darkness has a way of being revealed by Querry's spiritual malaise in the terms of its dialectical opposite.

The sense of Africa as a bright, sepulchral limbo inhabited by wraithlike *colons* of much the same color accounts for many of the novel's stylistic peculiarities. Speech acquires a certain limpness and lassitude in this hot, white world, an exhausted resonance that seems oddly toneless, as if it had actually been formed out of the opaque silence that frames it. Not only is the novel's style conspicuously neutral, in its spareness and detachment it seems always to be just on the verge of actually losing interest in what is being described. "This was somewhat the way in which the days passed" (4), the narrative voice yawns during the cabin passenger's voyage upriver. "This was a specimen of his days and nights," it adds later, in an account of Querry's first journey to Luc: "He had no trouble beyond the boredom of the bush" (34). The voice itself might well emanate from some weary phantom. Certainly the language of ordinary speech takes its cue from it by seeming to be somehow disembodied. Verbal communication becomes a matter of effort and difficulty in the world of this novel, a thread that is always in danger of being lost. In the first stages of Querry's stay at the mission, the simplest conversation becomes arduous even for the relatively gregarious Doctor Colin: "He paused a while for Querry to answer, but all that Querry found to say was 'I shall be glad to be of use.' The distrust between them deadened intercourse; it seemed to the doctor that the only sentences he could find to speak with any safety had been preserved for a long time in a jar in the dispensary and smelt of formaldehyde" (31). What speech in particular and language in general primarily reflect in an ambience of oblivion is a tendency toward a discontinuity of consciousness. It is as if even discourse aspired to the condition of suspension rather than of fluidity.

However much he might prefer to be altogether rid of his past, Querry is not quite an amnesiac, like James Callifer. But he does seem to suffer from a form of mental disconnectedness. One of the kinds of development that he resists is that which we ordinarily think of as narrative sequence: the development implicit in a flow of events that may be perceived to have some intelligible direction or *telos*. Events for Querry tend to be sequential only in the sense that they are strung out on a temporal line, one thing following without much connective significance on another. *A Burnt-Out Case* is a remarkably dilatory novel: the plot does not thicken for a long time, and as in *The Quiet American*, there is a good deal of waiting. But even this has less to do with suspense than with an aimless suspension, a state of metaphysical pendency or abeyance. The reality that Querry observes around him is often literally devoid of narrative meaning, its only organizing principle inhering perhaps in its labyrinthine form:

> On the other shore the great trees, with roots above the ground like the ribs of a half-built ship, stood out over the green jungle wall, brown at the top like stale cauliflowers. The cold grey trunks, unbroken by branches, curved a little this way and a little that, giving them a kind of reptilian life. Porcelain-white birds stood on the backs of coffee-coloured cows, and once for a whole hour he watched a family who sat in a pirogue by the bank doing nothing; the mother wore a bright yellow dress, the man, wrinkled like bark, sat bent over a paddle he never used, and a girl with a baby on her lap smiled and smiled like an open piano. (27)

The phantasmagoric character of the scene derives from its peculiar stasis, the sense that the rhythms of human existence have somehow been assimilated to those of the silent vegetable life of the forest, so that movement and purpose appear to be frozen. Everything in the jungle seems slightly grotesque, rather reminiscent in this respect of the domestic environment of Mr. Chou in *The Quiet American,* because the jungle is another kingdom of dream and death. Nothing happens here, or, to the extent that anything does, it does so only within the frame of reference, so to speak, of a kind of governing vegetative principle. This jungle with its exotic but alien reptilian abundance is almost a science-

fiction forest, and Querry might easily be on another planet—
one where growth and decay are simultaneous and indistinguishable, where the customary signs and signals of evolutionary
process do not appear. It is as though the sequential thrust of
evolution had been not merely suspended but actually reversed.

Although this phantasmagoria seems strictly ironic, signifying
nothing more than an ultimate human alienation from nature,
the irony is comprehended by a larger conventional framework.
If Querry is in the archetypal woody maze of romance itself here,
then the reptilian life of the forest is Medusan and the real doom
that it suggests is the one always threatened by a romantic limbo:
paralysis or petrification. The looking-glass world of dream and
death is romantic in more than just the exoticism of its atmosphere. Patricia A. Parker characterizes romance "as a form
which simultaneously projects the end it seeks and defers or wanders from a goal which would mean among other things the end
of the quest itself."[29] She argues in effect that the form may be
considered in terms of two basic narrative rhythms: the forward
linear movement of a central quest and a labyrinthine rhythm of
errancy or divagation from the goal of the quest. Implicit in any
quest narrative, in other words, is a type of antinarrative: a continuous, structurally subversive tendency toward what Parker
calls "dilation" or "deferral." In most quest stories, of course, the
emphasis falls on the sequential thrust; but some modes of romance, particularly the historically later versions of the genre,
tend to stress the rhythm of deferral. Perhaps the clearest example of this deferral is to be found in the characteristic theme of
Keats: "the fruitfulness of wandering, of the more circuitous
route."[30] Narrative circuitousness is generically ironic, however,
because of its inherent subversiveness: the ultimate form of
"ironic" romance would be a labyrinth of purposeless narrative,
a story entirely without *telos* and hence without significance. For
if the rhythm of sheer errancy can be said to lead anywhere it is in
the direction of suspension and silence, an indefinite deferral of
narrative meaning. To a considerable extent, *A Burnt-Out Case*
is so constructed that it approaches as closely as possible to such
a fictive limbo without actually ceasing to be a story. It is a dila-

tory novel because it is largely concerned with a process of dilation; to precisely the extent that he functions as the antihero of an antinarrative, Querry is a fictive cipher. Paradoxically, the only conceivable "end" of dilation and deferral would seem to be a state of immobility. Suspense is always in danger of becoming suspension, and the real danger for Querry is that of being metamorphosed, as the man in the pirogue appears virtually to have been, into a kind of tree himself.

Errancy or divagation tends to be perceived in narrative terms as "drift." One of Doctor Colin's earliest notions about Querry is that "perhaps here too was a man under obedience, but not to any divine or civil authority, only to whatever wind might blow" (30); and we are later told that "it is characteristic of Africa the way that people come and go, as though the space and emptiness of an undeveloped continent encourage drift; the high tide deposits the flotsam on the edge of the shore and sweeps it away again in its withdrawal, to leave elsewhere" (153). This kind of imagery suggests the romance of the accidental or random encounter in a world where almost anything might happen, a story about a labyrinth stylized emblematically as a wheel of fortune. But the apparently fortuitous realm of the antinarrative is actually characterized by an ineluctability which amounts to the sense of fatality. The Africa in which Querry finds himself turns out to be a place of discovery in the sense of "recognition." His affinity with Deo Gratias, for instance, is really based on the symbolic role of the leper as his mirror image. What Querry sees in Deo Gratias is a more fully developed version of the man in the pirogue: a human being who, like himself, is just about literally immobilized. The symbolic doubling of the two characters is thematically based, of course, on the idea that they are both burnt-out cases, but Querry's apprehension of this bond could hardly have been presented in more concrete and specific terms. During their first journey to Luc together, Deo Gratias behaves exactly like Querry's shadow, moving in an absurd, lockstep unison with him that Querry finds nearly as unnerving as the man's name. The figurative basis of this looking-glass effect is the way in which Deo Gratias's mutilations cause him to resemble an inanimate object. Again, Greene

73

is quite specific about this connection: the real significance of the affinity between the pair becomes clear only when they both stop moving. Deo Gratias "on his two rounded toeless feet" is "like something which had grown on that spot ages ago and to which people on one special day made offerings" (33). If the great trees are the "kings" of this vegetable world, as they are in *Heart of Darkness*, then Deo Gratias is to be regarded as a kind of totem king as well as a leper. Such an apotheosis would in itself be ironic and hence faintly sinister, but something more ominous is suggested beyond it:

> At long intervals, spaced like a layer of geological time, the forest dropped trees across the way. In the deep bush trees grew unnoticeably old through centuries and here and there one presently died, lying half collapsed for a while in the ropy arms of the lianas until sooner or later they gently lowered the corpse into the only space large enough to receive it, and that was the road, narrow like a coffin or a grave. There were no hearses to drag the corpse away; if it was to be removed at all it could only be by fire. (31–32)

What appears to be merely a random natural process, part of an unnoticeable vegetative drift, is pointedly apprehended here as a distinctly human vision of death: a totem king may also be a ritual or sacrificial victim.

A fictively labyrinthine world in which almost anything might happen is one where in fact only one thing is certain to happen. The sense of what might be termed the sheer fatality of death is remarkably pervasive in a novel in which few of the characters actually die. It is attributable to the tendency toward a certain figurative reductiveness inherent in antinarrative "dilation." Everything in a limbo or netherworld fades to a deathly pale sameness, so that death itself becomes the principle of ritual identity. Querry's flight into Africa is mirrored by the flight of the terrified Deo Gratias into the jungle, where what is fled merges, as it were, with what is found, quest and anti-quest becoming much the same thing. Querry's whole situation in the novel is mirrored again in the periodic glimpses that we are given of the old man who sits in his battered deck chair, waiting to die. This immobilized character is really the heraldic figure of the antinarrative: ironically enthroned, a king who is sick unto death, he has nothing to do with the action of the story, no function except to wait and to expire. Narrative divagation is suspension and suspension is immobility; but as a matter of narrative texture immobility means repetitive recurrence, a dreadful sameness of meaning which is ultimately the demonic identity of death. Querry's spiritual numbness is reflected not only in Deo Gratias's mutilations but also in the mortal sickness of the old man. The chair that seats this figure suggests an ironic kingship because he is powerless; in another context, however, his absurd "throne" becomes, as we shall see, one of the most potent symbols in the novel.

Everyone in *A Burnt-Out Case* is more or less trapped in the reductive dynamic of the antinarrative. The obnoxious Rycker tells Querry that he too has "buried" (37) himself, and his wife is even more clearly lost in the depths of the forest. The Rycker factory appears as an infernal place, so that in romance terms Marie Rycker becomes a maiden imprisoned in an underworld; and to the extent that her husband's moral unattractiveness is actually perceived as monstrous, she is increasingly revealed in the role of an ironic Andromeda. Even the priests who run the leper colony are isolated in a peculiar limbo of their own. Their mission bears such an inevitable resemblance to every other mission of its kind everywhere that they might as well be anywhere. It seems to consist of an arrangement of boxlike rooms or cells within which each of the fathers is inclined, understandably, to be somewhat fixated on the "minute differences" (166) between his own domestic setting and all the other such settings in the outside world that so closely resemble it. They are almost literally suspended in sameness. So, in the reductive looking-glass perspective, Querry's constant urge to go "deeper" or "further in" amounts in one sense only to an ironic quest that "ends" with a box at the center of a nest of identical boxes. The centripetal rhythm of the antinarrative always seems to lead to the same place. Even Doctor Colin has, in effect, buried himself as thoroughly as anyone else. But there is an active as well as a passive principle in the world of this novel. The work of the priests is valuable and important; Rycker, too, manages in spite of himself to supervise the production of something that could be described as useful. And in the case of Colin, purposeful activity becomes the very thing by which he is fictively defined. The doctor's own urge to go deeper is a professional compulsion to penetrate rather than to identify with an obscurity. In fact, his tenacious faith in his work tends to become a metaphor for nothing less than the intelligibility of narrative action, a faith in the sequential pursuit of a significant goal.

The total structure of the novel is based on a dialectic tension between antinarrative "drift" and narrative *telos,* the inherent antipathy, which Patricia A. Parker sees as the structural crux of romance itself, between the idea of errancy and that of quest. If Deo Gratias is Querry's antinarrative counterpart, then Colin is his narrative antitype: another reversed mirror image. The doctor is the novel's embodiment of narrative energy and purpose; working against leprosy, he works against petrification and silence. He has a not-unexpected interest in theories of evolution, and although he is an atheist Colin seems to be animated in this respect by something very like religious faith. He believes in evolutionary progress, the gradual development of the higher forms of life through the creative power of love. It is a faith in natural process as a genuinely significant sequence. In this context, Colin's perception of Querry as another "patient" amounts to a recognition of the nearly counter-evolutionary direction of the protagonist's journey: to choose to be lost is to choose death. Querry knows this, of course, as well as anyone, and in spite of his distaste for language, he manages to respond to Colin's exhortations to resume his profession as an architect with a note of murky protest: "At the end a half-sentence had been thrust out into the void—'I will do anything for you in reason, but don't ask me to try to revive . . .' like a plank from a ship's deck off which a victim has been thrust" (58). Querry normally sees himself as a betrayer rather than as a victim, but the metaphor of resurrection implicit in his "half-sentence" is proleptic of his whole situation in the novel. Resisting Colin's encouragements "to be of use"

(50), he hints specifically at a fear of awakening or coming to life. He clings to the status of antinarrative ghost or cipher; what he resists is narrative development.

The trouble with language from Querry's point of view is its tendency to become figurative: people have a way of speaking metaphorically and thus, since metaphors are the seeds of stories, expressing themselves in narrative form. But in an environment where discontinuous drift seems to be the only principle of movement, intelligible narrative sequence can only be an illusion. Querry's dislike of speech has to do with his sense of the inherent fictiveness of all language. To the extent that verbal communication is genuinely possible, it amounts at best to a matter of inventing and trading stories; more commonly, speech is simply a pack of lies. Language in any antinarrative perspective consists of illusory sequences of illusory events: it has exactly the substance and shape of dreams. But if Querry is disturbed by his own half-sentences, he is much more deeply disturbed by some of the larger narrative illusions thrown up by his mind. Shortly after sending his message to Colin, this man whose despair has driven him to lose himself in a tropical forest dreams that he is a disguised priest "in a cold country" (59) who is searching desperately for another priest in order "to make his confession and obtain wine with which to celebrate Mass" (59). The Querry of the dream, in other words, is a mirror projection or reversed image of the Querry in the antinarrative. Where the conscious protagonist fears revival, the sleeping dreamer fears death: the heavy medieval door of the priest's house, "studded with great nails the size of Roman coins" (59), suggests the lid of a coffin; the dreamer also longs for a final chance of escape, but in this case "escape" means an opportunity to celebrate love and the renewal of life. The sense of being overtaken by a disastrous doom when that last chance apparently eludes him is quite explicit: "He let out a cry like that of an animal in pain and woke" (60). Querry's dream vision of a fatal entrapment is suddenly displaced into the conscious awareness of his surroundings, of "the small white cell that his mosquito-net made, the size of a coffin" (60); and of course the first thing that he does in the morning is to arrange to have a desk and a drawing board made. The dream impels him to a self-conscious form of "revival." In an antinarrative world, the impulse toward narrative sequence is driven as it were underground, but it has its own subversive impact there.

The nature of Querry's conception of reality would not encourage him to attach much lasting significance to a "story" like the one about the disguised priest, but we soon discover that the reality, in fact, has actually become the reflection of the dream. Looking for the lost Deo Gratias in the jungle, Querry finally hears "a harsh animal sound" (65). Having located the leper by becoming the auditor of a cry of pain, he goes for help. But "Deo Gratias howled as a dog or a baby might howl. He raised a stump and howled, and Querry realised that he was crippled with fear. The fingerless hand fell on Querry's arm like a hammer and held him there" (66). The figure who is terrified of having lost his last chance is now, clearly, the immobilized African. Deo Gratias is Querry's mirror image here in the sense that he primarily reflects not the despairing man who wishes to be buried but the dreamer who longs to revive. The structure of the night episode in the forest is intricately informed by the structure of Querry's dream narrative. Even the voices of the chattering pious women from the dream are echoed by "the continuous chatter of the insects" (63) in the jungle; and Querry's earlier meditation about the forest's emptiness—"It had never been humanised, like the woods of Europe" (63)—is suddenly rendered ironic: the forest has been "humanised" by the presence of Deo Gratias in it and by the recognition of a common humanity implicit in Querry's discovery and rescue of him there. To be more exact, it has been humanized by its narrative function as the meeting place of two human dreams: Querry's, and Deo Gratias's fantasy about finding "Pendélé." Pendélé is not so much a place as a word; a legendary African Eden, it signifies a heart of light rather than of darkness and, because it derives from the memory of childhood, pertains more to the imagination than to reality. Deo Gratias comes to see Querry as a kind of savior who will lead him to Pendélé, and Querry adopts Deo Gratias's longing for the place as his own. Their two dreams merge because both are about revival. In terms of the antinarrative, Querry is identified with the African's leprous mutilations; now he himself identifies with Deo Gratias's absurd dream about a recovery of innocence. These woods are no less enchanted, obviously, than the forest of any northern fairy tale.

In this episode, Querry is more exactly than ever in the position of Conrad's Marlow because he actually searches for something. What he finds is Deo Gratias, and he is to spend the rest of his life "searching" for the Pendélé of the leper's story—a form, at last, of narrative action. In the context of the novel's allusiveness to the structure of *Heart of Darkness*, Deo Gratias may be regarded here as Querry's Kurtz: sharing the same horror, they may ultimately be said to speak the same language. The language of the fearful animal cry has its own hidden significance, and what the episode reveals is that the kind of development that Querry chiefly fears may be inescapable. Without realizing it, he makes an imaginative commitment to the form of a simple myth. Though the rhythm of the antinarrative has so far been the dominant one in *A Burnt-Out Case,* it begins to be superseded at this stage by the upward thrust or "revival" of narrative itself.

However, the most characteristic form that language takes in the Africa of the novel is that of speculative gossip and rumor: the pack of lies. Isolated people who are suspended in a world where nothing much happens have nothing much to do but to invent happenings. Rycker and his wife and Father Thomas and Parkinson make Querry into a kind of heroic legend, and they do this largely because their only alternative is silence, the abhorrent narrative vacuum. The stories that they devise about him reflect their own hopes and fears, so that he tends to become the savior-king of their personal fantasies: for Rycker and Father Thomas, he is a peculiarly modern saint, a St. John of the Cross lost in a dark and arid night; for Parkinson, Querry is another Schweitzer, the type of culture hero sensationally promoted by newspaper proprietors; and for Marie Rycker, he is a sexual celebrity, a virile rescuer from the pages of an unending magazine serial. They invent a Querry who quickly becomes, for each of them, a narcissistic projection; through this legendary character, in other words, it seems possible that they might recover the failing dreams of their individual lives. Such fantasy narratives are sentimental romances. They differ from the real story in which Querry has begun to be embroiled in the forest principally by virtue of certain structural elisions: because they stress Querry's power, these legends are all about quest and achievement and hardly at all about the suspension and terror implicit in the "dilation" of wandering. The true story of Querry starts with his relationship with Deo Gratias and it begins with their mutual impotence and helplessness: it is a story about petrification which exactly reflects the "line" of the antinarrative.

There can be no doubt, though, that when Querry sets off into the jungle he enters one of the realms of romance. Fully awake, he walks into a version of his own dream. At the same time, it is as if his ordinary waking consciousness had been almost forcibly suspended from the outset: "The sharp sour smell of chlorophyl from rotting vegetation and swamp-water fell like a dentist's mask over Querry's face" (63). This is another threshold image, and what it suggests, besides anesthetization, is that Querry is being swallowed up by a kind of green monster. He thinks at first that the forest is "empty" because it is devoid of familiar life, but it has an existence of its own, nevertheless—an insistent, overwhelming vegetable life which seems to subsume everything to itself. In the case of Deo Gratias, this does not mean merely the entranced vacancy earlier exhibited by the family in the pirogue; Deo Gratias, when Querry finds him, is "warm and wet like a hummock of soil; he felt like part of the bridge that had fallen in many years ago" (66). His petrification is literal: he has become virtually an inanimate forest object and his terror is hardly to be wondered at, especially in view of the fact that what originally drew him into the jungle was the mental picture of another sort of green world altogether. The finding of Deo Gratias makes Doctor Colin's views on evolution seem perversely optimistic: Querry examines feet that are described as "rocky" (66), and we are told that the knuckles pinning his own "felt like a rock that has been eroded for years by the weather" (66); it is as though the leper had suddenly evolved backward through eons of geological time—a reductive "progression" from human to animal to vegetable to mineral. In effect, the romance of "wandering" becomes a story about the slow process of vegetation.

The pervasiveness of the imagery of vegetation in *A Burnt-Out Case* has to do with something more than authenticity of atmosphere or mood. Vegetating is what nearly everyone in it seems to do, and not just in a manner of speaking. Rycker is described at Querry's first meeting with him as "the kind of plant people put in bathrooms, reared on humidity, shooting too high" (36). Even the predominant conception of verbal communication as a matter of spreading stories is figured in much the same terms: "The most monstrous rumours were easily planted and often believed. It was a land where Messiahs died in prison and rose again from the dead" (48). More specifically than in any other novel by Greene, the theme of *A Burnt-Out Case* could be described as the inevitability of the process of going to seed. The drift that characterizes Africa becomes the figurative vehicle of that process. Even Doctor Colin's evolutionary theories seem to hinge on this metaphorical pattern. Acknowledging evolution's tendency to produce evil men more frequently than saints, he tells Querry: "I have a small hope, that's all, a very small hope, that someone they call Christ was the fertile element, looking for a crack in the wall to plant its seed" (160). And he goes on to insist that "love is planted in man now, even uselessly in some cases, like an appendix" (160). Later, when Parkinson's stories begin to appear in the newspapers, Querry picks up the metaphor again as he broods upon the hopelessness of "silencing" (174) Rycker: "If he had to have a tormentor how gladly he would have chosen the cynical Parkinson. There were interstices in that cracked character where the truth might occasionally seed. But Rycker was like a wall so plastered over with church-announcements that you couldn't even see the brickwork behind" (166). What this kind of imagery suggests, of course, is the narrative archetype of fertility and renewal, a vegetation myth in which life always waits to burst out of the decaying shell of death. And implicit in such a story is the notion of an escape from bondage, for these walls with their desperately sought cracks and interstices are the perimeters of private jails.

The perspective of the *colons* in the novel returns us to Greene's image of the room as the safe domestic enclosure that is also a cage. The leper colony, for instance, is a haven, but as such it is inevitably sealed off from the darker life of the forest beyond it. For Deo Gratias, the sense of confinement becomes unbearable. Enclosed life is nothing if not hothouse life, and Marie Rycker, who has little more to live for than the escapist serial romances in *Marie-Chantal,* is virtually suffocated by a claustrophobia not much different in kind from the mutilated leper's feeling that "there wasn't enough air" (68) in the leproserie. In this perspective, the forest itself is characterized by both a dangerous immediacy and an elusive remoteness. The figure of the "wall," from the colonial vantage point, signifies the edge of the forest clearing: Marie Rycker's view of the indigenous life of Africa—an ambivalent blend of fascination and fear—is a series of liminal glimpses from an almost totally sealed room. She "stare[s] away at the dull forest wall," and the only visible path leading into the jungle is "closed with fibre mats for a ceremony no white man must see" (73). Everyone in the novel is confined, in some sense, to a personal cage. Querry's, we are told, is "cold and hard, like a grave without a cross" (90). Father Thomas's is a place in which "it needed an act of faith to know that the forest had not come up to the threshold. . . . Sometimes it seemed to him that he could hear the leaves brushing on the mosquito wire" (111). The view from a room like this suggests that the forest may be, again, a devouring giant, that it has a monstrous life of its own which roughly resembles human life but remains implacably inimical to it.

At the center of this whole structure of imagery lies Marie Rycker's recurrent phantasmagoric vision of a quintessential Africa glimpsed from a car on the road to Luc:

> In a village by the road stood a great wooden cage on stilts where once a year at a festival a man danced above the flames lit below; in the bush thirty kilometres before they had passed something sitting

in a chair constructed out of a palm-nut and woven fibres into the rough and monstrous appearance of a human being. Inexplicable objects were the fingerprints of Africa. Naked women smeared white with grave-clay fled up the banks as the car passed, hiding their faces. (73)

It is as if the forest were spelling out its own dark narrative about cages and vegetation. The story it tells frightens Marie, partly because, written in a language she does not understand, it is incomprehensible to her, but chiefly because its symbols, however "inexplicable," seem to convey some primal message that addresses her own predicament. In fact, whatever one makes of the passage without benefit of anthropological expertise, these enigmatic "fingerprints" are clues which speak indirectly to the fears of everyone in the story. The effigy in the rickety chair is almost certainly a fertility fetish—the women smeared with grave clay would appear to be ritual mourners—but it might just as easily be the presiding spirit of the world of the novel itself. As the representation of a man, it suggests a vegetation god or totem king whose authority is simultaneously absolute and absolutely contingent on the cycle of the seasons, a symbolic deity representing an ascendant life force which can be renewed only by a perpetually recurring descent into death. Like the old man who sits in his battered deck chair, this figure is ironic in its enthronement because it is powerless against decay. To be immobilized is to vegetate, and human endeavor in such a reductive context becomes merely the process of dancing in a cage above the flames of a fire which will ultimately consume it. In just this sense, Marie Rycker herself is at once free and imprisoned, a maiden in a tower who is painfully aware of her protected but confined life as a process of dying. Her view of the cage on its stilts is of something "strutting by the road like a Martian" (80) precisely because the reality evoked by symbols like these seems so alien; they mock all ordinary human dreams and aspirations. In Querry's case, the cage and the vegetable effigy are differently focused clues to the same fears. Querry is more afraid of revival than of death. He keeps insisting that he has come to an "end" but finds himself confronted at every turn by evidence of ends becoming transformed into new beginnings. If, like Deo Gratias, he wanders into the maw of a giant, he manages to emerge from it as well.[31]

As the rhythm of the antinarrative in *A Burnt-Out Case* is proleptic of death, so the principle of *telos* in the narrative structure itself is based on a continuous prolepsis of rebirth. When Colin remarks to Querry that he must have had "a bad night" in the forest with Deo Gratias, Querry replies: " 'One has had worse alone.' He seemed to be searching his memory for an example. 'Nights when things end. Those are the interminable nights. In a way you know this seemed a night when things begin. I've never much minded physical discomfort. And after about an hour when I tried to move my hand, he wouldn't let it go. His fist lay on it like a paper-weight. I had an odd feeling that he needed me' " (67). Querry saves the leper's life by joining him, so to speak, in the immobility of death. By doing so, the protagonist inadvertently provides those who are inclined to mythologize him with the basis for an extravagant new story, but the undeniable fact remains that it *is* like a "story." Events in this episode do indeed take an improbable literary form. Querry's account of the dark night in the forest echoes the kind of narrative, like the one in the background of *The Potting Shed*, that shows a hero who descends into a lower world of bondage and rises out of it again in triumph. Without realizing it, Querry becomes the harrower of a hell. The real significance of this "story" for him is that the salvation of Deo Gratias becomes the basis of his own salvation. So the limbo of the antinarrative is now identified in figurative terms as a place of fictive seed. Deo Gratias's need and the protagonist's response to it adumbrate a persistent *mythos* of resurrection within the central story of the novel, a rhythm in which darkness always yields to light. The tendency toward tragedy implicit in antinarrative dilation and deferral yields to the comedy of narrative renewal.

At this stage, both Querry and Deo Gratias are still not much more than ciphers, a pair of metaphorical corpses, but life is rekindled in them by virtue of the shared dream of Pendélé. The story of Pendélé remains a story, but other stories about anticipated recovery and revival now begin to proliferate, informing and illuminating the events of the main narrative. Colin explains, for instance, that the Simon to whom Deo Gratias prayed in the night was a man who "died in gaol nearly twenty years ago. They think he'll rise again" (68); and Querry replies, it would seem rather cryptically: "That word 'Pendélé' runs in my head" (68). The point about the story told to Querry in the forest, of course, is that Pendélé is a paradise that is "buried" or suspended there. And if Querry has also been buried himself, then his corpse still exhibits at least one of the signs of life: " 'You'll know where to look for me,' Querry said, 'if I should be missing.' An unexpected sound made the doctor look up; Querry's face was twisted into the rictus of a laugh. The doctor realised with astonishment that Querry had perpetrated a joke" (69). The comedy of proleptic resurrection runs very deep in *A Burnt-Out Case*, extending into some unlikely places. When Marie Rycker walks like a pre-destined victim to her marriage bed, we are told that her husband "looked like a drowned man fished up in a net—hair lay like seaweed on his belly and legs; but at her entrance he came imme-diately to life, lifting the side of the tent. 'Come, Mawie,' he said. A Christian marriage, how often she had been told it by her re-ligious instructors, symbolized the marriage of Christ and his Church" (84). This view of Rycker as a type of the biblical Bride-groom is deeply ironic as well as grotesque, but the parody here is constructed on the basis of an archetype of revival so persistent that it functions as a comic narrative pattern even in the depths of a hell like Marie's. The anecdote that turns up later in the novel about the confidence man who persuades a local tribe to give him their blankets "because they would be too heavy to wear at the Resurrection of the Dead" (154) depends for its effect on the per-sistence of the same kind of pattern. In a world ruled by death, the creative energy of life always tends to be characterized by a slightly absurd narrative ingenuity.

Querry's own sense of humor is, of course, somewhat limited, and there would seem to be nothing very funny in any case about the effigy in the chair. Querry is obsessed with extinction, not resurrection; like Thomas Fowler, he is attracted by the idea of death's permanence and "peace." The vegetable effigy does not horrify him in the same way as it horrifies Marie. Yet this scarecrow figure may be interpreted in comic terms too, as a reborn as well as a dying king. An ambiguous emblem of power, it is assertive of the fertility of nature, and what it signifies is the cyclical character of nature as a structure. This significance also pervades the structure of the novel. The narrative is full of circles and cycles: Querry has "come to an end" but detects the glimmering of new beginnings; he dreams of death and hopes to be buried beside Doctor Colin and his wife, yet he resumes his profession and designs a hospital for the leproserie.

There is as well the kind of cycle in which an old order yields to a new: although the father superior governs the mission with an apparently absolute and immutable authority, his benevolent reign is inexplicably terminated when the bishop replaces him with the unlikely figure of Father Thomas. This turn of events just about coincides with the completion of Querry's new building. Witnessing the superior's preparations for departure, Querry feels "like a stranger present at some domestic grief" (166): it is an occasion that suggests the demise of a beloved king. There is even the hint of another "throne" here in the chair "that had become unique by its unreliability" (167). As Querry stands apart from the group of unhappy priests, it becomes clear that his real emotional affinities lie with the man who has been deposed. He dreams that he is "with the Superior" (168) on the departing boat:

> In his dream the boat took the contrary direction to that of Luc. It went on down the narrowing river into the denser forest, and it was now the Bishop's boat. A corpse lay in the Bishop's cabin and the two of them were taking it to Pendélé for burial. It surprised him to think that he had been so misled as to believe that the boat had reached the furthest point of its journey into the interior when it reached the leproserie. Now he was in motion again, going deeper. (168)

The corpse being borne down this virtually subterranean river is the figuratively dead body of Querry himself. As the superior is now withdrawn from the action of the novel, so Querry has attempted a withdrawal from his own life; but although he has begun a "new" life, his act of self-abdication is not yet complete and he must somehow bury himself deeper still. Abdication implies kingship, of course, and while Querry has no literal authority like that of the superior, it is also true that he has in effect been symbolically enthroned in the various stories about him propagated by the other characters in the novel: he is uniquely elevated at the center of a labyrinth that is strictly fabulous, a maze of "lying" legends. But if he is thus a kind of constructed fetish himself, his fictive throne is insubstantial, no less "rickety" (190) than the chair which supports the grotesque effigy. The "unreliable" chair in the mission is an image with a surprising resonance. Like the superior, it will turn up in the novel again.

The most influential and certainly the most amusing of Querry's various hagiographers is Montagu Parkinson. A foreign correspondent for an English newspaper, Parkinson represents the greatest threat of all to the peace and relative anonymity that Querry has managed to find in Africa: he insists on resurrecting "*the* Querry" for the whole world to consider. This fraudulent cynic with a nose for profitable news has a long ancestry in Greene's fiction, but the significant fact about him in *A Burnt-Out Case* is that he is explicitly perceived as another of the protagonist's doppelgängers. From the moment of Parkinson's arrival at the leproserie, Querry recognizes him as a kind of personal counterpart. He arrives as a cabin passenger on the very boat that brought Querry, and his first appearance induces a displaced déjà vu sensation: "in the rumpled bed which Querry had somehow imagined would still bear, like a hare's form, his own impression, lay the naked body of a very fat man" (122). When they meet, Querry says: "you are a man like me" (138) and "we are two of a kind" (139). Later, he tells him, "I have been waiting for you, Parkinson, or someone like you. Not that I didn't fear you too" (146). By way of explanation, he adds: "You are my looking-glass. I can talk to a looking-glass, but one can be a little afraid of one too. It returns such a straight image" (146). What Querry has in mind, of course, is the notion that the journalist is another burnt-out case, but there is nevertheless something almost comically anomalous in his conception of this "mountain of flesh" (138) as his double. Greene is invoking a type of mirror relationship here that derives again from the novel's affinities with *Heart of Darkness*. Parkinson actually alludes to it himself in one of his absurd articles: "What is it that has induced the great Querry to abandon a career that brought him honour and riches to give up his life to serving the world's untouchables? I was in no position to ask him that when suddenly I found that my quest had ended. Unconscious and burning with fever, I was carried on shore from my pirogue, the frail bark in which I had penetrated what Joseph Conrad called the Heart of Darkness" (171). If Parkinson is his own fantastic version of Marlow now, then Querry becomes *his* Kurtz. Unlike the original Marlow, however, this chronicler ignores his subject's expressions of horror, converting him instead into the rather banal hero of yet another sentimental romance. Rycker and Father Thomas have made Querry into a fetish; it is Parkinson who completes the story by tidying it up and publishing it.

The story itself is highly conventional, about a man whose legendary sexual and creative achievements become transformed into a sort of spiritual prowess. In it, Querry is turned from a subject of envious gossip into an object of veneration, but the transformation really serves to clarify rather than to diminish his fictive status as a man of power; his appeal as a fertility figure is at once broadened and more sharply focused by it. Stories with this type of structure, however, are all apt to end in the same way: fertility gods are only fertility gods by virtue of being, at least implicitly, sacrificial victims as well. Even Parkinson begins to recognize that the shape his dispatches are taking implies a sequel with another kind of transformation: "I told you I was going to build you up, Querry. Unless, of course, as now seems likely, I find it makes a better story if I pull you down" (215). Parkinson is talking here about two distinct types of story that form the two halves of a single archetypal cycle, a continuous narrative "turning" or transformation which, considered dialectically, expresses the idea of transfiguration.

This kind of narrative cycle is what Doctor Colin might describe as a myth. "Sometimes," he says, "I think that the search for suffering and the remembrance of suffering are the only means we have to put ourselves in touch with the whole human condition. With suffering we become part of the Christian myth" (157). In order to come to life, Querry must first recover the power of feeling, which in this novel means the capacity for feeling pain: he must in a sense be capable of genuinely dying before he can be genuinely reborn. The prolepsis of death in the novel's antinarrative and the narrative prolepsis of rebirth belong to the same archetypal cycle. They are complementary parts of the same myth, and Querry is unwillingly cast as the divinity at its center, the immobilized cipher king who is doomed to suffer and die. But the real significance of the myth, like that of the fetish in the jungle, is the triumph of life, for the king redeems his kingdom with his death: the ultimate meaning of the Christian story is the resurrection of Christ.

Querry may be said to combine something of the roles of both father and son in *The Potting Shed*. He is an aging, impotent man who also acts as the heroic rescuer not only of Deo Gratias but of Marie Rycker. He carries Marie off like Perseus, though not, as she would wish, to marry her. Querry does at last what everyone else in the novel seems always to have done: he makes up a story. The narrative which eventually puts Marie to sleep in the hotel room in Luc is a surprise in several respects, not the least of which is that it is coolly, almost disinterestedly, autobiographical; up to now, Querry's infrequent attempts to account for himself have either been incoherent, owing to his distrust of speech, or, as in the case of his poisonous "outbreak" (158) to Parkinson, distorted by his own self-hatred. It is unexpected as well because it takes the form of a parody romance. Querry's intention is of course ironic, but since this is his longest single discourse in the novel, the structure of the fairy tale may be worth considering in some detail.

The most notable formal feature of the story is that it lacks a conclusion. Marie never learns what happens "in the end," as the customary phrase goes, to the "boy" (196) who becomes "a famous jeweller" (197). She does interrupt from time to time with some pertinent critical questions and comments: "When are you going to reach a climax? Has it a happy ending? I don't want to stay awake otherwise. Why don't you describe some of the women?" (199). But Querry is a dilatory narrator. If others tell stories about him that are characterized by purposeful action and achievement, the story he tells about himself is full of failed quests and dead ends. From one point of view, its ironies would seem simply to be underlined by the conspicuously romantic character of the fairy-tale context. In the larger context of the novel itself, however, what the shape of the story tends to suggest is that the narrator has some grasp of the formal principles of that mode of romance which focuses on the suspension of events rather than on their fulfillment. In its structure, Querry's story is not unlike a television soap opera: there is a good deal in the way of dramatic incident in it, though not much in the way of narrative *telos* or resolution, and it gives the effect of going on indefinitely. While Querry's immediate purpose is to calm Marie Rycker down and to suggest that her own life is not at the decisive watershed she imagines, the deliberate inconclusiveness of his open-ended parable points to a design of a different order.

Like the novel which contains it, Querry's story has both narrative and antinarrative dimensions. It is the episodic history of a man's growing disillusionment, and at the same time it reveals that this minimal sense of a process of "development" is itself an illusion. The account of the jeweler's art is neatly emblematic of the whole fictional procedure: "He made one gold jewel in the shape of an ostrich-egg: it was all enamel and gold and when you opened it you found inside a little gold figure sitting at a table and a little gold and enamel egg on the table, and when you opened that there was a little figure sitting at a table and a little gold and enamel egg and when you opened that . . . I needn't go on" (200). But Querry does go on. He proceeds to relate a story about, among other things, story making: this receding perspective of eggs-within-eggs-within-eggs constitutes the essential figurative pattern of all narratives, he is arguing, because it reflects the only possible view of human life that seems formally intelligible. All attempts to go "deeper" or "further in" lead back to the same place, and metaphors having to do with the exploration of labyrinths modulate inevitably into a fatalistic vision of perpetual recurrence and repetition. This is the vision of Robert Graves's "Warning to Children," in which the business of growing up is revealed in terms directly antithetical to those of growth or upward expansion, becoming instead a continuous process of deepening entombment, of being trapped within an indefinitely receding perspective of attractive "prospects" which turn out on exploration to be identically narrow cages. The "husky fruit" on the island tree in Graves's poem[32] is of course an ironic symbol of natural renewal, and the golden egg of Querry's story functions as an even more explicit embryo image of the same kind. But the jeweler is an artist, and his seed images are ironic emblems of resurrection as well as rebirth: "On the top of each egg there was a golden cross set with chips of precious stones in honour of the King. The trouble was that he wore himself out with the ingenuity of his design, and suddenly when he was making the contents of the final egg with an optic glass—that was what they called magnifying glasses in the old days in which this story is set, for of course it contains no reference to our time and no likeness to any living character" (200). Querry now loses the thread of his narrative for a time—he does cease, briefly, to "go on"—but as we are returned to the context of the larger "containing" story it becomes clear that his silence about the final egg expresses something more important in relation both to the outer story and to the one he is telling than merely the sort of temporary authorial bemusement induced by whisky. Within this narrative silence, a genuine resurrection of a kind is in fact taking place.

Earlier, when Marie objects to Querry's jeweler and his king by saying that she does not much like parables, or his hero either, Querry responds: "He doesn't like himself much, and that's why he's never spoken before—except in this way" (199). The narrator "is" himself the hero, in other words, and the parable his own "story." Again, there is that curious sense in which we feel that Querry somehow exists simultaneously in both the third and the first persons: his life is at once past and present; it is as if Querry's subjective reality can emerge only in terms of a kind of a priori self-annihilation, as if his "I" can come to life only by virtue of being objectified "in this way" as "he." And this sense amounts in this particular novel to the virtual transfiguration of a commonplace about the psychology of creativity. As Querry falls silent after his account of the nest of artificial Easter eggs, we are told that "he couldn't remember how long it was since he had experienced the odd elation he was feeling now" (200). In the context of the novel's rhythm of proleptic revival, his elation marks an awakening that goes beyond the occasional "rictus" of a smile or laugh: "It was, he began to think, a sad story, so that it was hard to understand this sense of freedom and release, like that of a prisoner who at last 'comes clean,' admitting every-thing to his inquisitor. Was this the reward perhaps which came sometimes to a writer? 'I have told you all: you can hang me now' " (201).

The passage echoes Thomas Fowler's sense of what *his* story amounts to at the end of *The Quiet American*. The story of Querry is "sad" because it is about failure and betrayal, but there is an access of new life for him in the act of telling it; and the rhetorical question about the writer's "reward" effectively re-minds us of the extent to which the confessional narrative form is increasingly conceived by Greene in romantic terms. The "un-finished" design of the protagonist's tale of himself as a burnt-out case is what makes it a romance: to tell an incomplete story may be to emerge from it, to complete it by recovering the identity that has been lost or petrified in it. All this is implicit in the nar-rator's first silence. And the silence that later descends when Querry breaks off his parable for the last time is genuinely epi-phanic. "I wish you'd told me a romantic story" (205), Marie complains before falling asleep; the whisky has run out and so has the narrative. The king of the story is dead so far as the jeweler is concerned, but the sun outside the window suddenly rises and there is an apocalyptic explosion of light which now transforms the closed ironic significance of the final egg. Querry is abruptly aware of nothing but renewal: "He sat on his bed and the light grew around him—it was the hour of coolness. He thought: the King is dead, long live the King. Perhaps he had found here a country and a life" (205). Besides being a distant star, the king is also, of course, incarnate in Querry's hero, and the total form of the cycle which underlies the novel's intimations of death and its intimations of rebirth is all at once illuminated.

Querry's sad but subtle tale is no less a romance in the telling than Parkinson's trite and mindless one. As a legend about creative power and aridity, it seems more plausible than Father Thomas's; as a fable about sexuality and the pride of life, it seems more realistic than Marie Rycker's; but, viewed in its frame, it presents the same kind of picture as both. The meaning of this novel is not separable from its structure, the receding, "double" perspective of story-within-story, archetype-within-parody. Querry's parable seems unromantic to Marie because her own perspective is limited by her role as a character in the framing plot; she cannot read Querry's silences. But the parable about a fall is, proleptically, about rising as well. If the looking-glass perspective reveals all places as the same place, then it reveals a corresponding "identity" of narrative forms. Within this kind of structure, all stories are the same kind of story. Even the villain reads *The Imitation of Christ*. In other words, there is an emerging narrative logic—what the superior finally refers to as "the pattern" (255)—which insists that Querry must actually die and that the story of his death must parody the story of the Passion. Indeed, his death has as much ritual inevitability about it as one could wish for. Before he is shot, a cycle ends and the order of things changes when Querry allows Rycker, ironically, to depose him as "God's important man" (251); there is even a sort of mock coronation just prior to the murder scene in which Rycker sits down heavily on the mission's "unreliable" chair and splinters "the weak back" (244).

It is impossible to say, though, whether all this is comedy or tragedy: the entire affair, as Father Jean remarks, seems "a little like one of those Palais Royal farces" (245); Querry dies laughing; the superior speaks in the final chapter of "a happy ending" (254). The climactic event is not tragic or comic but "absurd." This last word of Querry's might be said to refer not only to the manner of his death but also to the logic of the kind of "pattern" that culminates in this way. The ending of the novel is absurd in the way that all closure is more or less absurd. But unlike phenomenological absurdity, which derives from a breakdown or suspension of meaning, the absurdity of the narrative ending has to do with the fact that it constitutes the completion of a conscious design and thus has an informing significance. There is a genuinely creative absurdity implicit in narration itself, a dimension of storytelling that is endlessly and inescapably romantic. Querry's parable about the jeweler and the king may be ironic in intention, an antinarrative, but its ironies are ultimately turned upside down by the very act of narration, even if it is completed in silence. Querry's death is absurd because the story of Querry is ultimately a romance, completed in the same silence: " 'Absurd,' " he says, " 'this is absurd or else' . . . but what alternative, philosophical or psychological, he had in mind they never knew" (251–52). The point is not simply that he must die but that he must die in order to be reborn.

Like so many of Greene's earlier heroes, Querry is a Christ figure, but he is quite different in this respect, clearly, from protagonists like the whisky priest or Henry Scobie or even Pinkie in *Brighton Rock*. What distinguishes him at one level is his fictive emptiness, his role as a narrative cipher. Querry lacks belief or faith, even a faith, like Pinkie's, in the power of evil. He is a man who has lost himself, like Conrad's Kurtz, and he retains a certain hollowness of character almost to the very end. As a type of Christ, then, he may fairly be described as "ironic." But the absurdity of his position is also romantic, which means in this case that there is a peculiar resonance in the very silence of his hollowness. Without wanting to be, Querry finds himself involved in the narrative unfolding of a myth; but we feel that he is "unrealized" in the sense that his suspended existence in the novel always seems somehow embryonic, as if he is always waiting, without knowing that that is what he is doing, to be born. If we consider *A Burnt-Out Case* by standing back from it, to invoke the analogy of narratives and paintings once again, we find that the implications of the metaphor in the novel's title are reversed by the perspective of distance and that the shape of the story has something in common with the structure of one of Shakespeare's last plays: paradoxically, this novel about a flight into tropical Africa looks like a winter's tale; it is a story about a man who becomes a kind of frozen statue and it is also a story about the statue coming back to life again. Querry's "rictus" of laughter suggests the proleptic awakening of a corpse. What his death really implies is his resurrection. In other words, he is a Christ figure in the context of a perspective which reveals the story of God's Incarnation and Passion as a romance rather than as a tragedy. And the view from this distance suggests that Querry's redemption, as it is actually experienced by him, is best described as the type of revival that amounts to an instant of genuine self-recognition, the relief of a man who awakens from a nightmare and realizes, briefly, who he is. Querry is enveloped, as it were, in a myth of revival as a dreamer is enclosed by his dream or a fetus by the womb.

His preoccupations are ontological from the outset because his identity is the central thematic issue of the novel. The doubling technique which suggests that the action of the story is taking place in a mirror world becomes definitive of his loss and confusion, his numb sense of the endless dispersal of himself. This type of protagonist poses certain technical difficulties for the novelist, of course, not the least of which is that a hero who is nothing more than a cipher becomes a fictional as well as a real impossibility: a literally petrified or "hollow" or unborn man has no recognizably human existence of any kind. Querry's initial claims that he is unable to feel anything are obviously figurative, tokens of his metaphysical status as a symbolic corpse or phantom. But even a metaphorical cipher presents another problem: to a man who is "burnt-out," nothing further of any interest to him can really happen. He can, and in this case does, revive, but there is no realistic way of demonstrating his revival without implying that his near-catatonic and schizoid consciousness represents merely a kind of transient pathological state. But Greene means us to take Querry's claims about the disappearance of himself more seriously. He meets the difficulty with a strategy that might be strictly defined as poetic, the dramatization of the protagonist's loss of identity by means of a structure of archetypal imagery which locates what might otherwise seem to be only a psychological "problem" in the context of a cyclical romantic quest.

To recapitulate: the imagery of drifting seeds, which modulate into cells or cages, and the imagery of burial, which modulates into the condition of being lost in a labyrinth, define the process of descent and death; the cycle of ascent and recovery is translated into the terms of growth and escape and the vision of the labyrinth as an intelligible design. The apparently centrifugal drift of the antinarrative becomes transformed in narrative terms into the centripetal rhythm of implantation and the renewal of life. At the center of this fictive structure sits a dying and reborn king who presides over the buried life of a vegetable kingdom; nearby stands a cage which also appears to be a tower, a construct that could symbolize either confinement and suffering or genuine vision and understanding. The outlines of the mythic pattern are clear enough. Everything that happens in the novel is assimilated to it, including the dreadfulness of leprosy: the leper is the kind of literal outcast that Querry has figuratively become, a person who must experience numbness and the mutilation of himself in order to be "cured" or redeemed. In symbolic terms, leprosy is mortality, the condition in which living becomes indistinguishable from dying; even the jungle, where decay and growth appear to amount to the same thing, seems leprous. Querry's redemption derives, in other words, from the mythic structure of the "story" in which he is caught up, just as it is arguable that Conrad's Kurtz is redeemed by Marlow's story about him. And language itself is redeemed for Querry by virtue of his discovery of its redemptive powers: Querry "betrays" Rycker and "rescues" his wife not by seducing her but by telling her a fairy tale. It is almost as if the new life that Marie carries inside herself were engendered by the word rather than by the corrupt flesh.

A Burnt-Out Case is poetic in the sense that it is a fiction which bears some resemblance to a long and rather self-conscious poem. This self-consciousness has to do with the fact that the structures of imagery in it tend to call attention to themselves as structures, rather in the way that the account of the jeweler's Easter eggs calls attention to the shape of the story about him: the novel has the same quality of conspicuous fictiveness as *The Potting Shed*. We have already glimpsed something like it in the confessional story-within-story patterns of *The End of the Affair* and *The Quiet American*—Sarah's diary within Bendrix's narrative and the story of Fowler's guilt within his story about Pyle's suicidal folly—but this particular obsession with the structurally centripetal tendencies of fiction is otherwise a new phenomenon in Greene's work.

As a phenomenon, it precisely reflects the shift from ironic and tragic modes to the formal dominance of romance. For romance tends to present a world that seems absurd because it is purely artificial, a verbal universe that is structurally self-contained and self-referential. Yet this absurdity is also the projection of a vision of identity: a world in which everything is an archetype because everything is an image of everything else that exists there, so that the significance of each image, rather than deriving from any external reality, becomes an exclusively verbal matter of endless echo and allusion. The powerful attractions of romance are based on the compulsive logic that lies behind the centripetal symmetry. Greene is not so much intrigued by receding story-within-story perspectives for their own sake as he is compelled by the implications of the vision which underlies the design. He begins as a novelist with a sense of reality that is clearly, though unspecifiably, religious; this later becomes an explicit if slightly cranky Catholic Christianity, a view of life focused tragically on the story of Christ's crucifixion. The later novels would seem to represent a departure from it because the element of comedy suddenly assumes a new prominence and all the vexed doctrinal questions either recede or disappear. In fact, though, Greene's sense of reality remains as religious as ever. What has changed is his perspective: as the focus of his Christian vision shifts from the Crucifixion to the Resurrection, his "reality" becomes a place characterized by nothing so much as fictiveness. Calvary becomes the central *topos* in a story within a story within a story— and so on, a receding perspective of eggs and crosses. What the imaginative centrality of the myth of the Resurrection implies, in other words, is quite simply a vision of perpetual imaginative rebirth. Meaning is identical with structure in *A Burnt-Out Case* in the sense that the kind of renewal of identity which is the novel's theme becomes the kind of transformation which is inherent in its narrative procedure.

As a work of art, the jeweler's nest of golden eggs is meant to be a type of practical joke. The story about the man who makes it is also a joke, but of a different type. The two jokes share a principle of absurdity that is based on a principle of artificial recurrence and deferral of meaning. The difference between them has to do with perspective. From the tragic point of view, comedy must be irony, a form of dark escapism; from the point of view of romance, it is epiphany, a form of dawning recognition or understanding. In this novel, the ironic joke is contained and comprehended by the romantic one. The exuberant artifice of romance is the more genuinely creative form of absurdity to the extent that the principle of recurrence and deferral on which it is based is the more intelligible. When Greene speaks of having discovered "Comedy" he is talking about the kind of playfulness that is resonant of revival. It becomes the norm in his fiction now because the "escapism" associated with comedy tends also to be the very narrative "dilation" that is not only the deferral of an end but the germination of a new beginning.

FOUR

A Sense of Reality

This is an underground fate we suffer from here,
and that was a garden fate—but it all comes to
the same fate in the end. —"Under the Garden"

To the extent that fictional narration may be said to be an inherently romantic enterprise, the device of the subsidiary story that is contained within a central framing story tends to become a romance archetype in its own right. In other words, what strikes us most forcibly about this kind of formal device is not so much that a central narrative sequence has been interrupted as that the conspicuous fictiveness which characterizes the interruption signals a shift in structural arrangement from a linear to a more vertical design, a modulation of the narrative rhythm from a sequential order to a symbolic one. The convention of the pastoral interlude in heroic romance provides the clearest illustration of the principle. Typically, an inset pastoral story seems deliberately unrelated at first glance to the main heroic action, and the sense of the contrast between the two modes underlines the element of artifice in pastoral; at the same time, the usual function of such an inset fiction is both to offer a reversed or oblique image of some important motif in the main action and, in so doing, to provide a crucial new perspective on the less artificial world "outside" the interlude. Paradoxically, therefore, the subsidiary story has a kind of interpretive or shaping power over the narrative which contains it. The reason why the pastoral world belongs to heroic romance is that it is, almost by definition, a designedly fictive place. And the same principle applies in more obviously realistic contexts as well: Graham Greene's much-discussed use of dreams, for instance, has to do with the shaping or configurative dimension of the dream in the typical structure of his narrative; in this sense, his accounts of his characters' unconscious fantasies tend formally to constitute his own characteristic version of romantic pastoral. Any story within a story invariably has a way of signifying a degree of generic shift, however slight, away from the naturalistic and in the direction of the fabulous.

We have seen that the plot of *A Burnt-Out Case* hinges largely on the shape of the kind of fantasy dreamed up about Querry by the other characters; the total structure of the novel is really based on what happens when the stories that other people tell about him are perceived to intersect, as it were, with the story that Querry finally tells about himself. This may be only an elaborate way of saying that Querry becomes both a sacrificial victim and a reborn "king" because Greene's conception of fiction is one in which every story echoes or reflects an implicit framing story or myth about the inevitability of human sacrifice and redemption. But it does seem to be true that Greene has become increasingly interested during the latter stages of his career in the idea of narrative as a romance archetype in itself. He has recently complained about a "general refusal to grasp the importance of fantasy in my books,"[1] and it is probably fair to say that such a refusal stems from a persistent critical habit of continuing to read him, in strictly realistic terms, as the ironist or Christian tragedian that he appeared to be in the 1930s and 1940s.

The "entertainment" that immediately preceded *A Burnt-Out Case* is an instructive case in point. Philip Stratford has noted that *Our Man in Havana* (1958) is "a fiction about fiction-making."[2] This perceptive remark may be regarded as referring to the way in which that novel is a satire on the sort of paranoid scheming and plotting that characterizes geopolitical relations in general and the world of espionage in particular; it certainly offers a clue of a rather different kind to what Greene has in mind when he describes *Our Man in Havana* as a fairy story. The inset narrative here consists of the hero's ingeniously absurd reports about what appear to be mysterious military installations in the Cuban mountains, huge imaginary constructions actually modeled on a type of vacuum cleaner that he happens to sell for a living. As he devises his fiction, James Wormold sees himself, naturally enough, in the role of novelist, and his cast of characters is partly invented, partly based on the membership list of an exclusive Havana country club. At the outset, Wormold is presented in comic terms as something of a burnt-out case himself, a man trapped in the mechanical routines of a dull existence who views his real life as something locked away in his past. When, however, his imaginative exercises on behalf of the British Secret Service increasingly inspire him to more elaborate variations on the theme of his basic scenario, he recovers through them a vitality and sense of purpose that had seemed lost to him forever. The trouble with his story, of course, is that it inevitably has a devastating effect on the world in which he sets it: he revives from a state of figurative death only to find that he is at once plunged into the darkly romantic country of lurid and violent espionage fiction. Innocent people in the "real" world are threatened and even killed because of Wormold's fantasy narrative; his only friend, Doctor Hasselbacher, is brutally murdered; and an attempt is made on his own life. The framing story is quite literally shaped by the more "artificial" one inside it. From one point of view, the novel becomes yet another tale about a victim hunt, a moral fable that seems to point in a rather transparent way to the dangerous inadequacy of the romancer's perspective when it is brought to bear on the political complexities of life in the twentieth century. In that sense it is, like *The Quiet American,* a fiction about fiction making as a form of destructive meddling with what we call the real world.

But this view can also be regarded as significantly incomplete. In the novel of which he is the hero, Wormold inadvertently creates about himself a type of romantic inferno; yet the hypotheses on which his fiction is based are essentially no different as interpretations of reality from those to which virtually everybody habitually accedes: farfetched as his story may seem, the point here is that his political masters in London (like nearly everyone else) believe in it. If this were all there were to the novel, then it would be merely a species of parody romance, a satirical meditation on the nature of illusion. However, Wormold's journey into the realm of adventure fiction is not by any means over: he avenges Doctor Hasselbacher's death and his comic inferno is gradually transformed into a personal purgatorio, out of which he is eventually conducted toward a more genuine sense of his own identity by a lady named, evocatively, Beatrice.

This rather bald summary of *Our Man in Havana* may perhaps serve to indicate not only the extent of Greene's growing preoccupation with stories within stories, but also the way in which the configurative resonance of an inset story suggests to him a parallel hypothesis about the relationship between all fiction making and reality. *Our Man in Havana* is a fairy tale not just because it is a novelist's *jeu d'esprit* or even because it alludes faintly and indirectly to the structure of Dante's epic romance, but ultimately because it takes seriously the human tendency to interpret the world by the act of fictionalizing it. There is something important as well as absurd, as *A Burnt-Out Case* attests, in the activity of making narratives out of that which is manifestly not a narrative. Wormold's fantasies may be regarded as a prelude to the kind of thing that is so strongly, if inarticulately, deplored by Querry: the fact that people seem absurdly compelled to concoct stories. To the extent that all such narratives are romance archetypes, so Querry's objection implicitly goes, then all stories are nothing but idle romancing. But the hero of *A Burnt-Out Case* ends by devising a story of his own, and what the structure of the novel of 1961 suggests about the "entertainment" of 1958 is that the tendency to fictionalize the world offers a form of access to it that is potentially more significant and revealing than any other. The central narrative archetype in both novels is much the same: the protagonist gets lost in a world at the bottom of which, so to speak, he finds the basic feature of its reality to be an endless process of victimization, a process in which he is obliged to recognize his own complicity. In both cases, though, this recognition modulates into a perception of the process as one of deliberate ritual sacrifice, a narrative interpretation of events which turns the directionless wandering of the hero into a quest that ends with revival and recovery.

There seems, in other words, to be a kind of subtext in these two novels that might be formulated roughly as follows: if reality is what we make of it, then what we do characteristically make of it is narrative. In Greene's next book, this notion becomes the central theme. *A Sense of Reality,* published in both England and the United States in 1963, is not so much about reality, in fact, as about myth and dream. The organizing thematic principle in this sequence of four stories is that reality becomes intelligible only to the extent that it yields to some more-or-less coherent narrative view of it. Critics have generally failed to notice the centrality of the theme, preferring to comment instead on what they have usually regarded as the anomalous novelty of Greene's "experiments with fantasy." But romancing is quite specifically the subject as well as the method of each of these stories, and Greene's attitude to it is entirely consistent with his treatment of fantasy within his standard operative framework of narrative realism: private dreams have an extraordinary configurative resonance in the familiar world of alienated or unimaginative consciousness because they are the definitive human or imaginative versions of that world. For Greene, dreams are always in some sense the narrative animations of a reality that normally appears to be in a state of petrified suspension. This is a peculiarly romantic view of fantasy, and given the direction of his development during the preceding decade, there is nothing particularly experimental about its invocation in *A Sense of Reality.*

The hero of "Under the Garden," for example, is a mortally ill and disillusioned man of the world who searches in his childhood for an elusive, half-remembered "dream" or "game" or "legend" or "story"[3] that might make sense of an existence which now appears meaningless to him; approaching the actuality of death, William Wilditch seeks his own figurative kingdom of dream and death, the narrative archetype at the center of his life. "A Visit to Morin" deals with an exploration of a similar kind, although this time it is dramatized as a search for religious belief, something that had clearly become a problematic issue for Greene.[4] The narrator, who has idolized Morin since boyhood, evidently hopes that his meeting with the famous "religious" novelist will provide some sort of metaphysical illumination or certainty. What he actually gets is Morin's flat assertion that he no longer believes in

God. The story is constructed around the type of paradox that apparently characterizes Morin's own fiction: the novelist has lost his belief in God but retains his faith in the church. In fact, his faith in Catholicism is offered as the justification for his disbelief. The teachings and rituals of the church add up for him to a kind of cautionary tale: if a man avoids the sources of divine grace, then his belief will wither. This is exactly what has happened to Morin; involved in sin, he has stayed away from confession and communion, and belief has indeed died. But his very disbelief then becomes, in the most literal way, a sign of his faith in what might be termed the church's "story." As theology, this seems all very dubious and casuistical, but the point is that Morin's way of dealing with the emptiness of a real situation is to interpret it by means of a narrative structure that gives it meaning. It is important to notice that Greene carefully distinguishes here between belief and faith: if "belief" has to do with our attitude toward the data of real experience, "faith" refers to our attitude to myths and stories. Morin's view of Christianity is not so far removed from Doctor Colin's in *A Burnt-Out Case.* Faith, like Coleridge's "suspension of disbelief," seems to be the characteristic response of the imagination, and the structures of the imagination are now given a certain priority over those of ideology.

Greene seems to be arguing not only that the imaginative response is essentially different from the activity of giving or withholding credence but that it might in fact be dangerous to confuse the two. The leper in the third story, "Dream of a Strange Land," is destroyed because he takes to be reality what is actually a narrative illusion. The inset "story" here is the elaborate enacted fantasy in which the Swedish estate of an eminent leprologist is briefly transformed, in order to gratify the whim of a senile general, from its snowbound desolation into a Monte Carlo casino. For Greene, every fiction is a story about a victim and a betrayer, and from the outset of "Dream of a Strange Land" these two roles are evidently to be filled by the leper and the leprologist. The leper kills himself when he returns to the professor's house because he believes that he has somehow become hopelessly "lost" in a "strange" country. This is the *mise-en-scène* of the oddly sinister charade about the gambling casino, which appears to damn him by excluding him from it. But the ultimate revelation of "Dream of a Strange Land" is that the betrayer of the story is perceived as lost too: the inset narrative turns the leprologist into the same kind of stranger and victim as his patient, so that each becomes the mirror image or double of the other. In other words, as *Our Man in Havana* would tend to suggest, the shaping power of fantasy is inevitably destructive whenever people begin actually to "believe" in it. And credulousness of this kind seems, paradoxically, to be a function of age or experience rather than of innocence. Faith, in Morin's sense, belongs more characteristically to the perspective of the child. Wilditch's "dream" (or "game" or "legend" or "story") functions creatively because it is apprehended as myth rather than as reality—because Wilditch responds to it with the suspended disbelief of childhood rather than the credulity of adulthood. In this kind of context an excess of artistic "realism" might even be dangerous: perhaps the most sinister feature of the casino illusion is its peculiar trompe l'oeil effect.

The "innocent" character of the response of faith is exemplified allegorically in the last story in *A Sense of Reality*. "A Discovery in the Woods" is about some dwarflike children who belong to what is gradually revealed to be the world as it might eventually look after a nuclear holocaust. The story is also about the story which they devise in order to account for their discovery of the wreck of an apparently fabulous ship on a mountainside. The ship becomes the ark of Old Noh, a folk echo of the biblical Noah, who has evidently assumed a status of legendary primacy in this disaster-stricken world. Evidence of a real catastrophe is translated into the terms of the authoritative myth of the children's primitive tribal society, the conflation of a dim memory of a deluge fable with a story about a vanished race of giants. The impenetrable mystery of the actual ship yields to a fiction about an ark and a lost golden age, and even from the reader's putatively more sophisticated perspective, the story fits: the terror implicit in an inexplicable "real" phenomenon is both distanced and as it were prophesied by the interpretive force of the narrative archetype which seems most appropriate to it, so that the framing tale can hardly be distinguished from the one that is framed. The children's "sense of reality" is in fact the energy of a more innocent social imagination, a way of looking at the world from a mythic perspective that the maturer reader, it is ironically implied, has all but lost.

This last irony includes the suggestion that it was the very diminution of that kind of imaginative energy that brought about the terrible flood in which the ship foundered in the first place. There is a structural circularity about each of these stories: the technique of closure in each case involves a revelation of the type that returns us from the end to the beginning. And there is a corresponding circularity about the sequence as a whole. The young William Wilditch's adventure beneath the garden is prefaced by his discovery on the wall of a cave of some writing in which the only intelligible word appears to be "fish." Near the end of "A Discovery in the Woods" the children find a "design" on the bridge of the wrecked ship that is clearly the word "France"; while this design is literally meaningless to them, it is evocative and powerful as well, a sort of rune that may be "a clue to the time of legends" (138). To the reader, whose response is at a different level, it seems to be only an ordinary proper noun denoting nothing more than perhaps the ship's country of origin; but at the same time, in the context of the whole sequence of stories, the effect of the final rune is to evoke the earlier one: it functions as a revelation about the imaginative primacy of an enigmatic "first" word within a sequential structure of words. The recurrence of the image of the mysterious rune suggests a kind of quintessential romance archetype, a central fictive "word" which amounts to both alpha and omega at the heart of a larger narrative "code." The last story points back, as it were, to the first, because "Under the Garden" is the sequence's definitive story about looking for and finding the definitive story: the other fictions in *A Sense of Reality* are framed or structurally comprehended by it.

If our sense of reality is predominantly fictive, then the important question inevitably becomes: what kind of fiction is it that we make of the world? The answer in the present context seems to lie in the story recollected and reexplored by William Wilditch, a dream about a descent into a lower world and an emergence out of it. However, Greene now devises a slightly different version of an otherwise familiar narrative structure. In his search beneath the garden, not only is the young Wilditch defying an authoritative maternal figure who (like Mrs. Callifer in another tale about a quest under a childhood garden) disapproves of "fairy-stories" (23), but he is also looking for a father. Like the motif of descent and recovery, the theme of the search for the true father seems to belong almost generically to the mode of romance. The central reality of life for the older Wilditch is his own imminent disappearance from it; but that impending catastrophe is not in itself the principle of closure informing his own "sense" of personal reality. Death is not the important mystery for him. The essential mystery surrounding any romantic hero—and Wilditch is nothing if not the hero of his own story—is "much more likely," as Northrop Frye puts it, "to have been a mystery of how he got into the world than of how he disappeared from it."[5] The whole idea of a first and last narrative "word," that is to say, seems intricately bound up with the romance theme of progeniture: what it symbolizes is the mystery of identity, and the hero's quest becomes in a sense the search for his own genuine or original or proper name.

From one kind of perspective, "Under the Garden" could be regarded as a supremely daft fiction about a dying man who learns that he has spent his life looking for a woman whose photograph he once imagined that he saw in a newspaper story about a beauty contest, a woman known to him only by the appellation "Miss Ramsgate." But "Under the Garden" is of course a fairy tale; the glimpse of the woman pertains to the romance convention of the dream vision, and the absurd triviality of her name has more to do with what it conceals about her than what it reveals: her genuine identity is too "powerful," as Javitt would put it, to be translated into utterance. For this is a story much concerned with names and displaced identities. Its theme from the beginning is in fact the displacement of the identity of its hero.

Like Querry, William Wilditch is an aging man who has become radically estranged not just from the world in which he lives but from his own personal existence. Although the prevailing tone of "Under the Garden" is altogether lighter and more fanciful than that of *A Burnt-Out Case,* it seems nevertheless to be a story about a man suffering from a similar sort of dislocation of self: the imminent reality of death mirrors an a priori process of ontological petrification. So "Under the Garden" begins as another third-person fiction whose protagonist seems eminently suited, so to speak, to its narrative perspective; during the episodes dealing with the diagnosis of his cancer, it is as if Wilditch had lost possession even of his own body: his subjective sense of himself is overridden by its being transformed into the impersonal terms of a medical problem. And because his identity is suddenly imperiled, figuratively as well as literally, Wilditch's whole life is cast into doubt.

When he returns to the house where the summers of his childhood were spent, it becomes clear that he wants to find not merely some way of coming to terms with his past; he wants also to find the very William Wilditch who has somehow vanished. From his own viewpoint, the real mystery of "Under the Garden" is the mystery of the "real" Wilditch. He has not much more to go on than a vague conviction that the restlessness of his life appears to have been based, unspecifiably, on "what might lie underneath the garden" (16) at Winton Hall. The subject of the story seems at first to be his search for some decisive seminal event in his childhood, his attempt at a kind of psychoanalytic recovery of something deeply repressed in his private history. In a sense, of course, it is; we soon learn, though, that what in fact lies "buried" under the garden is not so much an actual as a fictive event.

The trouble with Wilditch's life is that it seems purposeless to him in the special sense that it lacks narrative significance: he has lost what might be termed the narrative thread of it. Wilditch is a displaced person precisely because his history as a rootless wanderer is the displaced version of some more meaningful account of errancy and exploration concealed inside it—"his dream, his game, whatever it was" (18). He is looking, in other words, for an inset story, for nothing less, as it happens, than the fictive archetype that has shaped his life. The "real" Wilditch turns out to be a dreaming child, and his dream is perceived as a type of narrative epiphany of which his actual life has turned into an aimless parody. The subject of the story becomes a form of exploration which reverses the usual direction of the process that Frye would call realistic displacement. It is about an attempt to recover the myth that informs a reality: in Christian terms, the narrative revelation of a word hidden within a word. The absurdity of "Under the Garden" in any realistic perspective actually stems from the fact that the story also amounts to a literary joke about realism: it turns certain habitual assumptions about the relationship between fiction and reality inside out.[6]

The young Wilditch's secretiveness about his "experience" under the garden is linked to his fear of his mother. Her hostility toward any form of imaginative exploration and her commitment to a narrowly empirical rationalism place her clearly on the side of what Morin would describe as "belief" rather than "faith." To the extent that Mrs. Wilditch could be said to have had anything like an imaginative sense of the world, her faith seems to have been in records of accumulated facts, the social scientist's text of statistics and graphs. She was evidently a realist, but her realism was just as evidently marked by an odd hysteria: professing a hatred of mystery, Mrs. Wilditch seems to have taken an approach to reality which actually expressed, in the context of the central theme of this sequence of stories, a predilection for certain forms of arcane concealment. Leafing through her heavily annotated copy of Beatrice Webb's *My Apprenticeship,* the older Wilditch is struck by the opaque dullness of the sort of narrative that is organized around endless catalogues of arithmetical abstractions: "Perhaps because his own life was coming to an end, he thought how little of this, in the almost impossible event of a future, she would have carried with her. A fairy-story in such an event would be a more valuable asset than a Fabian graph, but his mother had not approved of fairy-stories" (23). While this might appear to indicate a wholesome preference for truth over lying, the sheer turbidity of the view of life typified by auto-biographical books filled with graphs and columns of figures tends in fact to suggest a neurotic taste for evasion and mystification. Mrs. Wilditch's obsession with accumulations of statistics reflects not so much a dislike of mystery as a kind of pedantic devotion to it.

When Wilditch finally comes across his own published version of the story that he is looking for, he is angered as well as disappointed by it. " 'The Treasure on the Island' by W.W." has something of the same cloudy falseness as the graphs in *My Apprenticeship*. This story within the story—a brief, sentimental tale about buried treasure—is not quite as bad as he thinks, but his distaste for the schoolboy exercise is really based on the extent to which it distorts the truth of "the dream which he remembered" (26), the extent, in other words, to which it displaces that dream. The "real" story is much more bizarre: "Of course it had all been a dream, it could have been nothing else but a dream, but a dream too was an experience, the images of a dream had their own integrity, and he felt professional anger at this false report just as his mother had felt at the mistake in the Fabian statistics" (28). As a displacement of the real story, "The Treasure on the Island" obscures the reality of the experience by violating the dream's integrity. But in spite of her passion for factual accuracy, it is really Wilditch's mother who is the presiding genius of this kind of obscurantism in "Under the Garden." Wilditch quickly realizes that "The Treasure on the Island" amounts to a "cover-story" (28), an attempt to formulate his experience in a way that will not incur his mother's animosity. However, the story is a failure from that point of view as well: it infuriates her simply by being an instance of "creative" writing. Mrs. Wilditch's dislike of "The Treasure on the Island" derives less from a conviction that it deviates from some objective standard of truth than from the perception that it actually begins to approach a kind of truth that she fears. In the psychoanalytic perspective, Wilditch's mother represents the very spirit, as it were, of mystery and displacement. Apart from anything else, she has evidently displaced Wilditch's father. And the conspicuous absence of the father from his childhood world now becomes a sort of unspoken narrative in its own right.

As the older Wilditch proceeds to set down a more faithful account, the basic technique and narrative rhythm of "Under the Garden" begin to become clearer. The story moves toward the discovery of the "true" fiction behind a "false" fiction, or, more accurately, the narrative process of working back through a displaced version of experience to the archetypal one. Again, there is a centripetal shift from a framing to an inset story, a structural tendency to move from the third person to the first. "Under the Garden" proceeds, in other words, from the displacement of a mythic event to the event itself, and what this process signifies is the recovery of the living child who is figuratively concealed within the dying man. The story as a whole is of particular interest here in that its structure may be usefully viewed as a kind of model for novels like *The Comedians* and *The Honorary Consul:* its version of the recovery of the child is also, in the Wordsworthian sense, the recovery of a genuine father. It is a story about nothing less than the awakening of a human imagination.

Wilditch's first-person account begins, like the opening chapter of *A Burnt-Out Case,* with a journey by water. That the water is in reality only a small pond has no particular bearing on the archetype of the journey itself: the translation of the protagonist into a mysterious new world. Wilditch's "I" is a child whose heroes are explorers; his primary imaginative source or "text" seems to be a work called *The Romance of Australian Exploration,* another inset "silent" story, and as happens with all wanderers in such books, the first thing he does is to get lost. With his discovery of the "great oak of apparently enormous age with roots that coiled away above the surface of the ground" (31), the echo of Querry's journey into a particular type of labyrinthine underworld becomes quite explicit: "I was reminded of those roots once in Africa where they formed a kind of shrine for a fetish—a seated human figure made out of a gourd and palm fronds and unidentifiable vegetable matter gone rotten in the rains and a great penis of bamboo. Coming on it suddenly, I was frightened, or was it the memory that it brought back which

scared me?" (31). The coiling roots of the ancient oak are associated, in other words, with a dimension of reality quite different
from that suggested by the formal order and expansive peace of
the garden. The journey by water modulates to a journey under
the earth, and the netherworld that Wilditch now enters is not
only more intensely alive and fertile than the pastoral one above
it but more powerful and dangerous too. The recurrence of the
image of the vegetable totem from *A Burnt-Out Case*—in a recollected version that is specifically phallic—suggests that the oak
is a tree of death as well as life, that the territory beneath it is in
fact the archetypal locus of the spilling of life: a place of seed and
burial and being "lost," where the usual arbitrary distinctions
between living and dying have ceased to obtain. Wilditch is at the
threshold of an underworld that is at once the erotic, improbable
territory of dreams and a treasure-house of hidden or forbidden
knowledge. He is about to be initiated into certain underground
secrets; he undergoes a process of "natural" education.

This process is governed, as one might expect, by a Wordsworthian dialectic of alternating excitement and fear: his sense of
having found a new freedom is balanced by a sense of being
bound in a new captivity; his dream is at once an arena of quest
and a limbo in which he is held in a condition of suspension. The
evocations of *Alice in Wonderland* in the cave and underground
passage and of *Robinson Crusoe* in the solitary footprint on the
earth outside locate the oak tree clearly enough in the childhood
landscape of a familiar type of innocent adventure story. But the
night world below its roots is charged with a more ambiguous
energy, an elemental potency which has as much to do with the
forces of dissolution as with those of creation. The hole in the
ground is simultaneously a grave and a fabulous source of life,
both tomb and womb. Wilditch is traveling by way of these "actual" roots, that is to say, into the protean country of radical
figurative conception: the land of alpha and omega. Defying his
actual mother, he is in fact entering the terrain of an archetypal
mother, the sexual earth goddess who presides over a realm
where birth and death are inextricably linked. It comes as no
great surprise, then, that the first person Wilditch encounters is

the sort of witch or hag who is always inclined to haunt the night-mares of children.

But as a type of Proserpine, the squawking Maria cuts a rather incongruous, even comically grotesque, figure. In one sense, of course, she represents an undisplaced version of Mrs. Wilditch: a threatening but ultimately powerless maternal guardian or queen. She seems to be the keeper of the mysteries beneath the garden, and she takes an even keener and more jealous delight in the accumulation of treasure there than Javitt himself. She is sub-ordinate to Javitt, however, because genuine authority is invested in the king of this underworld, not the queen. Enthroned on his lavatory seat, Javitt rules. He is the undisplaced father figure of Wilditch's dream kingdom, and although "Javitt" is not his "real" name, the verbal echoes in it of "Yahweh" and "Jehovah" are sufficient to suggest a role of kingship with a much more authoritative resonance than that of, say, Pluto. Javitt is the cre-ative principle here, the ur-father, the original potent source. Since Maria acts essentially as her husband's servant, it could perhaps be argued that the young Wilditch's subconscious imag-ination has something of an antifeminist cast. Javitt, though, is no less grotesque a figure than his wife: if she sounds as much like a frog or duck as a woman, he looks as much like a tree as a man. While both would appear to be elemental nature spirits as well as people, Maria has at least the advantage, if that is what it is, of mobility. But she does seem less than human in some more fundamental way, and the significant physical detail in this re-spect is her roofless mouth.

Javitt rules because he can speak. The source of his authority is his articulacy. Talking almost incessantly, he seems to be the em-bodiment of the kind of fictional character whose existence de-pends on the manner of his speech. The young Wilditch is capti-vated more by his conversation than by anything else:

> He might be said to have talked me into staying, though if I had proved obstinate I have no doubt at all that Maria would have blocked my retreat, and certainly I would not have fancied strug-gling to escape through the musty folds of her clothes. That was the strange balance—to and fro—of those days; half the time I was

frightened as though I were caged in a nightmare and half the time
I only wanted to laugh freely and happily at the strangeness of his
speech and the novelty of his ideas. It was as if, for those hours or
days, the only important things in life were two, laughter and fear.
(44)

Javitt's rhetorical speciality is a type of proverbial wisdom which
draws equally on popular rustic and biblical lore, an associative,
discontinuous, and above all highly figurative style that oscillates
between the oracular and the commonplace:

> There was something of a monarch about him and something
> . . . of a prophet and something of the gardener my mother disliked
> and of a policeman in the next village; his expressions were often
> countrylike and coarse, but his ideas seemed to move on a deeper
> level, like roots spreading below a layer of compost. I could sit here
> now in this room for hours remembering the things he said—I
> haven't made out the sense of them all yet: they are stored in my
> memory like a code uncracked which waits for a clue or an inspira-
> tion. (43)

Javitt presents a picture oddly compounded of both banality and
sublimity. It is almost as if a kind of childish literalism had been
brought to bear on some mysterious figure from a poem by
William Blake. And the analogy is not perhaps too farfetched, for
what the strangeness of Javitt's speech suggests is a vision of language as pure metaphor, a view of the verbal imagination conceived as mysterious or oracular—its utterances "like a code un-
cracked"—because it is repressed or buried alive. In sexual
terms, the boy descends to a world that is symbolically female
only to find it governed by a principle of creativity that is symbolically male, a brooding and immobile ancient of days whose
source of power seems to be his gift of the gab. Javitt is the king of
this underworld because his talk seems kingly. He is the archetypal father of Wilditch's own imagination because he is the progenitor of an original "word." The younger Wilditch falls in love
with an image of the king's daughter and his quest becomes an
unsuccessful search, lasting nearly a lifetime, for a mythical princess; the real object of the older Wilditch's quest, which takes the

form of a process of recollection in a sort of tranquillity, is to decipher a code, to realize the significance of Javitt's original word in the time that remains to him. He must discover who Miss Ramsgate really "is," but her identity depends, before anything else, on what "Miss Ramsgate" might really mean.

"Under the Garden" is a story much preoccupied with questions about words and meanings. The bleak comedy of the opening scenes derives largely from the ways in which speech and language are used to avoid rather than to facilitate communication. Wilditch's relations with Doctor Cave and Sir Nigel Sampson, for example, are actually based on fairly elaborate but familiar enough techniques of verbal indirection—not saying what is meant and saying what is not meant, hearing what was unsaid and not hearing what was said. Words themselves in such a context tend to acquire both a portentousness and a curious opaqueness or impenetrability. Doctor Cave, we are told, sometimes "toll[s] his words like a bell" (10). Javitt's is not the only kind of speech in the story that could be described as "dark." But where Doctor Cave and Sir Nigel are pompous, solemn, and dull, Javitt is amusing and interesting. The movement of the story as a whole is from the displaced meanings of words toward an original or archetypal verbal significance. This is of course why Javitt seems so obsessed with the importance and "power" of "first" (51) words or names. But his obsession has a specific contextual bias: Javitt's own style is anecdotal as well as proverbial, and what it reflects is a propensity for words as narratives. In all his sayings, explanations, and accounts of things, he always takes a firm, if sometimes obscure, narrative line. Wilditch is captivated not just by what he says but by the very fact that everything to Javitt is a story. The bond between the old man and the child has to do with an affinity of perception: they share an exuberantly fictive sense of reality. The centripetal movement in "Under the Garden" toward some sort of verbal archetype is really the impulse to discover the radical first word of a radical first story. And this original story, it is implied, takes one of two basic forms: what we might call the "pastoral" or what we might call the "heroic."

In the course of urging the young Wilditch to read aloud "a piece" of "news" (38) from a newspaper that is almost fifty years old, Javitt remarks with a certain characteristic inscrutability: "We are deeper here than any grave was ever dug to bury secrets in. Under the earth or over the earth, it's there you'll find all that matters" (39). This seems at first to be just the sort of gnomic utterance that he is given to make from time to time for no apparent reason, but its relevance becomes clearer when the boy raises the expected objection about the age of the paper. "News is news," Javitt replies, "however old it is"; he goes on to insist that "news keeps. And it comes round again when you least expect. Like thunder" (40). The buried "secrets" of his previous observation would seem to refer, in other words, to the element of typicality in the verbal arrangement of recorded events. His conception of a news "story" is clearly that of some recurrent narrative type. In fact, his response to the specific item actually read to him—"Garden fête at the Grange" (40)—suggests that what he really assumes is that stories of this kind are archetypal rather than simply typical. "Was it a good fate or an evil fate?" (40) he enquires, and when the boy answers that the phenomenon in question was of a different "kind," Javitt proceeds to clarify his position on any and all stories featuring words which sound like "fate": " 'There's no other kind,' he said. 'It's your fate to read to me. It's *her* fate to talk like a frog, and mine to listen because my eyesight's bad. This is an underground fate we suffer from here and that was a garden fate—but it all comes to the same fate in the end' " (40).

This may seem to be archetypal criticism gone berserk, but there is a remarkably exact logic nonetheless in the subterranean drift of Javitt's ideas. In effect, he offers a clue to his code. If "news" can be regarded as the periodic recurrence of certain archetypal narratives, then "all that matters" under or over the earth is an awareness of the archetypes, the original buried "secrets" themselves that may be said to be the basis of any coherent sense of reality. "News" in this sense would be the metaphorical ground of the real world, a treasure hoard of first and last words into whose meaning the boy is being offered a form of initiation.

There are "garden" fates and there are "underground" fates, but the important thing is the idea of fate itself. A phrase like "the same fate in the end" might seem to refer to the real finality of death, but if one's "fate" is also the governing archetype of one's life then it means not so much a conclusive event as a kind of original story: a first myth, the design of an ur-narrative. Fatalism in Javitt's perspective has to do with ends as principles of narrative closure rather than as foregone conclusions: "There's no need to talk of dying down here" (42), he says, not just because he himself appears to be deathless but because death itself has no real or ultimate power in a world that is purely mythic. One's fate is one's own "story": what Javitt implies is that this story always has some integral connection with a larger original story. All fates are "the same" in the sense that they belong to the same mythic design.

The total shape of the rather shadowy ur-narrative to which Javitt points may only be guessed at, perhaps, but he does suggest that it can be partially glimpsed in two distinct literary genres: the type of story that takes place "over" and the type that takes place "under" the earth. A "garden fate" is presumably pastoral, while an "underground fate" would presumably belong to heroic romance. He hints, to put it baldly, that stories which project a lost paradisal age of innocence are linked in some significant way to exploration or quest narratives which project a world of fabulous but perilous adventures. Since Wilditch has literally left a garden to enter an underworld, the connection would seem to have a particular interest for him. From the point of view of literary criticism, of course, the link is in one sense obvious enough: the pastoral world tends to be a reversed image of the heroic one. But Wilditch is not a literary critic. What he finally comes to is a dream within his dream, a central "story" at the heart of the entire receding, centripetal perspective of stories within stories, an ur-dream which is not, strictly speaking, a narrative at all. "In my dream within a dream," he says, "someone laughed and wept" (65). The dialectic of joy and fear, of the sense of freedom and the sense of constraint, culminates in a wordless synthesis in which the two polar modalities of all imaginative experience are at once enacted. The alpha and omega of the story of William Wilditch turns out to be the sound of happiness and the sound of sadness. The pastoral world is a prelapsarian place of ease and joy, and the heroic world an arena of dangerous action where people are liable to come to grief, but his inmost dream suggests that there is some sense in which the two basic contraries of human response might be seen as first and last states of mind, reflecting each other like twins—*l'allegro* and *il penseroso*—and somehow expressed concurrently by a single mysterious identity.

Wordless epiphanies, however, are ultimately in the province of mysticism rather than of critical commentary; in any case, visions of promise more substantial than this are vouchsafed to Wilditch. There is, for instance, Javitt's legendary daughter. Or, more exactly, there is her picture in another old newspaper. The image of Wilditch's beloved has much the same aura of both sublimity and banality as that which surrounds her father, the same absurd blend of high romance and homely realism. Javitt tells him that she is now "over" the earth, a person who actually lives for the time being in what we would call the world of ordinary experience, but he also says that she will prove virtually impossible to find there. The facts of her elusiveness and her disguise point to another form of displacement: Miss Ramsgate is evidently the unattainable object of the most quixotic type of erotic yearning, an impossible courtly love goddess. However difficult she might be to identify in the world of ordinary experience, though, her identity in this subterranean kingdom seems less shadowy. A type of Persephone above ground, she is more simply the original fabulous princess of every fairy tale, one form of the object of every romantic quest. "Miss Ramsgate" exists, in short, as a metaphor, one of the buried secrets of the world: she is the vision of a paradisal garden that has been lost and of the beloved as the bride who must be sought and recovered. She represents the figurative embodiment of that truth in beauty which is the principle informing and redeeming the general daftness of all quixotic dreams and searches. The important thing about her is not her absence from the story nor the spuriousness of her "existence" anywhere else but the fact that she is always waiting to be found and revealed. The absurdity of Wilditch's infatuation and lifelong search becomes in another sense the real token of his faith, a guarantee of the integrity of all romantic aspiration and hope.

Miss Ramsgate is envisioned more substantially, certainly more concretely, in Javitt's "treasure," the hoard of faery wealth with which she is figuratively identified. The treasure amounts to nothing less, we are told, than "all the riches of the world, its pursuits and enjoyments" (65). There is nothing merely abstract or narrowly allegorical about it: "If this was a dream, these were real stones. Absolute reality belongs to dreams and not to life. The gold of dreams is not the diluted gold of even the best gold-smith, there are no diamonds in dreams made of paste—what seems is. 'Who seems most kingly is the king'" (64). The treasure trove is every bit as metaphorical as Javitt's daughter and its real-ity just as indisputable. We are in the world of imaginative iden-tity now, which means in effect that the narrative archetype of the search for buried treasure has the same mythic source or struc-ture as the narrative archetype of the search for the beloved. The point is important, for the paradox of this dream treasure's "ab-solute reality" is crucial to the older Wilditch's comprehension of his own quest. He cites Hardy, the least sentimental of poets:

> If I have seen one thing
> It is the passing preciousness of dreams;
> That aspects are within us; and who seems
> Most kingly is the King.[7]

What Wilditch suggests, or perhaps realizes for the first time, is that it is precisely the figurativeness of dreams which gives them a kind of metaphysical priority over the world of waking reality. This is the priority surmised in another context but in similar terms by Wallace Stevens:

> Let be be finale of seem.
> The only emperor is the emperor of ice-cream.[8]

Javitt's treasure is really the trove of the imagination; the jewels are neither more nor less than a legendary store of words. The

point is not that ordinary reality should or could be ignored—
such a notion would make nonsense of Greene's whole career—
but that only the private fictions we call our dreams can illumi-
nate the familiar darkness of our experience. If all stories, even
the most ironic or tragic, may be perceived ultimately as romance
archetypes precisely *because* they are stories, then the ultimate
romance is that of fictiveness itself. Wilditch's quotation from
Hardy could also refer, in a slightly different way but with as
much aptness, to the story of Querry; it bears just as much epi-
graphic relevance again, as we shall see, to the fates of Brown and
Jones in *The Comedians*.

Javitt's treasure "is" also Miss Ramsgate. This particular identification seems to point primarily to the idea that all arduous
questing might be a treasure hunt in the sense of amounting to a
kind of wandering in a wilderness in search of a promised land.
The link between pastoral and heroic modes is traditionally one
in which a fabulous golden age from the past tends to be projected into the future as a metaphor for the end and goal of the
hero's errancy; the pastoral constitutes an interlude which offers
the glimpse of an infinitely more desirable sort of reality than that
with which the hero normally finds himself stuck. But this
glimpse is always a matter of "seeming" only, a Pisgah vision: the
paradisal prospect will inevitably fade or the hero will realize
that he must don his armor again and resume his quest. Wilditch's glimpse of Javitt's daughter has determined the shape of
his life; but his wandering has led him nowhere. The "pre-
ciousness" of the treasure, though, inheres in its fictiveness, which
means that Miss Ramsgate's absolute reality is archetypal rather
than actual. From this perspective, the idea of the search in a
wilderness becomes the effort of the imagination to find the lost
or secret world that might constitute its genuine home. Since its
genuine home in this story is an archetypal one, it is to be found
"under" rather than "over" the earth.

There are, in other words, two different journeys or searches in
"Under the Garden." There is the boy's progress through his own
dream, which reaches a "climax" (66) with the revelation of Miss
Ramsgate, and there is the older Wilditch's quest for the story of

the dream itself, which is achieved through an effort of faithful recollection. Since Wilditch has failed to find his promised land, the recovery of the dream as a whole becomes the more important "end" here. The significance of the dream seems entirely bound up with the figure of Javitt: the ultimate focus of Wilditch's narrative is not the rather indistinct Miss Ramsgate but his relationship with her father. The object of his quest as a process of recollection becomes the recovery of that questing imagination which, in one sense, the prophetic Javitt symbolizes. Hardy's poem suggests, however, that the real significance of all dreams lies in the unconscious imaginative power of the dreamer, an idea which suggests in turn that the questing imagination is symbolized here in another sense by the boy. The relationship between Javitt and the dreamer who dreams him is that of metaphorical identity. In psychological terms, this identity could be described as familial, but the old man is more than a mere paternal surrogate: he is also Wilditch's spiritual progenitor. The movement of "Under the Garden" is from displacement to mythic archetype, and the central narrative archetype of Wilditch's dream is the discovery in an underworld of the true father.

If Javitt is "king," the boy is his prince and heir. Immobilized on his own lavatory seat, Javitt bestows on him a "golden po," which he describes as "the least of my treasures" (47). As an item of treasure, the chamber pot belongs to a vision of the plenitude of creation, but that plenitude is by nature figurative and hence protean: it signifies the abundance of a reality that is in a constant process of dissolution as well as of creation. The world below the garden is a "lower" one in every conceivable respect: a kingdom of roots because it is the region of archetypes, the teeming metaphorical source of things, and at the same time a kind of metaphysical bog to which the forms of all created things return. The implications of the "thrones" are of course scatological; the "prince" is a young child and his perception of creativity tends to be projected in sexually infantile terms. But besides being a rather basic emblem of flux, Wilditch's "golden po" might just also be a sly, punning dream echo from another remembered story.

In the sixth book of the *Aeneid*, the hero persuades the

Cumaean sibyl to take him down into the underworld. This type of journey seems, as we have seen, to be a narrative archetype central to the whole body of Greene's later fiction. But Wilditch's descent in particular constitutes a more specific kind of echo of the perilous expedition recounted by Virgil because it is evidently undertaken with the purpose of finding a dead father. Aeneas carries with him a protective talisman which enables him to cross the Stygian river: the golden bough from the fabulous oak tree that is sacred to Proserpine. He offers it to her in Hades as an act of propitiation. Wilditch's golden po, though distinctly humbler, certainly has something of the same sacramental and talismanic significance. As the boy prepares his escape from Javitt's kingdom, the old man urges him to take it with him "as a souvenir" (67). "You've got to have something when you start a search," he says, "to give you substance" (67). Wilditch picks up the po and Maria comes squawking out, making a dive for it "with her bird-like hand" (67). She pursues him, witchlike, through the subterranean passage, but when the boy finally reaches the surface of the earth his talismanic souvenir has disappeared: "Perhaps—I can't remember—I dropped the gold po at the entrance of the tunnel as a propitiation to Maria" (68). It is at this point that his narrative concludes and we are returned to the daylight reality of the third-person story.

If the Virgilian echoes in all this are to be taken seriously, it should be noted that Wilditch's gesture of propitiation, unlike Aeneas's, coincides with his emergence from the netherworld. The implication of Javitt's remark about the golden po giving substance to Wilditch's search is really that the world "over" the earth can also be regarded, figuratively at least, as another kind of "under" world. Wilditch's journey is unfinished, in other words, because the ordinary reality of the framing story represents a new arena of romantic quest. When he returns in the third-person story to the pond and the island, the protagonist finds beneath "the blackened remains of an oak" (74) an object that turns out to be "an old tin chamber pot" (74), colorless except for "a few flakes of yellow paint" (74). This is intended to be a sign not that the dream was after all an actual rather than a

fictive phenomenon, but rather that the process of Wilditch's actual emergence from a lower world is only now beginning. His
real journey and search are as fictive as Miss Ramsgate herself,
and the sense of the protagonist's paradoxical revival and recovery at the end of "Under the Garden" has to do with what the
chamber pot represents rather than with what it is. "Perhaps
years ago, when the paint was fresh, he had discovered the pot,
just as he had done this day, and founded a whole afternoon-
legend around it. Then why had W.W. omitted it from his story?
. . . He had a sense that there was a decision he had to make all
over again. Curiosity was growing inside him like the cancer.
Across the pond the bell rang for breakfast and he thought, 'Poor
mother—she had reason to fear,' turning the tin chamber-
pot on his lap" (75). "W.W." had omitted it because his own
literary effort represented a propitiatory offering that was in fact
identical with it. The golden po is the buried archetype of the
dream, the very thing that he had attempted to conceal from his
mother by offering a displaced version. In the terms of the story's
allegorical structure, it amounts to a secret or "first" name.
Aeneas's golden bough signifies, among other things, a royal or
transcendent identity; the golden po signifies, among other
things, a transcendent identity which had been lost. For Wilditch, recovering this item of buried treasure becomes a matter of
arriving where he started and knowing the place for the first time.
He recovers his inheritance; in finding Javitt again, Wilditch finds
himself.

The battered chamber pot in "Under the Garden" constitutes a
bathetic but entirely concrete image of the fictive integrity of the
story, a reverberative word in an archetypal idiom. The recovered
golden po is the symbolic talisman of Wilditch's own "kingship,"
and his impending death may then be read as inevitable in just
the sense that the death of Querry is inevitable. But the idiom of
romance here belongs to Javitt, and the "real" Javitt is deathless.
He has specified that the po is the least of his treasures; his own
heraldic device seems to be the rune of the fish, which is also of
course the emblem of Christ. The mysterious letters which the
children find on the "ark" in the last story in this volume suggest

that language itself somehow represents a kind of hidden life that lies embedded, so to speak, in the silence of death; in Christian terms, the identity of Christ would be the first word which is ultimately concealed or encoded in all language.

Whether as Christian divinity or as the allegorical embodiment of the verbal imagination, Javitt at any rate rules. His domain is certainly a more fanciful place than we might have expected from a novelist like Greene. While it is true that *A Sense of Reality* does not amount merely to an experimental anomaly in his oeuvre, it is also true that it is not in Greene's usual mode: "Under the Garden" can hardly be regarded as any sort of mimesis of ordinary, in the sense of familiar, experience. However, it would be a misleading oversimplification to view these stories as evidence that narrative realism has been abandoned in favor of absurdist fantasy. What Greene seems to be exploring here is the experience of dreaming, or, more precisely, the configurative resonance of inset fictions in a fictional world of waking consciousness. We have noticed that dream and reality are always inextricably and significantly linked in Greene, that the way in which the world of waking consciousness is perceived in his novels tends to depend on the shape of his characters' unconscious fantasies. This is as true of *A Sense of Reality* as of any of his other fictions. In any case, the structure of each of these stories hinges on a type of narrative revelation or discovery that is entirely realistic. If, for example, the narrative archetype of "Under the Garden" is in one sense the sixth book of the *Aeneid,* in another it is the image of that most humbly ordinary of real objects, a chamber pot. What really matters is the name that the object is given in the story. Still, the emblematic pattern of a descent into and an emergence out of an underworld seems to have a kind of thematic priority over the realistic texture of the context in which it is envisioned. It can be more legitimately said of *A Sense of Reality* that it reflects the development of Greene's interest in romance structure for its own sake and in itself—perhaps at the expense of a more habitual concern with the daylight reality of what we normally think of as Greeneland.

The shaping power of an inset fiction stems from its structural centrality. In "Under the Garden" it is as if Greene had set out quite deliberately to isolate and elaborate the centrality of a particular form of narrative. For Greene, Wilditch's dream would seem to be not only an interesting story but *the* interesting story. If an inset fiction is always to some extent a romance archetype, then this fable about the discovery of a sort of phantom identity in a kind of hell begins to look like the archetypal text which informs the structure of all his later novels. The sixth book of the *Aeneid* comes clearly into focus here because the customary "fraternal" role of the characteristic figure of the doppelgänger now modulates to that of a figurative paternity. This is a metaphorical shift which has some significant implications for the direction that Greene takes in his next three novels.

F I V E

The Comedians

When I look back on that afternoon, it seems to
me we had been granted the distant sight of a
promised land.

He did the place no outrage to liken it to an
hotel. —Henry James, "The Great Good Place"

Although Greene had traveled to Haiti twice during the 1950s,
privately noting the extremes of domestic poverty and foreign
profligacy which characterized the life of that country under the
rule of President Magloire, it was not until a visit in 1963 that the
place really awakened his imaginative interest. He discovered
that Haiti under François Duvalier was no longer the paradise for
wealthy tourists that it had once been and that now, for the vast
majority of its citizens, it had become a land in the grip of a
nightmare which seemed to bring it into a kind of metaphorical
alignment with the lowest and most desolate regions of Greeneland itself. The despotic "Papa Doc" governed with a cruel, ca-
pricious violence unknown in Haiti since the days of the "emperor" Christophe; brooding inside a presidential palace from
which he rarely emerged, Duvalier instituted a reign of terror that
was administered by his notorious "Tontons Macoute" and re-
sulted in the transformation of a merely conventionally corrupt
Caribbean republic into an almost Kafkaesque zone of darkness.[1] Haiti by 1963 had become a social and political disaster
area of a type that might have been designed to strike a special
chord of response in a writer like Greene: he found himself once
again in a particularly vivid version of his own characteristic
dream of hell.

First published in 1966, *The Comedians* was initially conceived in a spirit of reactive anger and with the desire to expose

and undermine the evil which Greene saw embodied in Duvalier: "*The Comedians* is the only one of my books which I began with the intention of expressing a point of view and in order to fight— to fight the horror of Papa Doc's dictatorship."[2] In this respect, as a matter of fact, the novel had a slightly more successful impact than is normally the lot of fictions marked by an aggressively polemical "point of view." François Duvalier was evidently enraged by *The Comedians;* the book even elicited a deranged counterblast in which Greene stood charged as a "liar, a *crétin,* a stool-pigeon . . . unbalanced, sadistic, perverted . . . a perfect ignoramus . . . lying to his heart's content . . . the shame of proud and noble England . . . a spy . . . a drug addict . . . a torturer."[3] Needless to say, the shame of proud and noble England was immensely gratified. But if the original motivation behind *The Comedians* was polemical, the actual shape of the completed novel suggests that its formal affinities lie as much with the patterns of burial and regeneration in *A Burnt-Out Case* as with, say, the more overtly "political" design of *The Quiet American.* Greene returns now to the descriptive immediacy of the first-person perspective in a clearly realistic context, but his narrator's story begins, like William Wilditch's, with a journey by water, a sea voyage this time that figures as yet another mythic passage to another underworld.

The account of this journey is constructed around a fairly elaborate complex of mythopoeic echoes. Although there is nobody quite like Javitt's Maria in sight now, a couple of legendary females do hover unobtrusively but persistently in the background. The ship which carries Brown, Jones, and the Smiths from Philadelphia to Port-au-Prince is named the *Medea,* and that jealous and ambiguous sorceress becomes the appropriate emblematic genius presiding not only over the "crossing" of these passengers with their "interchangeable"[4] names but over Brown's story as a whole. In a humbler sense, of course, the presiding spirit of the voyage is only the ship's prim Dutch captain, but the captain of the *Medea* is overseen, so to speak, by the image of another woman, the photograph of his stony-faced wife—she with the "iron-grey waves in her hair" (234)—whom Brown recognizes at once as a type of

Medusa: "Perhaps she gave him confidence: she would have given me a paralysis of the will" (24). A vessel with powerful mythological connections on the maternal side, then, the *Medea* also seems to be descended from Sebastian Brant's *Das Narrenschiff*, for she is clearly a ship of fools as well. From the outset, in other words, the novel invokes a whole series of stories that would appear to have some distant but nevertheless important ancestral relation to it. For what Greene offers here is another fiction much concerned with the business of fiction and fiction making. Beneath the informal surface of the narrative, *The Comedians* turns out in fact to be a remarkably and sometimes rather self-consciously "literary" novel. Despite the plainness of his manner and his ironic, conversational tone, Brown reveals himself to be a cannily allusive narrator. Repeatedly citing Wordsworth and Baudelaire, for example, he appears to share Thomas Fowler's taste for the literature of the nineteenth century. None of these references is merely incidental or peripheral, but perhaps the most salient of all the allusions in the novel is a kind of metonymical invocation of a title by Henry James.

During the final night of his ghostly vigil in his Haitian hotel, Brown tries to distract himself from loneliness and the imminent dangers of his last journey with Jones by reading James's "The Great Good Place." The story, though, does not have quite the desired effect:

> I wanted to forget that tomorrow was Monday, but I failed. "The wild waters of our horrible times," James had written and I wondered what temporary break in the long enviable Victorian peace had so disturbed him. Had his butler given notice? I had built my life around this hotel—it represented stability more profoundly than the God whom the Fathers of the Visitation had hoped I would serve; once it had represented success better than my travelling art-gallery with the phoney paintings; it was in a sense a family tomb. (274)

While the image of the family tomb may at first glance be a bit obscure, it seems clear enough that Brown is simply suggesting that his hotel had once been his own "great good place." However, this apparently trivial association of ideas acquires a peculiarly insistent resonance throughout the rest of his story, gathering a kind of cumulative narrative momentum that seems almost independent of both Brown and Henry James. Later, for instance, speaking apparently of the cemetery in which they are obliged to spend the night, Jones emerges briefly from sleep to remark to Brown "that this was 'a good place'" (291); Brown says that he "could see nothing good in it, but in the end I slept as well" (291). Later still, in Philipot's account of Jones's death, we learn that he had again "found what he called a good place. He said he'd keep the soldiers off till we had time to reach the road" (307); and finally, there is the voice of Jones describing his "part" (312) in the vaudeville routine of Brown's last dream: "'I've got it now. I have to say—just look at these bloody rocks—"This is a good place," and everyone laughs till the tears come. Then you say, "To hold the bastards up?" and I reply, "I didn't mean that"'" (313). The relevance of "The Great Good Place" to *The Comedians* is further underlined in a slightly different perspective by an echo of the only phrase which Brown has quoted from it— Doctor Magiot's ultimate epistolary reference to "the wild world we live in now" (312). What all this signifies, in effect, is that the title of the Henry James tale—almost as it were single-handedly—generates a sequence of echoes which reverberate outward from the simple metaphorical association triggering Brown's meditation on his empty hotel until they encompass virtually the entire meaning of the novel.

Deliberate reverberative allusiveness is an inherent function, of course, of romance itself. We have already noticed that the peculiarly literary or artificial quality of romance stems in part from the fact that it tends to be so intensely self-referential. The phenomenon of allusiveness in the genre is so commonplace that it is usually regarded as a convention which need not, for one reason or another, be examined too closely. Milton invokes Spenser and Spenser invokes Chaucer; Ariosto cites Boiardo, Tasso cites Ariosto; and so on: this is the kind of thing that romancers invariably do, and that, it seems, is that. But as even the first couple of chapters of *The Comedians* attest, it is also the kind of thing that sophisticated modern novelists frequently do. At its simplest, the deliberate fictive echo is usually a rhetorical expedient which gives point to a specific theme in a narrative or which lends an additional dimension of "authority" to it. But in more complex contexts, an allusion to another fiction can have exactly the same effect as the lengthier device of the tale within the tale: a subsidiary story in a narrative, that is to say, is sometimes no more than a definitively resonant echo of someone else's narrative. And an allusion in this circumstance, like the reverberativeness of "The Great Good Place" in *The Comedians,* tends to become nothing less than a conspicuous fictional archetype.

Since the rhetorical function of the particular sequence of echoes that we have just remarked seems to be that of metonymy, an apparently fortuitous passing reference to the title of a Henry James tale turning out to be something approaching an inset fiction in its own right, then the tale itself perhaps calls for some further consideration. "The Great Good Place" concerns an eminent man of letters, one George Dane, who is suffering from nervous exhaustion and a degree of associated depression that verges on despair; through the agency of a mysterious, unnamed "young man," he is somehow transported to an arcadian refuge where he recovers his health and sanity.[5] Dane's initial agitation is revealed to be what might now be called an identity crisis; what he recovers, in fact, in the elysium that gives the story its title is the sense of his own imaginative integrity, the very identity that had been in danger of engulfment by "the wild waters" of his troubled age. Dane's "good place" is primarily a garden, a formal pastoral pleasance which he contemplates from a bench in a cloister. The architecture rather indistinctly glimpsed in the background suggests a church or monastery, or, at any rate, some form of retreat from the wildness of the world that would ordinarily have an ecclesiastical signification: Dane finds that he has become a member of an informal band of "Brothers." However, this paradise seems to be something more than a sort of celibate Eden; it expresses an ideal of civilization as well as pastoral ease. While the place has certain affinities with the nineteenth-century institution of the spa, for example, it is also like a perfect country house or London club, furnished, moreover, with the world's ideal library.

It is, in short, whatever Dane or any of the other "Brothers" wishes it to be—including, incidentally, the world's ideal hotel. But in the story's dénouement, we learn that George Dane has actually been asleep all the while and that the "gift" of the great good place bestowed by the young man has been a dream. James's intention does not appear to be ironic: the protagonist evidently emerges from his dream as a genuinely restored, and in that sense a new, man. Located specifically in the desiring world of unconscious fantasy, the "good place" exists, in other words, as an archetypal or imaginative source of ontological recreation and renewal.

James's story is echoed by Greene's novel in at least two obviously significant respects, one of which has already been glanced at here: that of the potency of the idea of the "good place" itself. For the desire to realize a dream of paradise has always been, clearly, a central motivating force for Brown as well as for Jones. Brown's ambitiousness concerning the hotel that he has inherited from his mother, for instance, is identified from the outset as just such a "dream" (83). It is more banal, of course, than George Dane's, pertaining as it does to the stereotype of the kind of pastoral retreat normally featured in travel brochures for tourists. But as a dream it holds no less importance for Brown than Dane's does for himself. The second affinity between the two fictions, though it appears initially to be unrelated to the dream of paradise, is even more striking: the only other character in "The Great Good Place" who seems actually to be possessed of a name is Dane's butler, and his name is Brown. While James's butler does not exactly "give notice," as Greene's protagonist impatiently conjectures, he does in another sense experience a radical change in status. Toward the end of Dane's dream, Brown the servant suddenly appears to him as a "Brother" in his own right. The Brown of *The Comedians,* whose fate in life has always apparently been bound up with some role of service—whether to God, to the customers in the restaurants where he has worked, to the guests in his hotel, or, more simply, to the idea of fortune—undergoes a similar transformation in his perception of his relationship to Jones. He begins his narrative with a sense of himself as a fairly clever soldier of fortune and of Jones as a confidence man of a much lowlier and seedier type, but he ends it with the recognition that he has in fact met his "unknown brother" (289). And one of the grounds of this fraternal relation is that Brown and Jones share the dream, at once banal and sublime, of finding an island paradise: they are brothers in a mutual fantasy of arriving at a great good place.

Brown's story is prefaced by a quotation from the poem by Hardy that was cited in "Under the Garden":

> . . . aspects are within us; and who seems
> Most kingly is the King.

This epigraph has scarcely less allusive significance than the tale by Henry James, for as we have seen, the subject of Hardy's poem is the importance of dreams and dreaming. The two allusions may even be regarded as crucially linked: the gift of the dream in "The Great Good Place" is granted by a young man; the title of the poem by Hardy is "A Young Man's Exhortation." Fantasies about paradise seem to belong peculiarly or even archetypally to the province of youth: visions of blessed islands spring from the innocence of what Greene's Morin would describe as faith rather than belief. But the bloom of youth and innocence has long since faded not only from the person of George Dane but also from the Brown of *The Comedians*. There is, of course, a certain egalitarianism in the kingdom of dreams: all dreamers are, as such, equally "immature," and to the jaundiced, conscious eye of experience, any dream of paradise must be, to say the least of it, absurdly optimistic. While the Haiti of *The Comedians,* to take the example at hand, looks paradisal enough at a distance, a closer perspective reveals it as a type of hell. But even the most apparently unambiguous arcadian vision tends to have its darker underside. "A Young Man's Exhortation" is balanced in its exuberance by an underlying poignancy in the title, the hint that the hopeful view expounded by the poem's speaker will inevitably be modified by age and suffering. Even in Henry James's, or more accurately, George Dane's version of elysium all is not quite as rosy as it might seem.

Although James's story, hinging as it does on the hero's emergence or waking "up" from a lower or submerged state of being, belongs primarily to the mode of romance, this does not mean that it lacks the dimension of irony. George Dane's experience of his paradise seems, in the first place, to be curiously solipsistic and passive, a matter, more than anything else, of sitting and watching and "appreciating." This is very much what might be called a literary gentleman's idea of nirvana. Moreover, it involves a muted but unsettling note of absorbed, almost narcissistic, self-congratulation. The whole idea of a pastoral refuge of course presupposes the idea of an escape from some less desirable reality outside its boundaries, but the experience of paradise is not, presumably, supposed to be chiefly about avoidance. An element of narcissism in Dane seems to be built in, so to speak, to the idyllic prospect of his dream. For his view of the garden contains some significant subliminal "echoes" of his own fearful preoccupation with the failure of his powers and his sense of an impending doom. Although the setting in which he finds himself is by no means unattractive, it does at times evoke the picture of a rather different, more sepulchral kind of place. The peace which so delights Dane may also be seen as the equivocal peace of the churchyard. The "Brothers," that fraternal band of the blessed who appear to be much of a certain age, may also be regarded as a phantom legion of the dead. The case should not be overstated—James does not push the darker element in the story very hard—but it can certainly be made: the milieu into which Dane "falls" when he falls asleep might not be an underworld exactly, but it represents a view of the earth much closer to its actual surface than that which he has been accustomed to contemplate from the high window of his study. And if *The Comedians* is seen as a story organized around the theme of "The Great Good Place," this ironic, sepulchral undertone finds a resounding amplification in the wider world of the novel.

The voyage of Brown, Jones, and the Smiths to Haiti presents a recapitulation in a more realistic framework of the emblematic design of "Under the Garden." Beneath the surface of an idyllic island lies a darker and more sinister country, in this case a land of terror and suffering that lies under the spell of an evil sorcerer, a place where all action becomes dangerous: the typical country, in short, of heroic romance. This design is elaborated technically in two ways, both of which pertain to the matter of narrative perspective. In pictorial terms, the island is idyllic only to the extent that one could regard it with some impossible degree of detachment: "Distance lends enchantment to the view" (108), Petit Pierre giggles at one point, ironically adapting Wordsworth to the paradox of an accursed paradise; the closer one actually gets to the life of Haiti, as the Smiths learn to their dismay, the more the place resembles an obscene charnel house. And this doubleness of perspective is reflected in a slightly different way by the narrative stance of the storyteller. Brown is always uncomfortably aware that the point of view from which he tells his personal tale inevitably lacks the comprehensiveness of a more objective or "serious" account of Haiti. There are, in effect, two distinct stories in *The Comedians:* what Brown sees as the private comedy of the narrative with which he is most intimately concerned, and a larger, continuous public nightmare lying just behind it. In fact, this background text suggests a kind of contemporary *Inferno,* a tragic tale which, whenever Brown is obliged to look at it, has the effect of diminishing the scale of significance in his own personal narrative to the Lilliputian dimensions of pettiness and triviality.

Brown actually perceives his story, in other words, as precisely that type of subsidiary fable set within a wider implicit discourse which has by now become the characteristic central feature of Greene's whole conception of fiction. More precisely still, Brown regards his story as a play within a play: a drama in which the characters evidently cannot help behaving as if they were enacting a rather mechanical farce that happens to have been set, unaccountably, in a context where the very antithesis of farce would seem more appropriate. Speaking of his affair with Martha Pineda, for example, while he contemplates the corpse of Doctor Philipot, he says: "we were only a sub-plot affording a little light relief" (62); musing on his own capacity for sincerity when he lodges with the British chargé d'affaires a protest about the imprisonment of Jones, he remarks that he "felt a little like the player king rebuked by Hamlet for exaggerating his part" (113);

about Martha and himself again, he decides: "We belonged to the world of comedy and not of tragedy" (176). The structure of *The Comedians* is informed by the absurdity of the contrast between, on the one hand, Brown's account of his experiences as a "story" and, on the other, the nightmarish historical "reality" which frames it.

In the role of the narrator, then, Brown exhibits a peculiarly acute sense that his personal identity has become as it were fictionalized by his own narrative. The experience of finding himself defined, as the protagonist of his tale, in terms of the absurd artifice of that tale is embarrassing and disconcerting. But the artifice stems only in part from his view of the sequence of events which he recounts as a comedy within a tragedy. His sense of his own fictiveness also derives from the fact that his narrative about himself—the story in which he is the central figure—increasingly reveals certain emblematic patterns of a kind usually evinced by fiction rather than by "real" autobiography. The sheer ordinariness of his name, for example, would seem to preclude the possibility of a significant role for him in any literary adventure, but because his name is Brown he is disconcerted from the outset, returning from New York to his empty hotel in Haiti, to learn that his fellow passengers on the voyage are named Smith and Jones. The absurd coincidence, like the portentous Greek name of the prosaic little Dutch ship, seems to point either to a practical joke having to do with names or to the artifice of fiction. While the sea voyage offers Brown an interlude of unaccustomed peace and security, the fact that he is traveling on a vessel called the *Medea* suggests both an ironically grandiose prophetic allusion to his own jealous disposition and also the idea that he is fatefully embarked on a romantic journey for which his own name seems inadequate. And as adventurers, his fellow passengers are equally unlikely. Brown is particularly disconcerted by "Major" Jones because he cannot help but glimpse in him a distorted image of himself: the drifting gambler and confidence man down on his luck. The Smiths are more respectable than Jones but no less eccentric, and the figures of Baxter and Mr. Fernandez seem just lunatic enough to confirm Brown's unexpressed but palpable suspicion that he has become a character in some mock-heroic fable about human folly, the obscure, ironic point of which appears to be directed at himself.

Because one of Brown's basic assumptions about his life has always been that it is essentially patternless, the sudden appearance in it of the elements of a literary design takes him by surprise. Disconcertedness turns to horrified bemusement when he arrives at his hotel in Port-au-Prince and discovers that the Haitian minister for social welfare has just killed himself in the empty swimming pool. When he decides at this stage to provide the reader with a *"curriculum vitae"* (64) he does so in the spirit of one pinching himself to make sure that he is really awake. Brown's account of his own life seems to be at least partly motivated by a wish to reassure himself that his personal history is actually as formless as he has always assumed. To the extent that there has ever seemed to be anything resembling a consistent theme or central motif in Brown's career, it has been the theme of the dominance of fortune and the motif of the main chance: the various directions that his life has taken over the years have apparently been followed only in accordance with the random dictates of luck or hazard. Like many another Greene character before him, he is committed to nothing except being a gambler and a wanderer, and in late middle age, his most notable achievement appears to be that he has managed to avoid achieving any sort of distinction. It is a career that Querry might well have envied.

As a boy, we learn, Brown rebelled against his upbringing in a Jesuit academy by bluffing his way into a Monte Carlo casino, winning at roulette, and finally losing his virginity to a mysterious older woman. He then embarked, with the aid of a natural acting talent, on a series of jobs in England ranged on a sliding scale of legitimacy from waiter to confidence artist, a sequence of progressively shadier pursuits interrupted only by a rather grander period as a British intelligence officer during the war. When one of his confidence schemes was suddenly endangered by the threat of public exposure, Brown happened to hear from his long-lost mother, who also happened to be dying; made his way at last to Haiti; and inherited the hotel which she herself had fortuitously acquired by a kind of confidence trick of her own. It is evidently a story about nothing so much as the preeminence of chance. Even the commonness of Brown's name suggests an accidentally bestowed anonymity which, like the adventitiousness of his British nationality, allows him to drift through the world unhindered and largely unnoticed. But because any personal history, however undistinguished, amounts as well to a narrative interpretation of reality, even a drifter's-eye view of the world is inevitably informed by certain elements of literary design. And the central element of this kind in Brown's autobiography has a curiously medieval ring: his view of the world that he wanders is essentially one of a vast casino, "a vision of grown-up life" as "the palace of chance, where anything at all might happen" (68). The organizing metaphor in Brown's curriculum vitae is what would have been known in the Middle Ages as a vision of the house of Fortuna.

His account of his early life begins as a story about abandonment: forsaken by his father, he is also abandoned for many years by his mother. He himself abandons a putative religious vocation. In spite of this latter defection, though, an ideal of some role of ritual service seems to have been ingrained in him, persisting in a surprisingly tenacious way throughout his career: he abandons the idea of serving God but becomes an oddly slavish follower of fortune instead. A world where anything at all might happen must, as Querry learns in *A Burnt-Out Case,* be a world in which only one thing is certain to happen, but of course Brown does not devote himself to drifting and gambling simply in order to assure himself of the supreme reality of death. The gambler's dream is the dream of paradise. Even the most cynical of lottery addicts will attest that the hope springing eternal in the breast of any follower of fortune is the fantasy of "making" a fortune: a dream of the recovery of some imagined condition of ease and freedom from care. The object of gambling can only be the attainment of bliss. As a female goddess, in other words, Fortuna has the allure not just of an ideal maternal figure who offers special protection to her devotees but also of a beautiful woman who always holds out the promise of some apocalyptic erotic consummation. In both capacities, she is inevitably remote and elusive: her emblem is conventionally the perpetually turning wheel, a symbol of frustration in which the gambler's effort to decode an underlying principle of predictable recurrence becomes an obsessive devotion to the very circularity which enslaves him. Brown's curriculum vitae makes it clear that his life has been shaped or determined by his first sexual experience in the sense that that encounter symbolizes for him the fortuitous realization of the great dream of paradise. The older woman in the Monte Carlo hotel room becomes the personification of fortune because she embodies the crowning fulfillment of his first experience of "luck" at the roulette wheel. Brown's sexual initiation on the white bed in the white hotel room represents an epiphanic recovery of the mother who has apparently abandoned him. And as the quasi-magical appearance in the room of a majestic white bird would tend to indicate, the whole experience is more profoundly "religious" for him than anything that he has encountered in the Jesuit academy. It constitutes an early, definitive glimpse of the great good place. But fortune's wheel never ceases its turning, and almost everything that subsequently happens to Brown seems to be a falling away from that visionary apogee, a movement downward into a harsher world where abandonment again becomes the principal theme.

Brown's psychology as a gambler is evidently that of the orphan's Oedipal longing. All women in this perspective tend to acquire an unusually heightened significance because they are all potential agents of redemption. So the shadowy figures of the classical enchantresses invoked in the early chapters of the novel come into slightly clearer focus: both Medea and Medusa embody the most basic and the most ambiguous power of female attraction in this context—they are women whose allure may mean destruction. Beneath the dream of paradise lies a dream of hell. If the experience of sexual initiation represents the zenith of the cycle of Brown's fortunes, then its nadir is the experience of death. Doctor Philipot's suicide in Brown's hotel becomes the occasion of the curriculum vitae because it recalls the death of a previous Haitian victim. Marcel, the "big black beast" (87) who serves Brown's mother right up to the moment of her death in "her great brothelly bed" (101), is clearly a kind of dark, doomed

Adonis. Brown's mother is also perceived as an earth mother, and although Marcel dies by his own hand, it is also as if her lover had in fact been swallowed up by her. Marcel and Brown are rivals because, figuratively speaking, they are brothers, and the symbolic focus of their rivalry is the hotel itself.

When Brown finds his mother at last, the metaphor of the turning wheel that shapes his own unconscious conception of his life becomes something other than the emblem of the apparent randomness with which fortune bestows her favors. He attains his inheritance; he *arrives*. His mother's gift of the Trianon suggests to him that he has finally completed the broken circle of his own destiny. He perceives Marcel's surrender of his interest in the hotel as an "abdication" (86): Brown has finally come into his rightful kingdom, and Marcel's rapid decline following on the death of the "countess" heralds his own ultimate ascendancy. Inheriting his mother's bed, he again recovers his potency in another bed in another room in another hotel; his chance meeting with Martha Pineda in the Port-au-Prince casino becomes the renewal of an earlier encounter in an older casino. And the vision of the whole world as a vast palace of chance modulates, in the psychoanalytic perspective, into the vision of an enchanted hotel, so that the recovery of an Eden or of a lost golden age translates into the terms of a discovery of a "new" world, a magical arcadian place which, for Brown, becomes the transfiguration of one of the most familiar types of erotic subtext in the literature of the tourist brochure:

> Few in the good days drank anywhere else but the Trianon, except for those who were booked on round tours and chalked everything up. The Americans always drank dry Martinis. By midnight some of them would be swimming in the pool naked. Once I had looked out of my window at two in the morning. There was a great yellow moon and a girl was making love in the pool. She had her breasts pressed against the side and I couldn't see the man behind her. She didn't notice me watching her; she didn't notice anything. That night I thought before I slept, "I have arrived." (55)

This sexualized tourist paradise presided over by the spirit of a spellbinding woman with an inexhaustible hunger for love symbolizes the "making" of Brown's fortune in the very precise sense that it represents the realization of an endless erotic dream. The figure of arrival is one of consummation; Brown has again glimpsed a promised land.

The fact remains, though, that he takes possession of this great good place as a kind of outsider or voyeur. Brown's ascendancy and his new career are based upon the decline and fall of his mother's last lover: he remains uncomfortably aware of Marcel's role as sacrificial victim. Brown's mother may be inexhaustible, but her lovers are not: like Marcel or Brown's father, they die or disappear. Fortune's wheel keeps on turning and the vision of paradise remains elusive, appearing briefly and then forever receding into the distance like some tantalizing mirage. On the night of his mother's death, Brown dreams that he is walking, dressed as an altar boy, by the side of a moonlit lake; the water draws him like a magnet, but when he reaches it he finds that the lake has retreated from him until it exists "only as a gleam on the far horizon of . . . [a] . . . desert of small stones, which wounded me through a hole in my boots" (80). This is, of course, a version of Brown's life as a failed priest and a wanderer, but it is also the story of the perpetual desolation of the gambler, an image of the flat, endless, empty wilderness which looms eternally in the foreground of every chance prospect of paradisal fulfillment. The wheel turns, and the epiphany of the girl in the swimming pool turns to an epiphany of death: when Brown travels to Haiti for the last time he discovers that his swimming pool has become a grave. The mutilated corpse of Doctor Philipot signifies not only that a larger tragedy has intruded into Brown's private comedy but also that there is some mysterious, inextricable link between the kind of story that Javitt would regard as the exemplification of a "garden fate" and the kind that he would recognize as an "underground" tale. When Brown sets out for his Haitian hotel in the *Medea*, he does so with the hope of seeing it again in its aspect as a sunlit "illustration from a book of fairy tales" (52); what he actually finds when he gets there is the "Charles Addams house" (52) in a grotesque night world.

The Comedians may be read, like the underworld episode in the *Aeneid*, as a book of the dead, for the world that lies under the garden in this novel is perceived quite specifically as the country of death. Haiti becomes a kind of infernal necropolis, a vast burial ground where the fates of Marcel and Doctor Philipot seem to be peculiarly normative. Because of the cruel contempt in which human life is held by Papa Doc and his Tontons Macoute, death seems more than usually ubiquitous here. And this ubiquity has an important figurative dimension as well. The vision of Haiti is classically Hadean: not only are the inhabitants of this country terrorized, brutalized, and maimed, the context of their suffering is such that they have been deprived of the power of any sort of action except the most mechanical and compulsive; they have been robbed of genuine or substantial human identity. The legless beggar in Duvalierville may be regarded as exemplary: the horrifying futility of his attempt to flee from the vengeful "justice of the peace" (180) suggests the narrative ethos of the nightmare, the type of suspended animation of what is in fact an antinarrative in which the protagonist can only await his doom. Life in these circumstances is arrested in a kind of limbo, the marginal, twilight existence of the spellbound and paralyzed victim or of the shade trapped in hell. It is the night world of the anonymous sufferer who literally vanishes from human sight in what amounts to a never-ending curfew. Above all, this is the country of the walking dead.

One of the reasons why Brown and Martha Pineda are so troubled by a mutual sense of almost hypnotic compulsion in their love affair is that they are like a pair of zombies in a Haitian cemetery, two of the living dead inexplicably obliged to couple in a dance which seems to them both absurd and repellent. When Brown returns to Haiti, he is almost as dismayed by this sense of his and Martha's erotic helplessness as by the discovery of Doctor Philipot's body. He returns not to the fulfillment that he had hoped for but to a renewed "abandonment": what has actually been lost now, of course, is the sense of his own personal autonomy. If he appears to be equally distressed by the apparently unimportant disappearance from the hotel of a private souvenir or keepsake, that dismay is actually less incongruous than it seems in that the "small brass paper-weight" that he has lost is "shaped like a coffin, marked with the letters R.I.P." (55). The allegorical direction of the *Medea*'s nautical course could hardly have been made more explicit: returning "home" to find that his coffin has gone, Brown is upset precisely because he is now doomed *not* to rest in peace. If his hotel is his own great good place, it is also his own tomb, a ghostly house haunted ultimately by himself alone.

The dream of paradise is associated with the figure of an "enchanting" but elusive and sexually promiscuous mother. The complementary dream of hell is dominated by the figure of an equally spellbinding but more unambiguously sinister father: the dictator, Duvalier, is not known as "Papa Doc" for nothing. Although he never appears in the novel, Duvalier's presence hovers over the sepulchral night world of the background text like some brooding incubus. His authority derives largely from his legendary reputation as a kind of ultimate voodoo priest or *houngan*, one with the power to raise the dead for his own dreadful purposes. For this is a world under the spell of a great necromancer who, although he is unseen, is always everywhere, like a terrible parody of an omniscient God. Papa Doc may be regarded as the chief zombie in a country of zombies. With his neon-lit heraldic signature, "*Je suis le drapeau Haïtien, Uni et Indivisible*" (51), he represents the same blanket principle of demonic tyranny as Blake's "Covering Cherub." He is popularly viewed in Haiti as a vampire, which means primarily that his dark hegemony can be sustained only by the blood of his victims: as a paternal figure or "king," he is the giver not of life but death, which means in effect that his strength comes from his subjects in the sense that he feeds on them. "In this island," Doctor Magiot remarks to Brown, "the Catholic prayer is very apt—'The devil is like a roaring lion seeking whom he may devour'" (102). Papa Doc Duvalier has fathered a land of death because he is himself the personified embodiment of death as a paradoxically living or active power, the last word, so to speak, in bloodthirsty cannibalism.

The essential paradox implicit in any narrative about an underworld is of course that while the inhabitants of such a region are figuratively buried they also have the kind of figurative life usually attributed to phantoms and ghouls: the imaginative perspective tends to reveal them as dead men who are unable to lie down, as we say, in peace. Symbolically, death "possesses" its victims in a kind of active parody of the life-force. To take a relatively early and obvious instance of this principle of symbolism in Greene's work, Pinkie in *Brighton Rock* is an underworld figure whose career becomes intelligible only in the light of his all-consuming appetite for destruction. And the affair between Pinkie Brown's namesake and his mistress in *The Comedians* is clearly one in which Eros has modulated to Thanatos: Brown and Martha are impelled in their relation to each other by exactly the impulse that has shaped the destinies of Marcel and Doctor Philipot. Their love tends to be described as a morbid fever or an inexplicable sickness. They are "lost souls," for the dynamic of their relationship stems from the ethos of their environment. This is a situation that would seem to be intrinsically devoid of the possibility of narrative development. By the standards of logical discourse, in fact, any "book" of the dead is inherently absurd, almost a self-contradictory proposition. However, the principles of literary symbolism have their own peculiar consistency, and the narrative elaboration of a world of death-in-life normally proceeds according to the logic which inheres in the paradox that it is a world of life-in-death as well. If Papa Doc can be seen as a vampire or as a roaring lion seeking whom he may devour, then resistance to him becomes the essentially symbolic gesture of protecting the graves of those who are buried from his renewed depredations.

The conception of symbolic resistance in this context makes no more sense by the standards of logical discourse than the notion that death itself has some sort of monstrous personal vitality, but it is a conception nevertheless central to a structure of symbolism deeply rooted in the conventional idiom of romance. Again, the sixth book of the *Aeneid* may be regarded as the definitive narrative archetype here. Even the most cursory reading of the account of Aeneas's descent into the underworld reveals a near-obsessive preoccupation with the importance of certain types of ritual consecration: the Cumaean sibyl tells him at the outset, for example, that he cannot begin his journey until he buries the body of a fallen comrade with all the appropriate funeral rites;

and at the bank of the Stygian river, Aeneas finds that a great host of the dead are refused passage into Hades because they have not for one reason or another been buried with due ceremony in the world above. The essential rite of passage in the kingdom of death is clearly that of the commemorative obsequy, and the soul of the person who has been deprived of a consecrated burial seems to be left literally nowhere. What has actually been "lost" by a lost soul in this circumstance is his unique identity as a human being. In the classical epic tradition, the account of the elaborate funeral of the renowned warrior becomes a rhetorical commonplace precisely because it represents an assertion of the continuity of human identity in death. And while our perception that death is what robs us of our identity may seem obvious to the point of absurdity, it has a profound imaginative resonance in all literary conceptions of hell.

The narrative focus of *The Comedians,* the theme to which the novel returns again and again, is the theme of the importance of sanctifying the dead. We are told in the opening sentence of "the modest stone that commemorates Jones" (9), and by the time Brown reaches his conclusion, in which he himself begins his new career as an undertaker, that memorial has assumed a significance which seems considerably more than modest. Similarly, while the mysterious Mr. Fernandez is perceived initially as a kind of tragicomic simpleton, his role in the novel eventually modulates to something that approaches the idea of a secular priesthood. The figure of the undertaker becomes important because the raising of tombs represents a sacred trust undertaken by the living on behalf of the dead. The thing that is being entrusted to him is the symbolic preservation of an identity. William Faulkner's *As I Lay Dying* represents perhaps the most ambitious and complex modern treatment of this theme: all the members of Addie Bundren's family are compelled to be her companions as well as her undertakers, almost forced as it were against their wills to accompany her underground. In *The Comedians,* the "kidnapping" of Doctor Philipot's corpse epitomizes the peculiarly gratuitous brutality of Papa Doc's regime in that Doctor Philipot is thus denied a proper funeral. Apart from the popular belief that Duvalier in his role as Baron Samedi wishes to reanimate and then enslave the dead in the cellars of his palace, there is something uniquely grisly about the activity of body snatching. Designed to inspire an indeterminate terror, it seems also to represent an ultimate assault on human dignity. If Brown's hotel is a tomb, then at least it symbolizes the integrity of a familial identity, but one of the most horrifying aspects of the figure of death as a devourer is that this integrity is exactly what it devours. The essential condition toward which life tends in Papa Doc's Haiti seems to be that of a uniform, sinister anonymity. Papa Doc himself is virtually invisible; his agents, the Tontons Macoute, are indistinguishable from one another behind their dark glasses; the population at large has become an aggregate of faceless cripples. This is a society organized in terms of a parodic vision of identity. So the ordinary impulse to bury the dead safely and with appropriate ceremony becomes a serious challenge, almost an outright threat, to the very raison d'être of an absolute social authority which aspires to the creation of a world inhabited entirely by zombies. The ritual of the funeral in *The Comedians* takes on an emblematic significance which is closely connected to the larger motif of heroic action as political resistance; the whole theme of the revolutionary struggle that seems doomed to failure takes us from the text of Brown's narrative to the narrative that lies behind it, and its emblematic form turns out, in fact, to be a quixotic gesture of defiance in a cemetery.

There are two main strands of figurative design in this novel: the symbolism associated with mothers and the symbolism associated with graveyards. Since the structure of Brown's narrative is implicitly informed by the figure of the wheel of fortune, these two strands are of course closely interwoven. The narrator himself never arrives at any consistently conscious recognition of the link between them: "There were no heights and no abysses in my world," he tells us near his story's conclusion, "—I saw myself on a great plain, walking and walking on the interminable flats" (312). But behind this image of a horizontal lineality, an echo perhaps from the dream of the receding lake in the desert, lies the image of the turning wheel with a golden garden place at its zenith and at its nadir a grave. In the perspective of romance, they are the same place: his mother's hotel is at once a paradisal retreat and a mausoleum. Brown's metaphor of an interminable flat wilderness, like Thomas Fowler's vision of the landscape of Vietnam, represents the way in which an endless circularity might appear to someone who happens to be trapped inside it: a prospect not of heights and abysses but of a perpetual treadmill.

Every female character in *The Comedians* tends to be presented in terms of a maternal role that is usually conceived as protective. Aside from Brown's actual mother and the woman in the Monte Carlo hotel, the most important mother figure is of course Martha Pineda. From the beginning, Brown recognizes her son, the chubby "Angel" with his unangelic addiction to bourbon biscuits, as his "real rival" (97). In a moment of retrospective insight, he even acknowledges that "it was not Martha's love for me which held me, if she did love, it was her blind unselfish attachment to her child" (151). The real nature of Brown's dream of love becomes clearest when he is being consoled by Martha just after having been beaten up by the Tontons Macoute:

> I could not remember a time when we had been so alone and so at peace. The long hours of the afternoon faded behind the mosquito-netting over the bedroom window. When I look back on that afternoon it seems to me we had been granted the distant sight of a promised land—we had come to the edge of a desert: the milk and honey awaited us: our spies went by carrying their burden of grapes. (204)

But even the formidable Mrs. Smith shares something of this maternal consolatory function. When Mr. Fernandez bursts inexplicably into tears during the ultimate festivities aboard the *Medea*—an occurrence which, as we later learn, has to do with his belief at the time that his own mother is dying—Mrs. Smith soothes him and assuages his apparently unaccountable grief. "She might have been a mother," the narrator remarks, "comforting her child among strangers" (41). And later, when Captain Concasseur seems on the point of actually shooting Brown, Mrs.

Smith strides fearlessly to the rescue and demands that he hand over his revolver. In the face of her wrath, the sadistic Concasseur is briefly reduced to a kind of shamefaced infancy: "As though he were guarding a precious object from an angry mother, he buttoned the gun back inside his holster" (203). Madame Philipot is also perceived in terms of this protective maternal role, and even Mère Catherine, the old brothel keeper, is characterized as the kindly mother of her girls.

In general, the women in the novel display more courage than the men; and when the men do behave with some spirit, there is often the suggestion of the blurring of gender that occurs so frequently in romance. The captain of the *Medea* may be a prim "hausfrau" (233)—"an old lady," as he seems to Brown, "disturbed in her hotel room" (230)—but he deals authoritatively enough with the officer of the Tontons Macoute who swaggers aboard in search of Jones. And of course Jones himself is almost literally metamorphosed for a while into a rather grotesquely flamboyant female character; he brings the warmth, we are told, of "a kind of domesticity" (260) into the chilly Pineda household: Brown becomes jealous, suspecting him of being Martha's secret lover, but Jones's role in the familial life of the embassy seems in fact to be that of an ideal housemother.

However, the imagery of this kind of feminine warmth and protective vitality is consistently linked in one way or another with the imagery of death. Brown is no sooner reunited with his mother than she expires, and his account of her funeral becomes the account of his real introduction to the life of Haiti. The cemetery in which she is buried resembles nothing so much as a city built for a subterranean race of dwarfs: her grave looks "like a hole dug for drains in a town street, for all around were the little houses the Haitians constructed for their dead" (83). Figuratively speaking, the tomb and the cemetery constitute, respectively, the real domestic and social settings of the novel; the iconography of the necropolis is everywhere. A Haitian village, for example, is described in the following terms:

> In the small yards the family tombs looked more solid than the family huts. The dead were allotted mansions of a better class than

the living—houses of two storeys with window embrasures where food and lights could be placed on the night of All Souls. . . . In a long yard beside the road there were rows of little crosses with what looked like tresses of blonde hair looped between, as though they had been ripped from the skulls of women buried below. (281)

This is an iconography that pervades the texture of Brown's narrative in even its most subsidiary rhythms:

An occasional candle burned over a little group bowed above their rum like mourners over a coffin. (153)

Or:

I watched before every turn for the light of another car, but Port-au-Prince was as empty as a cemetery. (238)

Again:

The hotel had need of paint and repairs, but what good was there in spending the labour without the hope of guests? Only the John Barrymore suite I kept in good order like a grave. (100)

Or, in a more meditative vein:

I wondered whether the world would ever again sail with such serenity through space as it seemed to do a hundred years ago. Then the Victorians kept skeletons in cupboards—but who cares about a mere skeleton now? Haiti was not an exception in a sane world: it was a small slice of everyday taken at random. Baron Samedi walked in all our graveyards. (141)

Seen as it were from a distance, Brown's narrative becomes the revelation of an almost continuous process of lowering a corpse into a grave.

But the corpse is not necessarily safe from violation even there. A sudden rainstorm interrupts the funeral of Brown's mother, and the gravediggers as well as the mourners run for cover: "I didn't know it then, but I know now that the diggers would not have returned before the morning to cover up my mother's coffin, for no one will work in a cemetery at night, unless it is a zombie who has left his grave at the command of an *houngan* to labour during the dark hours" (83). The novel's vision of a society that amounts to a community of the dead is also, in emblematic terms, a vision of a funeral service continually menaced by the threat of a dreadful suspension. For the world ruled by Baron Samedi is one in which the dead are raised as ghouls in a demonic parody of the Christian resurrection of the body. In this context, the metaphor of revival has to do not with the awakening power of love but with the appetite of a kind of ultimate depravity: Papa Doc is "hungry for the dead" (195); when Hamit's body is discovered, there is a general local panic because of the feeling that "one body was not sufficient to make a feast-day for Baron Samedi" (268). Doctor Magiot explains that Doctor Philipot may have chosen to die in Brown's hotel because of the hope—based on the proverbial reputation of the Englishman's home as an inviolable castle—that his corpse might then remain undisturbed; there are, however, no safe havens.

Doctor Magiot himself is as much an underground figure as anyone else in the novel, and not just in the sense that he represents the subversiveness of a forbidden political ideology. Like Brown's, Magiot's house is also a family tomb, in his case a specifically Victorian mausoleum that contrasts oddly at first glance with his Marxism. As a revolutionary activist, in fact, Doctor Magiot seems somewhat unusual in a number of respects. He is a conspicuous anachronism not only in the Haitian but in the wider modern context, a representative in various respects of the buried life of the past: exemplifying a bourgeois solidity and formal courtesy which seem inseparable from his nineteenth-century domestic environment, he is repeatedly linked as well with the aristocratic dignity and stoicism associated with the ancient Roman *imperium*. Like Javitt, Magiot has the quality of statuesque immobility, a noble stillness of bearing that somehow exhibits all the virtues of whole vanished cycles or buried strata of civilizaton. As an underground figure, he differs from Brown in the sense that he looks less like a zombie than like a timeworn monument. Observing him "in his Victorian sitting-room," the narrator says: "Doctor Magiot was not in a humour to talk, but his silence was as monumental as his conversation. When he said 'Another glass?' the phrase was like a simple name carved on a tombstone" (269). In the iconography of the graveyard, perhaps the most significant image is that of the monument which is also a statue, the inscribed memorial which embodies or preserves the identity of the person who lies beneath it.

Northrop Frye has pointed out that statues and pictures tend to "turn up near the beginning of a romance to indicate the threshold of the romance world."[6] In this context, they are usually liminal symbols of the narrative idiom of suspension which characterizes the theme of descent as the rhythm of errancy in that world—emblems of an arrested motion which mirrors the sense of powerlessness or paradoxical immobility increasingly experienced by the wandering hero or heroine. *The Comedians* presents a fictional setting almost as cluttered with statuary as Magiot's house seems to be with Victorian bric-a-brac. At the threshold of Brown's narrative stands not only Jones's memorial stone but also all those gray public monuments to forgotten "frock-coated politicians" and "equestrian generals" (9) with which it is so pointedly contrasted. The figure of the monumental statue, obscure and not so obscure, sometimes merges with that of the maternal protectress. When, for instance, Madame Philipot vainly tries to prevent the hijacking of her husband's coffin, Brown notes that "she stood with her arms out like a bad patriotic monument to a forgotten war" (130). Even Brown's ambitious dream about the hotel that he has inherited takes the form of the realization or attainment of a kind of monumental prize: "*Exegi monumentum aere perennius*" (65) is the Horatian tag from his school days which surfaces in his mind on the day of his mother's death. His habitual place of rendezvous with Martha in Port-au-Prince is the statue of Columbus: a monument to the discovery of the New World as the figurative prospect of a recovered Eden or promised land. Statues are inevitably cynosural; existing to be looked at, they symbolize the theme of the centripetal gaze. "We sat and stared," Brown remarks, "at the statue which stared at America" (92). And what Frye calls the "naive and involving stare"[7] which always seems to be the quintessential visual perspective in romance is evoked even more clearly by the novel's various pictures and paintings.

These range in importance from the pictorial vignettes captured in a series of postcards designed for tourists and the faked works of art—"a picture can represent a fortune" (69)—by which Brown once made his living to a collection of genuine Haitian paintings that he has inherited along with his hotel. Again, the central theme here seems to be that of arrested motion. On his first arrival at the Trianon, Brown observes that the "walls were hung with pictures by Haitian artists: forms caught in wooden gestures among bright and heavy colours" (75). The pictorial vision always hints at a darker petrified world underlying the paradisal one. There is, for example, the painting by Philippe Auguste

> of a carnival procession, men, women and children wearing bright masks. Of a morning, when the sunlight shone through the first-floor windows, the harsh colours gave an impression of gaiety, the drummers and the trumpeters seemed about to play a lively air. Only when you came closer you saw how ugly the masks were and how the masquers surrounded a cadaver in grave-clothes; then the primitive colours went flat as though the clouds had come down from Kenscoff and the thunder would soon follow. Wherever that picture hung, I thought, I would feel Haiti close to me. Baron Samedi would be walking in the nearest graveyard, even though the nearest graveyard was in Tooting Bec. (275)

This description recapitulates the rhetorical structure of the novel as a whole: viewed closely, the absurd comedy of Brown's love affair both with Martha and with his resort hotel modulates to an arrangement of "wooden gestures" around the motionless centripetal figure of a symbolic corpse. In this perspective, the motif of the naive involving stare shifts to the background text and becomes the accusatory gaze of Captain Concasseur and the Tontons Macoute: the visual equivalent of the process of victimization is a menacing glare in which the victim is held or caught in the sense that he becomes totally known.

The Philippe Auguste painting represents the *pompes funèbres* of a ceremonial interment. But it takes the aspect of a carnival procession because of an element of genuine comedy in it, and this element has to do, as we have seen, with the way in which the symbolism of the funeral tends to incorporate a subversive dimension of social defiance or resistance to authority: here it is the representation of a ritual in which death itself is being ritually mocked. In figurative terms, everything that happens in *The Comedians* happens in a cemetery, so that virtually every event described by Brown has something of the aspect of the ceremonial interment. The voodoo ritual which ends with the disappearance of Joseph, for example, is perceived quite explicitly in just these terms: Brown says that he felt as lonely after the voodoo ceremony "as a man in a strange hotel after a friend's funeral" (198). However, the climactic occurrence at this "funeral" is not the lowering but rather the symbolic raising of the corpse. Through the agency of the martial god, Ogoun Ferraille, the crippled Joseph and the limping Henri Philipot are suddenly transformed from the pathetic immobility of their roles as "comedians," in the sense of helpless puppets, to a new active and heroic status as guerrilla warriors. Joseph in particular is like a monument come to life:

> Someone came forward with a machete and clamped it in Joseph's wooden hand as though he were a statue waiting completion. The statue began to move. It slowly raised an arm, then swung the machete in a wide arc so that everyone ducked for fear it would fly across the *tonnelle*. Joseph began to run, the machete flashing and cutting; those in the front row scrambled back, so that for a moment there was panic. Joseph was no longer Joseph . . . where was his injury now? He ran without a stumble. (197)

Joseph has in effect been reborn, and the structure of the imagery suggests the recovery or reanimation of an identity hitherto frozen or suspended. This new identity finds expression in a form of action which has a clearly political significance. It has become a kind of critical truism to note that Greene's political sympathies by this stage in his career are with the radical left, but his flirtation with Marxism needs to be located in the appropriate romance context. As a revolutionary figure, Doctor Magiot represents a heroic norm in the novel: he too is like a statue waiting for a sword to be clamped in his hand; but he exemplifies the energy of revolution in the Blakean sense that he embodies a buried life which is always waiting to be resurrected, a repressed but genuinely imaginative or civilized power that will eventually erupt to consume the forces of tyranny and death. The element of revolutionary romanticism in Greene's later work may or may not be politically naive, but its literary roots are in any case profoundly traditional and sophisticated.

In romance terms, there is a crucial shift in focus in *The Comedians* from the pastoral to the heroic, from Brown's story about his hotel and his love affair to the world of the public nightmare lying behind it. This shift is centered on the clownish but irrepressible character of Jones. Jones shares with Brown the gambler's dream of landing up on a paradisal island; even more deeply embedded in his life, though, is a dream of military glory. In realistic terms, his fantasy about being an expert guerrilla leader seems no less absurd than every other feature of his history. But then the realistic perspective is one in which all dreams are always quixotic: the genuine source of affinity among Brown, Jones, and the Smiths—what is actually symbolized by the "interchangeable" anonymity of their names—is that they are all literary dreamers. Each of them lives with the hope of realizing some more-or-less eccentric vision of utopia. What they share, in other words, is a distinctly fictive sense of reality. The trouble with Mr. Smith's project of establishing a vegetarian center in Port-au-Prince is that it reflects a hopelessly inadequate view of the real conditions of life in Haiti: it is a private narrative rather than a plausible public enterprise, and for that very reason, both Brown and Jones come to recognize Mr. Smith as a type of spiritual "father" (212–13). Brown's dream of persuading Martha to leave her family and of creating the supreme tourist pleasure dome in the Caribbean constitutes essentially the same kind of quixotic fantasy, as does Jones's pipe dream about "Sahib House" and "the Desert Island Bar" (216–17). These are all strictly imaginary versions of elysium, literary pastorals of a highly conventional order. But behind the surface of Jones's vision of himself as a lotus-eating "sahib" lies a more deeply rooted narrative about his exploits as a guerrilla hero; and, as it happens, this dream is one which the dreadful reality of Haiti might just accommodate.

The pastoral in heroic romance tends to be properly an interlude, an oblique image or figurative projection of the end of the quest rather than an end in itself. Almost by definition, the pastoral vision of the great good place is a dream, a mirage like Brown's perpetually receding lake. If the pastoral *is* viewed as an end in itself, then what tends to happen, typically, is that the reverie of ease and freedom turns into a nightmare about some form of petrification and loss of identity: *otium,* to use an older terminology, becomes *accidia.* Brown, for example, always finds himself in the position of glimpsing an image of fulfillment that forever eludes him, so that he becomes suspended in a kind of spellbound immobility in which he is in every sense lost. Alone in his hotel, he has another dream, and his cherished anonymity is now transformed into a sort of dreadful invisibility:

> I was a boy kneeling at the communion-rail in the college chapel in Monte Carlo. The priest came down the row and placed in each mouth a bourbon biscuit, but when he came to me he passed me by. The communicants on either side came and went away, but I knelt obstinately on. Again, the priest distributed the biscuits and left me out. I stood up then and walked sullenly away down the aisle which had become an immense aviary where parrots stood in ranks chained to their crosses. Someone called out sharply behind me, "Brown, Brown," but I was not certain whether that was my name or not, for I didn't turn. "Brown." This time I awoke and a voice came up to me from the verandah below my room. (225)

Brown's loss of his "name" and the image—which we have met before in *The Third Man*—of the parrot as a mocking echo bird tell us a good deal about the dangers implicit in what might be called pastoral narcissism. Brown's narrative perspective has always been, like Fowler's in *The Quiet American,* consistently and profoundly solipsistic. He is, as Martha tells him, a "novelist" (249) whose characters are all projections of his own anxieties. Brown has only one story, his dream of his own good place, and he is evidently captivated by or locked into it. Paradoxically, this obsession with a private pastoral vision which seems unattainable has led him to the edge of a kind of self-annihilation. But the last voice to call his name in his dream, the one that wakes him up, belongs to Jones; and Jones's life is governed by another type of story, one in which the vision of an island paradise constitutes an interlude in the hero's quest rather than its real goal.

While Jones's story is all about heroic action, it remains of course a fiction, and a remarkably narcissistic fiction at that. The episode in his career which corresponds to Brown's dream about his uncertainty over his name is his meeting in Burma with a commando whose great talent was the ability to smell out water in the jungle: "when he told me that," Jones tells Brown, "it was like someone calling me by my real name" (289). He adopts the talent as his own and thus assumes his guerrilla identity. Until now, however, this has always been a literary identity, a purely imaginative role. When the purser of the *Medea* looks up Jones's birth sign in an astrological almanac he finds: "An artistic temperament. Ambitious. Successful in literary enterprises" (221). Jones's life as an amiable fraud has been one long series of literary enterprises, but the only confidence trick that will turn out to be really successful is the story he devises which concludes with his own martyrdom. He reverts, with the failure of his scheme to swindle Captain Concasseur and Papa Doc, from his "Sahib House" story to the private narrative that is imaginatively prior to it. As the pastoral dream recedes, Jones commits himself at last to the heroic one, and Brown discovers to his astonishment that this is a literary enterprise with a genuine shaping power over the seemingly intractable reality which forms the setting of the novel. Jones's entire life and, indeed, the Haitian Hades in which he finds himself are in effect transformed by what appears to be no more than an idiosyncratic fantasy.

The power of the fantasy, however, derives from the way in which its structure conforms to the shape of things as they are in the country where it is enacted. Haiti looks like a paradise but is actually a hell; Jones's last "literary enterprise" takes the conventional romance form of the abandonment of an illusory garden world in favor of a heroic descent into a world of death. It is a descent from which he does not himself emerge alive. In the figurative idiom of the novel, Jones relinquishes the escapist dream of paradise in order to undertake a journey to a graveyard. Like

William Wilditch, he goes underground, taking Brown along with him: the metaphorical direction of the arduous trip from Port-au-Prince to the cemetery near Aquin is downward, a journey in a sense into the desert landscape of Brown's first nightmare. Like Wilditch again, he takes his own romantic talisman along with him as well—the cocktail case from Asprey's which becomes the symbolic focus of all the keepsake imagery in the novel, such as Brown's paperweight coffin and his mother's memorabilia. And although we have no reason to suppose that Jones may be a religious man, his last literary enterprise is above all a Christian romance, for he is to become a sacrificial victim whose death proves redemptive, a quixotic but authentic harrower of hell. What is more important from his own point of view, the end of his quest is his personal discovery of a "good place." At the very bottom, so to speak, of the pictorial vision of Haiti, we are given a glimpse of paradise that takes the form of a reversed image of the prospect at the surface: Jones's discovery is of a kind of Calvary. Brown's last dream on the last page of *The Comedians* suggests that "the great good place," the only place where human identity becomes genuinely recoverable, is the place of death.

On the face of it, this seems a rather morbid conclusion even from a Christian viewpoint. In fact, of course, the essential thing about the idea of the good place is that it exists and thrives in the imagination. "Who seems most kingly is the King," and the few square yards of boulder-strewn wilderness where Jones dies are his real "kingdom": they amount quite simply to the way that a promised land might appear in the heroic rather than the pastoral perspective. While Brown recognizes Jones's death as an act of martyrdom, he himself is no martyr, and the heroic perspective is not one that he could long sustain. Driven by the same death wish as everyone else in his narrative, he is nevertheless a born survivor. Brown's role in Jones's story becomes that of the most ambiguous of figures in Greene's mythology, the role of Judas: he makes the journey to the cemetery possible and, at the same time, knowing as he does the odds against his "brother's" survival in the mountains with Henri Philipot's tiny band of guerrillas, he acts as Jones's betrayer. But Brown is also one of those whom

Jones redeems. The central metaphor of redemption in *The Co-medians* is of revival in the sense of an emergence from a state of spellbound suspension, an awakening from the sort of zombie-like trance which characterizes Brown's last days and nights in his "family tomb." Because of Jones, he goes down to the ceme-tery near Aquin, taking what Doctor Magiot describes as "that dangerous journey which we all have to take before the end" (311); and his escape from Haiti into the Dominican Republic then becomes a figurative ascent, an escape from death that is also a kind of rebirth. Moreover, Brown's new vocation turns out, ironically, to be another version of the one that he had aban-doned in the Monte Carlo casino: in this novel, the offices of priest and undertaker are much the same. Like Thomas Fowler, he recognizes that his real role in his own narrative is to be his savior's chronicler, so that his story is ultimately the verbal equiv-alent of Jones's memorial stone, the translation of a monument into living speech.

With the revelation of the narrator as a man who has risen from the world of the dead in order to honor the dead, Brown's narrative comes full circle. From beginning to end, his career is informed by the figure of the turning wheel. Because he is without "roots," Brown sees himself as one of the "faithless" (304), of whom he says, "We have chosen nothing except to go on liv-ing"—and here he quotes Wordsworth—" 'Rolled round on Earth's diurnal course, / With rocks and stones and trees' " (304). His choice of allusion is both curious and revealing. The refer-ence is to the Lucy of "A Slumber Did My Spirit Seal," who has in fact departed the living to join the dead. However, the paradox around which this poem is constructed is that Lucy's death means that her life has passed into the consciousness of the poet, whose task then becomes to speak for the rocks and stones and trees. For the speaker, the girl's departure represents a painful awakening from the state of slumber in which he himself existed while she was alive: nature ceases to be a kindly, nourishing mother and becomes an indifferent, mechanically wheeling cycle that symbolizes his own sense of loss and alienation. Superim-posed on this figure of the turning wheel, though, is the image of the awakening from inarticulacy: in becoming Lucy's chronicler, the poet emerges from silence, converting the mute forms of nature into those of language. So too in *The Comedians:* Brown undergoes the same kind of painful revival. And like the speaker of Wordsworth's poem, he finds that he is both "faithless" and at the same time imbued with a new fidelity to the dead. Brown begins as an orphan in search of a mother, a man who spends his life looking for a great good place, but he comes to the realization that such a quest has led him into a fateful circularity; his story concludes with a dialectical thrust out of the process of circularity, an upward movement of the wheel which turns on the figure of a statue coming to life in a cemetery. And at the end of it all, he receives a letter from a dead man: Doctor Magiot is now literally as well as figuratively entombed. Brown begins by looking for his mother and ends by finding a dead "father"—not the great necromancer of the novel but his antitype, an underworld "sorcerer" who "exorcis[es] death" (102).

Doctor Magiot becomes Brown's spiritual father not just because he is, like Mr. Smith, a congenial paternal figure, but because Brown inherits the subversiveness of his "faith" (312). While this could be read as a belief "in the future of Communism" (193), it is, more broadly, a faith in the ultimate triumph of life over death. The figure of the maternal protectress is associated with the narrative rhythm of errancy or suspension; the figure of the true father is associated with the narrative thrust of significant action which leads forward in heroic romance to the goal of the quest. Aeneas goes down into Hades because he wants his father's blessing before setting out to found a new Troy. The upshot of Brown's relationship with Doctor Magiot is less dramatic: the only form of heroic action available to him becomes the assumption of a certain imaginative attitude, a commitment more passive than active to a spirit of resistance which, in the immediate practical sense, is certainly futile. In any case, Brown is no guerrilla hero. But in joining the firm of Mr. Fernandez he becomes in his own way a man who inherits a paternal "craft." Like his real father, he makes an escape; like Doctor Magiot and the speaker in Wordsworth's poem, he learns to exorcise death by speaking for the dead.

Language in this sense becomes a type of monumental action. The world of the novel's "reality," the background text that "contains" Brown's narrative, is not so much tragic, in fact, as unintelligible: Papa Doc's regime presents a vision of human suffering without meaning; it is a tale signifying nothing but horror. Moreover, the trouble with the narrator's story about his own dream of paradise is not only that it has no impact on that vision of unredeemed pain but that it tends to be assimilated to it. But in telling Jones's story about finding *his* good place, Brown makes the larger reality intelligible. The dream of heroic action ceases to be the most subsidiary of the novel's interior narratives and becomes its supreme fiction. An intractable reality yields to an imaginative interpretation of it; meaningless suffering is suddenly assimilated to the story of martyrdom and redemptive sacrifice. And the fiction assumes a paradoxical priority over the reality: in ceasing to be merely a subsidiary fantasy, the discovery of the good place becomes an archetype in the sense that it informs the narrative as a whole. Generating the novel's meaning, an apparently irrelevant fiction in which a man falls asleep, dreams, and then wakes up again becomes progenitive in that it turns out to be a first and last "word"—like a rune carved on a stone or an inscription on a tomb.

The missing father in Brown's story is not so much his real father as a dead man who must be found and resurrected in his own imagination. We have noticed that Doctor Magiot's strength and integrity derive from the way in which his political radicalism seems so profoundly based on a view of "civilization" that is centered on the past: a statuesque man who looks and behaves like a Roman "senator" (251) and who lives in the kind of house where, after dinner, Brown has the feeling that "we should have joined other members of the Browning Society for a discussion of the *Sonnets from the Portugese*" (270) clearly exemplifies something more than an eccentric Haitian version of Marxism. He seems to represent a principle of continuity between past and future: in effect, he embodies the buried imaginative life of the past and offers it as a genuinely radical basis for a possible future. He is "anachronistic," in other words, in much the same way as Henry James seems anachronistic when Brown comes upon the line in the story about "the wild waters of our horrible times." The fact is that the times are always horrible. Doctor Magiot's faith, no less than Henry James's, is in the civilizing and redeeming power of the human imagination. The real revolutionary heroes are the heroes of art, and the missing father of Brown's narrative is found whenever he "resurrects" one of those artists who give him a kind of access to his own story—not just Henry James and Hardy, but Baudelaire's vision of an "*île triste et noire*" (189) and Wordsworth's poems about the forms of nature as awakened spirits and all the other ancestral voices from various literary enterprises that tend to reveal the landscape of the narrative as a world of dream and death: a place in which a huge array of captive ghosts waits to be released.

Brown's real name is only "Brown" after all. Like Thomas Fowler's, his story is intended to be no more than a kind of confession and a kind of memorial. But for all his cynicism about monuments, the image we are left with is that of a monumental statue shaped or carved out of language. Doctor Magiot in his last letter implores him not to abandon "faith," which means nothing less in effect than a faith in the possibility of a new world. Brown stares at a huge statue which stares at a strictly romantic notion of such a world. The true father of his story is an ancestral archetype of the imagination: the figure of a sleeping giant. The giant dreams of a lost golden age and a promised land, but such a dream is available only to the kind of faith which regards Brown's own literary enterprise with that "naive and involving stare" specifically elicited by the mode of romance.

SIX

Travels with My Aunt and The Honorary Consul

"We might almost have been doing a
literary pilgrimage."
"Hardly literary," I said.
"Oh, you're your father's son. . . ."
—*Travels with My Aunt*

Yet another father, Doctor Plarr told himself, are
we never going to finish with fathers?
—*The Honorary Consul*

A voice explained the story in a prose touched
with the dignity of the unrecallable past.
—*The Honorary Consul*

Of all Greene's later novels, *Travels with My Aunt* (1969) is perhaps the most obviously romantic in conception. With its plot
about a retired English bank manager who, after a succession of
bizarre adventures, finds a new life as a smuggler in Paraguay and
a new bride in the person of the fifteen-year-old daughter of the
local chief customs officer, it exploits many of the most familiar
conventions in what might be termed the quixotic-picaresque
tradition of popular comic romance. This element of the "popular"—the extent to which Greene seems quite happily to have
adapted a highly conventional, indeed formulaic, type of narrative design—is undoubtedly the source of much of the wide-
spread critical uneasiness about the novel. Many commentators
have found it difficult to take *Travels with My Aunt* seriously.
The consensus seems to be that it represents a reversion to the
earlier mode of "entertainment," that it is merely playful or even
"escapist" in spirit: one critic has recently grumbled that *Travels*

with My Aunt is "the only one of . . . [Greene's] . . . novels that verges on deliberate silliness."[1] The very popularity of romance as a genre has always, of course, tended to leave it exposed to this kind of charge. But the romancer in the present case is hardly a vulgar hack, and the interesting fact in this connection is that Greene himself, disagreeing strenuously with the critics, takes *Travels with My Aunt* very seriously indeed. "I consider it," he says, "one of my best books."[2] This, from the author of *The Power and the Glory* and *A Burnt-Out Case,* suggests that we need to look rather more closely at some of the romance formulas around which the novel is constructed, to investigate the possibility in fact that the almost "deliberate silliness" of this sort of narrative might actually represent the superficial *visibilia* of a profound sort of seriousness.

Travels with My Aunt exhibits certain characteristic features both of the traditional picaresque novel and of the type of story usually designated as a fairy tale. In its picaresque aspect it proceeds according to a conventional narrative rhythm which can best be described as a movement between two poles of experience: a gradual shift from a setting which is ordinary and familiar to one that is strange and exotic, a journey in the course of which the traveler leaves the safe but dull predictability of home in order to discover the sometimes violent excitements of a new country where anything at all might happen. The two poles are different "worlds": Henry Pulling's suburban England and Aunt Augusta's international subculture represent distinct and apparently discrete fictive territories. But in its aspect as a fairy tale the novel presents these two worlds as linked in the kind of relation which we ordinarily think of as that between reality and dream: like the territory of the Freudian unconscious, Aunt Augusta's world is legendary as well as real, impinging upon Henry's Southwood with the force and effect of myth. In this perspective Aunt Augusta herself becomes a mythic figure—if not actually a "wicked fairy,"[3] as she only half-jokingly suggests, then certainly an elfin character who appears from and returns to a mysterious and morally ambiguous dream kingdom. What gives this realm its character as a country of total unpredictability is the undisguised and continuous flow of erotic energy which could be said to inform it. Henry's elderly aunt is consistently associated with the classical goddess of love, and her interest in venery runs much deeper than, say, the passion for Venetian glass—"Venice once meant a lot to me" (21)—which constitutes one of the first clues to her mythic identity. In her maternal role, she is also a kind of earth mother. As an exotic, faery Venus, then, she becomes someone much more considerable than Henry's "aunt." The mystery of Henry's birth in the picaresque context derives from the hoary convention of the foundling plot, but in the fairy-tale perspective this protagonist is not simply a foundling: he is in effect a changeling, and as such, he returns in the end to his real mother and his "real" home.

All this does seem of course to be essentially playful or fanciful. But Henry Pulling's text is oddly littered with various enigmatic images of a decidedly more somber and troubling kind. There is, for instance, his account of his first farewell to his aunt's black lover in Paris: "I got into the taxi and drove away. Looking through the rear window, I could see Wordsworth standing bewildered on the pavement edge, like a man on a river bank waiting for a ferry. He raised his hand tentatively, as though he were uncertain of my response, whether I had left him in friendship or anger, as the traffic swept between us" (93–94). In view of Wordsworth's hitherto comic role in the plot, this sudden vision of him as, almost literally, a lost soul seems at the time inexplicably ominous and disturbing. The same unexpectedly dark perspective is brought to bear on him again, a few pages later, when Henry and his aunt leave for Istanbul on the Orient Express: "I stood at the top of the steps as the train began to move out from the Gare de Lyon in short jerks and Wordsworth followed it down the platform, wading through the steam. He was crying, and I was reminded of a suicide walking out fully dressed into the surf" (110). In the framework of comedy, these are curious, anomalous-seeming revelations about the ebullient Wordsworth, although of course his ultimate fate in the story may be said, retrospectively, to account for them. Still, the playfulness at the novel's surface has been abandoned for an effect that is clearly sinister in tone yet at the same time obliquely symbolic in the sense that its significance remains at least temporarily uncertain: it is as if an entirely new frame of reference had been abruptly invoked. Similarly, Henry's description of his visit with his aunt to his father's tomb at Boulogne is prefaced by an apparently unaccountable episode involving a dead boar, a brief piece of conspicuously irrelevant reportage that has much the same effect of the ominous compounded with the figuratively enigmatic: "A shop advertised '*Deuil en 24 heures*,' and a wild boar, hung outside a butcher's shop, dripped blood, and a notice pinned on the muzzle read, '*Retenez vos morceaux pour jeudi*,' but Thursday meant nothing to me, and not very much to Aunt Augusta" (181). Scenes like these tend to work against the grain of whimsy in *Travels with My Aunt*. Like the sheer ruthlessness which marks Mr. Visconti's eventual entry into the novel's action, their appearance is at once somehow unlooked for and darkly evocative, as if they represented distinct but puzzling echoes from a different type of story altogether. In one sense, this is precisely the case.

While the central romance archetype in this novel is the familiar journey or quest in an increasingly exotic landscape, its conventional context here is primarily comic. However, even the most popular romance formulas have a way of expanding or referring beyond themselves to more complex contexts and, in the process, acquiring dimensions of meaning which may subvert any initial simplicity of intention. It should also perhaps be noted at this stage that not all romance conventions are necessarily "popular." We have seen, for example, how the use of literary allusions in fiction can have a specifically romantic function, so that the idea of fictiveness itself has a tendency to become a romance motif of a fairly sophisticated kind. Greene's own growing habit of allusiveness is nowhere more evident than in *Travels with My Aunt*. In a text dense with literary reference, the narrator cites a range of his (and his father's) favorite authors that gives his narrative something of the flavor of a nineteenth-century anthology: Blake, Sir Walter Scott, Wordsworth, Tennyson, and Browning. Henry Pulling's taste (always following his father's lead) is for the great Victorians in particular, and for reasons that will become clearer as we proceed, it reflects the importance of Greene's own predilection for that historical period.

Each of the echoes from each of these authors has much the same kind of function as the reference to "The Great Good Place" in *The Comedians:* it serves as a type of inset "story" with a significant informing or interpretive effect on the structure of the narrative in which it is invoked. All the stories within his own to which Henry alludes may be regarded as hinging on the kind of contrast that we have just observed between two different fictive worlds, one more or less "realistic" and the other more or less "romantic," which exist at the same time in a relation of almost symbiotic interdependence. Scott's *Rob Roy* and Wordsworth's "Immortality" ode, to take the most frequently cited instances, are both concerned with the movement between these two worlds as a symbolic journey between two contrary states of mind, two antithetical modes of perception. Like Frank Osbaldistone's, Henry Pulling's travels take him from a secure but imaginatively constricted view of human experience to the vision of an adventurous freedom which is explicitly associated, in its richness and strangeness, with the fictive realm of what French criticism would describe as the *féerique.* Similarly, like the speaker in Wordsworth's poem, Henry seems to recover the vision of an original metaphysical splendor which had been obscured and all but annihilated by the shades of his own particular prison house. But travels into the country of romance are not of course without their pitfalls, nor is the end of the romantic journey necessarily the same thing as the achievement of the quest. The narrators of *Rob Roy* and the "Immortality" ode find themselves curiously distanced if not actually alienated from the kind of vision which they describe; and Henry Pulling finds that his travels could also be regarded as a descent into hell.

Perhaps the most striking pattern of literary reference in *Travels with My Aunt* is its continuous allusiveness to Greene's own work. Without "knowing" it, Henry reconstructs and recapitulates much of Greene's career as a novelist. Most vividly recalled are certain features of the worlds of *Stamboul Train, Brighton*

Rock, and *A Burnt-Out Case,* but this pattern of self-referential allusion is so extensively diffused as to encompass what might be thought of as the Greene canon in its entirety. The novel can virtually be read as a sort of fictional autobiography, including in its range of Greenean reference even such important "influences" as Marjorie Bowen's *Viper of Milan.* In part, of course, this kind of thing is clearly an aspect of the more general narrative playfulness—a matter, depending on how one reads it, of either whimsical self-mockery or "deliberate silliness." But more important, in the context of the total pattern of allusiveness in this novel, what Greene seems deliberately to be doing here is invoking his own characteristic idiom. In other words, the novel is self-referential chiefly in the sense that it alludes to the structure of the kind of romance that Greene has himself been writing for years. To the initiated reader there is something resonantly familiar, for example, about the figurative prospect of Aunt Augusta's abandoned lover as "a man on a river bank waiting for a ferry" or as "a suicide walking out fully dressed into the surf." In their immediate setting such images may seem bizarre and incongruous, but they are also peculiarly recognizable in the sense that they are peculiarly idiomatic: they belong, unmistakably, to the dialect of Greene's total fictive universe. And in that context their meaning is clear enough. All unknowingly, Henry Pulling is describing a doomed man, a designated scapegoat or victim.

Putting it at its simplest, it is as if Greene were invoking one of the central figurative codes of romance itself: Wordsworth (the character rather than the poet) is perceived as someone who waits, unable to join Henry in a passage or crossing in which Aunt Augusta plays the role of pilot, at the outer threshold of an underworld. For the most significant fact about the milieu with which Aunt Augusta is associated is that it can be seen, almost as it were iconographically, to lie "underneath" the everyday or garden-variety reality of Henry's Southwood. From the picaresque point of view the narrative movement from one kind of world to the other is realistic primarily in that Henry's progress is presented in linear or horizontal terms, one phase of his travels following sequentially on another; but in its aspect as a fairy tale the novel exhibits these two realities in a figuratively vertical relation. Henry's travels conclude, from this point of view, with the type of journey by water that we have witnessed before, a river voyage which is also a pilgrimage to a mysterious nether kingdom. And this lower world is the archetypal place of death as well as of dreams, Thanatos as well as Eros.

To the extent, then, that Henry's travels may be seen as a journey of descent, the mythopoeic basis of the novel's action can be generalized as follows. Under the suburban garden where the hero cultivates his dahlias lies a world which looks very much like Southwood's polar antithesis: an ethos whose sole governing principle is the primacy of human desire. Where Southwood is tame, inhibited, and prudent, Aunt Augusta's milieu tends to be lawless, almost Dionysiac in its worship of impulse and the pursuit of pleasure. Morally reprehensible by Southwoodian standards, this lower world is nevertheless palely reflected by the world of the suburban garden in the sense that gardens derive whatever life they have from whatever lies underneath them. As a psychological construct, that is to say, the emblematic design which shapes the novel is based on the Freudian model: with all her exuberance and appetite, Aunt Augusta is clearly the embodiment of sheer erotic energy; she erupts into the confines of Henry's existence like some irrepressible force from a familial id. But she can be envisioned too, of course, as a "wicked" fairy. For the world into which she emerges is one where this kind of energy is disconcerting and tends to be dealt with by being imperfectly suppressed, so that it becomes a place peopled by characters who are identifiable largely by the various absurd and compulsive ritual habits into which their own individual energies appear to be locked. Exemplifying the sort of mechanical or puppetlike behavior that Greene usually has in mind when he talks about "comedians"—Major Charge with his starving goldfish and his lunatic imperialism, the admiral with his obsessive but unfocused rage, Henry himself with his dahlias—the populace of Southwood might easily comprise the dramatis personae of some contemporary comedy of humors. At the same time, the reasons for repressiveness are not hard to find: erotic energy has its destructive as well as its creative dimension. The goddess of love has always been a highly ambiguous figure, attractive but also fickle and dangerous, and so is Aunt Augusta. If the central myth of the erotic life is the story of Venus and Adonis, then the world from which Aunt Augusta appears must also be considered as the archetypal hell of love's archetypal victim: the subterranean kingdom of a martyred fertility king.

Like Marcel in *The Comedians*, the black lover of the narrator's mother in this novel becomes a type of doomed Adonis. At his death, he is also perceived by Henry Pulling as a type of literary or mythic "father": poor Wordsworth's death occurs, specifically echoing the fate of the narrator's father in Tennyson's "Maud" (from which Henry has just been quoting to his future bride), in a "hollow" behind a "little wood" (315–16). For there is a paternal as well as a maternal principle at work in the structure of *Travels with My Aunt*. In mythic terms, Adonis is the slain father of all life because he is the seasonal vegetation god who is annually sacrificed in order that the spring might return—the symbolic basis of the grotesque vegetable totem in *A Burnt-Out Case*. But the paternal figure in this novel also takes a much more particular human form. The real mystery surrounding Henry's birth is not so much the identity of his mother (that becomes obvious to the alert reader, if not necessarily to Henry, quite early on) but rather the real identity of his father. As he progresses in his travels, Henry feels increasingly curious about and affectionate toward the sleepy man who was also the unfailingly ardent lover who died in Boulogne in the arms of Miss Paterson. And the figure of the father who has disappeared and whose true nature becomes the genuine object of the hero's quest can now be said to be the central symbolic character not only of Greene's fictive universe but of Henry Pulling's personal one as well. Once again, we find that the pattern of a novel's allusiveness brings its basic structural archetype into focus: the quest for a "royal" progenitor in an underworld.

The narrator of Tennyson's "Maud," for instance, finds that he has in a sense rejoined his father by undergoing a form of ritual death and burial.[4] Wordsworth's "Immortality" ode becomes a quest story (in this kind of context) in which the narrator discovers that the lost or buried "child" he seeks is actually "the father of the man."[5] And Scott's *Rob Roy*, besides being the favorite novel of Henry's father, presents Henry Pulling with the prospect of a literary counterpart or double: Frank Osbaldistone also lives in the shadow of a father figure who is himself shadowy and elusive; going about his father's business, what the narrator of *Rob Roy* really seeks is self-definition. The implications of all the literary echoes in *Travels with My Aunt* invite more judicious and thorough exploration, but their significance seems clear enough in its general outline. The wild boar that hangs outside the butcher's shop in Boulogne—together with the emblem, "Mourning in 24 hours"—is suggestive not so much of an obscure Catholic feast day as of some atavistic feast of lamentation for Adonis. This allusion to the legendary death of a legendary ur-father may be only glancing and oblique (and indeed playful), but it serves to indicate the direction in which Henry's travels are taking him. He is following in his father's footsteps.

Boulogne represents a critical watershed in Henry's progress because the visit to his father's tomb signals the beginning of his shift of allegiance from one of the two worlds in his story to the other. At the beginning of this particular journey, he tells us: "The English side of the Channel lay bathed in a golden autumn sunlight . . . and I would gladly have given all the landscape between Milan and Venice for these twenty miles of Kent. There were comfortable skies and unspectacular streams; there were ponds with rushes and cows which seemed contentedly asleep. This was the pleasant land of which Blake wrote, and I found myself regretting that we were going abroad again" (174). But the excursion ends with the jealous quarrel between Aunt Augusta and Miss Paterson; and Henry returns alone to an England that "lay damp and cold, as grey as the graveyard, while the train lagged slowly from Dover Town towards Charing Cross under the drenching rain" (194). His sense of desolation is due partly to his aunt's sudden abandonment of him and partly to his new identification with his father. In both his loss and his new discovery, Henry almost literally enters his dead father's world: the disappearance of Adonis means that the golden autumn has given way to the bleakness of winter, so that when Henry looks out the train window on the return journey it is not a green and pleasant land that he sees "but my father's grave in the smoky rain and Miss Paterson standing before it in prayer" (195). Envying his father's "inexplicable quality of drawing women's love" (195), Henry finds when he gets home that it is in fact he himself who has become a kind of dead man. In an effort to assure himself of his own reality he goes to one of Major Charge's political meetings, but he learns there that the identity he has always taken for granted has palpably vanished: "Like a waiter on his day-off I passed virtually unrecognized. It was an odd feeling for one who had been so much in the centre of Southwood life. As I went upstairs to bed I felt myself to be a ghost returning home, transparent as water. Curran was more alive than I was. I was almost surprised to see that my image was visible in the glass" (196). He has in effect become his father's shade or phantom. But Henry has never been an ardent lover, and although his new identity is to be realized in Aunt Augusta's world rather than in an English garden, the archetypal form it takes is slightly different from that of the ritually slain victim.

The rhythm of descent in the novel culminates with Henry's arrival in Paraguay. There he finds himself living in a house that reminds him of his father's tomb (259), and there too he meets the man who might be termed the novel's ultimate father figure, the notorious Mr. Visconti. Henry has at last reached the heart of the lower world of dream and death. However, Aunt Augusta's new (and old) lover is of a distinctly different type from all the others: not only is Visconti no dying god, he is a ruthless survivor, an ancient and cunning soldier of fortune whose charm can only be described as deadly. What looks like criminality to the various police forces of the outside world appears to Aunt Augusta as the epitome of sheer energy and imaginative exuberance; no matter how Henry (or indeed the reader) may feel about it, Mr. Visconti is the essential embodiment of all that she loves and admires. Henry, on the other hand, can never quite shrug off his own sense of Visconti's reptilian monstrousness, his vision of the man as not only a viper but a rat—as a whole implicit zoo of unattractive beasts, a nightmare creature whose protean guises are never quite human. Visconti does have an unmistakable animal magnetism, but then so in her own way does Henry's mother. He seems, in short, to be a kind of male counterpart of Aunt Augusta, a connoisseur of erotic experience who may also be "one of the life-givers" (191) but who can just as easily bring death as well. His mythopoeic role in the novel has to do with the story that could be regarded as the inversion of the legend of Venus and Adonis. For the reversed mirror image, so to speak, of the myth about a maternal goddess who must be perpetually pleasured by a perpetually dying youth is the story about a maiden who is surrounded by ravening monsters. The novel's structure evinces an Andromeda pattern, that is to say, as well as an Adonis pattern. The motif of the disappearance of a father can also modulate to the motif of the little girl lost, the figure of a victim who is female—a "daughter" rather than a "son." And in terms of this Andromeda design, Henry's real identity turns out to be closer to that of Perseus in the classical legend. Henry's ultimate role combines the figure of a resurrected Adonis with the heroic (and specifically English) character of St. George.

Henry Pulling's erotic capacity seems to be for the type of paternal love that seeks to rescue and protect. He befriends and sustains Tooley on the Orient Express and spends much of the rest of his narrative worrying about her. At the Christmas Eve service in St. John's Church, he sits in a pew below a stained-glass window which "shows Christ surrounded by children" and beneath which the text is "Suffer little children" (204). A son in quest of his father, he goes down to an underworld and finds himself imprisoned there, both literally and figuratively. At the end of it all, he even dreams of his own death:

> I dreamt that the rabbit-nosed man was feeling my pulse and telling Mr Visconti that I was dead of the fluke—whatever that might mean. I tried to speak out to prove that I was alive, but Mr Visconti commanded some shadowy figures in the background, in a jumbled phrase from *Maud,* to bury me deeper, only a little deeper. I tried to cry out to my aunt who stood there pregnant in a bathing

dress, holding Mr Visconti's hand, and I woke gasping for breath and for words and heard the sound of the harp and the guitar playing on. (315)

If Henry's father is a type of the slain Adonis, then Henry himself might be seen simply as the father reborn. He wakes from his dream feeling "oddly elated to be alive" (315) and committed at last to Aunt Augusta's and Visconti's world. But he emerges as well to discover the corpse of Wordsworth in the hollow behind the little wood, and his final act in the novel signals a renunciation of the fateful pattern of erotic murderousness which characterizes that world. Wordsworth has chosen one kind of romantic part; Henry Pulling chooses another. He befriends and then engages himself to marry yet another vulnerable girl child. The final allusion in the novel is to Browning's *Pippa Passes:* Maria is not exactly a maiden in distress, but like Pippa, she does seem to exemplify a kind of potent innocence in the heart of a country where innocence is by no means the norm. And reading Browning together "in the warm scented evenings" (319), she and Henry present an oddly touching Victorian cameo, a picture which seems faintly absurd only because it is set against the background of General Stroessner's Paraguay. The novel concludes, in other words, with the sense of Eros as a quixotic but nonetheless potentially redemptive goodness in a corrupt world. Against all odds, Henry Pulling ends up not just as a type of Adonis but as a type of Christ.

In our consideration of the romance conventions in this novel we are brought back once more, then, to the matter of the conspicuous fictiveness which seems so central to romance as a narrative structure. If *Travels with My Aunt* is to be read as a realistic story, its tendency is certainly toward a "deliberate silliness"; but if Henry's travels constitute "a literary pilgrimage" (156), as Aunt Augusta suggests, then the realistic reading itself becomes absurd because it is wildly inappropriate: the kinds of meaning suggested by a linear plot are always being modified if not actually subverted by the various patterns of literary allusiveness on which it turns. Again, Greene seems to be pointing in the direction of his idea that what underlies any conceivable "sense of reality" is some archetypal structure of words. The idea is illustrated neatly by Aunt Augusta's story about the traveling company in Tunis who played *Hamlet* in Arabic: "Someone saw to it that in the Interlude the Player King was really killed—or rather not quite killed but severely damaged in the right ear—by molten lead. And who do you suppose the police at once suspected? Not the man who poured the lead in, although he must have been aware that the ladle wasn't empty and was hot to the touch. Oh no, they knew Shakespeare's play too well for that, and so they arrested Hamlet's uncle" (64). For our interpretations of real events, in other words, even the most unimaginative among us tend to rely on the idiom of the kinds of fiction which seem to fit the occasion.

The "traveling" world, of course, is quintessentially fictive. In a slightly grotesque way (she is after all an elderly lady) Aunt Augusta embodies the ardent energy of Eros, but what this actually seems to mean in practice is that she tells a great many stories. Eros is genuinely or creatively absurd in the sense that it is a designing and shaping power, so that its tolerance for artifice tends to be antipathetic to the spirit of realistic mimesis as the representation of things merely as they are. Reality by itself, on the other hand, seems absurd in the opposite sense: for Greene, as we have noticed, it is usually envisioned as some form of suspended animation—an unintelligible condition of petrification or silent immobility. In *Travels with My Aunt* this kind of wordless suspension seems to be one of the features of life in Southwood. The loneliness and isolation which characterize the lives of the inhabitants of that world have much to do with a general fearfulness about language. The admiral's apoplectic speechlessness, for example, reflects a wider social inexpressiveness, an anxiety about communication that is based on an anxiety about the idea of genuine community. People in laconic Southwood do not ordinarily say what they mean, or not aloud anyway, as Henry realizes to his embarrassed chagrin when he contemplates his encounter with the beautiful but deaf woman who once consulted him about her financial affairs. Misunderstandings and failures of communication are the norm here; they are usually perceived in comic terms, but as the halting, formal correspondence between Henry and Miss Keene demonstrates, they can be sad or pathetic too. Against this kind of background, stories represent ways of escape: the articulate disposition of words means, among other things, fluidity and movement, and it accounts for the way in which Henry's father seems actually to have lived as much as possible in the world of Walter Scott's novels, as well as, more generally, in the peculiarly abundant verbal universe of Victorian literature. Literary allusiveness is important in this novel because the world that lies beneath the suburban garden can be seen as a shifting kaleidoscope of interrelated fictions. The impulse of Eros is toward community, and one of its basic expressions, besides sexual love, is the sort of verbal structure that seeks to assimilate an erotically unintelligible reality to its own purposes.

Life in Southwood tends toward isolation and silence rather than community, and the dominant image associated with it is that of imprisonment. The world of Major Charge and the admiral and Miss Keene with her tatting has an intensely claustrophobic quality. Henry's own memory of the teller's cage in which so much of his career was spent merges imperceptibly into the Wordsworthian vision of the "prison-house," modulating again into his own vision of the domestic cell inside which, as he comes to realize, his father was trapped. The ultimate symbolic form of this prison image is of course the graveyard at Boulogne. Aunt Augusta's world, on the other hand, seems to be characterized chiefly by the imagery of freedom and mobility—everything that is involved in the whole idea of "traveling." And yet when Henry reaches Paraguay, we find that the motifs of imprisonment and silence become dominant once again. Henry is briefly incarcerated in the local jail; later he has a nightmare about his own interment; Visconti's house is like his father's tomb; and indeed the exotic new world of Paraguay itself is also described as an "ancient world of silence" (264). In this connection, Henry alludes perceptively to Tennyson's "Lotos-Eaters" as well as to the burial theme in "Maud." In fact, Paraguay is both prison and tomb precisely because it is represented as a literary reflection of Southwood. Or, more accurately, Southwood is to be figuratively regarded as a pallid and colorless mirror image of Paraguay.

If the quest for the father in this novel is a form of literary pilgrimage, it follows that the literature of nineteenth-century England increasingly acquires the status of something like a definitive mythology. The Victorian world, as expressed in its novels and poetry, has a unique cultural authority for Henry Pulling. It is in terms of this literature, for example, that he tries to interpret the underworld in which he ultimately finds himself. For Henry, Stroessner's bizarre and cruel domain becomes a curiously "Victorian" country, a mysterious land but one which lends itself, oddly enough, to a whole series of Tennysonian readings. "It was as though," he says, "I were safely back in the Victorian world where I had been taught by my father's books to feel more at home than in our modern day" (316). The names of the Paraguayan national dances "sound very Victorian" (311), Henry remarks to the chief of police, who, enjoying himself at Mr. Visconti's great party, eats "like a good trencherman in a Victorian illustration" (312). The city of Asunçion itself, with its "yellow Victorian station" (309), is described as "a very Victorian town" (258). And while this view of Paraguay may seem naive as well as eccentric, it does have an exact metaphorical logic of its own. For the world under the garden in this novel, as the figure of the "rabbit-nosed" man would in any case tend to suggest, is also a looking-glass reality. In "Victorian" Asunçion, Henry tells us:

> One soon ceased to notice the cars—they were an anachronism; there were mule carts and sometimes men on horses, there was a little white castellated Baptist church, a college built like a neo-Gothic abbey, and when we reached the residential quarter I saw big stone houses with bosky gardens and pillared porticoes above stone steps which reminded me of the oldest part of Southwood, but in Southwood the houses would have been split into flats and the grey stone would have been whitewashed and the roofs would

have bristled with television masts. In place of the orange and ba-
nana trees, I would have seen neglected rhododendrons and thread-
bare lawns. (258)

The important thing about Paraguay from Henry's point of view
is that it is like a more intensely alive version of the world from
which he has come, a mirror image of that world, but an image in
which it is time rather than space that has been reversed. In symbolic terms, Paraguay represents the mythic source of Henry's
being, the fictive Victorian world to which he and his father really
belong.

In the sense, then, that Henry's travels take him to a definitively mythic or archetypal country, the real significance of traveling becomes entirely fictive. It is not that there are no prisons in
Aunt Augusta's world—on the contrary, she and Mr. Visconti
always seem to be only a step or two ahead of the law—but that
traveling, properly regarded, is an imaginative process, an expression more than anything else of human aspiration or desire.
Aunt Augusta's story about Henry's Uncle Jo becomes the exemplary fiction here: the dying bookmaker who manages to tour
most of the world by moving each week to a new room in the
crumbling Italian *palazzo* to which he has been confined also
succeeds in triumphing, however briefly, over the condition of his
own mortality. And his nephew, at the end of another journey,
emerges from a suffocating dream about being buried alive with
a new appetite for life.

Romance tends to be popularly thought of as an escapist genre
concerned chiefly with the adventures associated with erotic experience. As a matter of fact, its "escapist" tendencies can be seen
almost as a direct function of the degree to which it is preoccupied with the world of Eros. The dialectic of confinement and
fictive escape in *Travels with My Aunt* is worth stressing, for the
central narrative motif—the story about a search for a father
who has vanished into the prison (or tomb) of a looking-glass
"Victorian" world—reappears in Greene's next novel. *The Honorary Consul* is anything but playful and presents a very different
view indeed of General Stroessner's Paraguay, but it is also a

novel about escape—in a sense which makes it inappropriate, for once, to regard "escapism" as a term of dismissive abuse.

Published in 1973, *The Honorary Consul* can be read as a "political" fiction of the kind hitherto most clearly exemplified in Greene's oeuvre by *The Quiet American;* but like *The Quiet American,* it can also be read as a romance. Though less insistently so, it is as thoroughly mythopoeic a novel as the one that immediately preceded it. In fact, whereas *Travels with My Aunt* is formally organized around nothing much more substantial than what might be called the grammar of Greene's own characteristic dialect, together with certain related echoes from the literature of the nineteenth century, *The Honorary Consul* may be said to be shaped by a literary idiom that derives from nothing less than the legendary source of Western civilization itself. The novel invokes the most central Western myth of all: the story about a son who, by dying for it, redeems the world that his father has made, a hero whose sacrificial death has the effect not only of appeasing the father but of rescuing a rather elusive female figure who is at once both mother and bride. The novel's explorations of contemporary political problems in South America are intricately bound up, that is to say, with its Christian symbolism. And although the context of this symbolism is recognizably (if not always conventionally) religious, it is, at a profounder level, peculiarly fictive too. Behind the central Christian story here lies a whole complex of legendary secular narratives about fathers and sons, most notably the one about Oedipus—though not so much in its classical form as in the modern Freudian version, which treats the themes of parricide, incest, and filial guilt primarily in terms of the psychodrama of unconscious fantasy rather than in those of waking reality. Eduardo Plarr's psychological predicament is familiar to us in one sense simply because it has the cultural resonance of a certain type of almost contemporary "popular" story. But the novel is informed by older legends as well: the story about a "false" or usurping king, for example, and the related one about a "true" but impotent king whose realm has become a wasteland.

The figure of the usurper in *The Honorary Consul* is the Paraguayan dictator, General Stroessner, who functions as much the same kind of sinister father figure as Papa Doc in *The Comedians;* the impotent king in this context becomes the father who has vanished, Eduardo Plarr's actual father, or at any rate his ghost, and the wasteland is of course Paraguay itself. That country tends to be envisioned now not as Henry Pulling's freakish Victorian wonderland but as a place of drought and desiccation. "Our people do not starve," Father Rivas tells Charley Fortnum, "—they wilt."[6] Describing Stroessner's technique of isolating political prisoners, Aquino explains to Eduardo Plarr that the general "plants his victims out in separate pots with insufficient earth, and they wither with despair" (231). As this remark also suggests, the imagery of the wasteland can modulate to the imagery of imprisonment and entombment. We are told that Paraguay is the country where Doctor Plarr's "father was buried—whether in a prison or a patch of ground he would probably never know" (12). Because the foreground action of the novel is set across the border in Argentina, this arid Paraguay on the other side of the Paraná River has something of the specifically mythic or fictive about it as well: the world of the father figure, to put the matter in psychoanalytic terms, is almost inevitably the terrain of dream and unconscious memory rather than of immediate reality. Eduardo Plarr's outward taciturnity masks an ongoing interior monologue which focuses obsessively on the mourned absence of his father and the unwanted presence of his mother. In that sense, he is almost (but not quite) as much a novelist as his friend, Doctor Saavedra, almost (but not quite) the narrator of his own story.

That story is organized around the same figurative motif as that which informs the story of Henry Pulling's travels: a kind of waking dream or fiction, with certain "Victorian" associations, about a "true" father who lies imprisoned in an underworld. It is this mythopoeic construct that allows Eduardo Plarr in his role as his father's son to identify with Henry Plarr in his role as a captive, for the senior Plarr's buried life as Stroessner's prisoner is, in oedipal terms, one of filial subservience. The dream or fiction may also be regarded as a "poem," an emblematic extended metaphor which defines the most basic of all South American political realities. "The first poem I wrote in prison," Aquino tells his own captive, Charley Fortnum,

> was about the first prison of all—the one we all of us know. Do you know what Trotsky said when they showed him his new home in Mexico? They had made it secure from assassins, or so they thought. He said, "This reminds me of my first prison. The doors make the same sound." My poem had a refrain, "I see my father only through the bars." I was thinking, you see, of the pens in which they put children in bourgeois houses. In my poem the father went on following the child all through his life—he was the school-master, and then he was the priest, the police officer, the prison warder, and last he was General Stroessner himself. I saw the General once when he was touring the countryside. He came to the police station I was in and I saw him through the bars. (150–51)

In the psychoanalytic context, the relationship between fathers and sons is inevitably hostile. And if Eduardo Plarr identifies with his father as a political victim, what this means at a more private and personal level is that he regards him as an antagonist or rival.

Doctor Plarr's view of Paraguay on the first page of the novel is of a country behind "bars" (9). But these are the bars, in Aquino's terms, of Plarr's own prison as well: if the doctor is locked out of his father's world, then he is also in some sense locked into a private one. The imagery of confinement and constriction becomes as definitive in fact of the novel's actual Argentinian environment as it is of the unseen Paraguay beyond the river. The domestic worlds of all the main characters are invariably perceived as places of incarceration. Plarr's apartment is "as bare and truthful—almost—as a police station cell" (176); Doctor Humphries has a "small room" whose window opens on "a patio which contained one dusty palm and a dead fountain" (19)—an ironic parody, if ever there was one, of the paradisal enclosed garden; Charley Fortnum's consulate is characterized by an unexpected emptiness and bareness (58); and Doctor Saavedra's room in a building which seems to be "an extension" (201) of the adjacent prison has a cramped "bareness" (203) about it that reminds Plarr of "the inextinguishable hunger of his literary obsession" (203). Even the more elaborate domestic settings have something of this claustrophobic, prisonlike character: the courtyard of Senora Sanchez's establishment may be "airy" (66) and the brothel more spacious than its counterparts in Buenos Aires, but the rooms there are nevertheless "small cells" (66); in Charley Fortnum's comfortable house in the country Clara is "like a bird which had been bought in the market in a makeshift cage and transferred to one at home more roomy and luxurious" (87); Plarr's mother's apartment is "kept almost as airless as the dome over the wax flowers" (173), while her favorite tea shop in the Calle Florida resembles a noisy "aviary" (176). The essential reality of the novel's actual setting derives, in other words, from a basic metaphor of reflection: Paraguay is again the mythical looking-glass world here, and when Eduardo Plarr broods about his own sense of self-division—"I'm only half English and that half is in prison or dead" (61)—he is like a man with amnesia puzzling over his image in a mirror. But the metaphor of reflection can work in another way as well: if Plarr feels caged and helpless, powerless to find and free his father, he also feels guilty; he feels in effect that it is he himself rather than General Stroessner who has usurped his father's identity and his life.

The themes of oedipal guilt and of the actual powerlessness of sons who live in the shadows of absent fathers are paradoxically linked throughout the novel. To the extent that he can be viewed objectively, Henry Plarr perhaps looks less like a hero of the political left than a henpecked husband who might have been more relieved than anything else to send his wife away to the safety of Argentina, but he has a remarkable mythic potency in his son's memory for all that. As an Englishman in South America he comes from what seems to be a kind of fairy-tale land, one, moreover, which always tends to be associated in Doctor Plarr's mind with the world of Victorian fiction. In that sense he has a genuine mythic power for his son—as a father who really does seem to be a sort of magical "king"—and yet at the same time he is curiously unreal: there is a quality of profound helplessness about him, an oddly mechanical passivity that almost precludes the possibility that he could be restored, as Eduardo Plarr wishes, to genuine life. At the most literal level, in other words, the elder Plarr can be regarded as a king who has been displaced by his own son. It is perhaps not surprising, then, that Doctor Plarr's world appears to be almost entirely peopled by such fathers and such sons. It is certainly not surprising that Plarr should feel uneasy and guilty about his affair with Charley Fortnum's bride: even more than Doctor Humphries and Doctor Saavedra, Charley is a natural father surrogate for Plarr—a well-intentioned but ineffectual older man whose absurdity in the role of "honorary" British consul reveals him even more clearly as a type of impotent king. (Not for nothing does Charley worry drunkenly that the flagstaff outside his consulate might be "leaning over a bit too much" [54].) And his wife in this context is evidently the antitype of Plarr's mother: perhaps especially in her pregnancy, Clara embodies the kind of beauty that has all too obviously gone to seed in the obese Senora Plarr. The oedipal pattern is repeated again in Charley's accounts of his relationship with *his* father, and the story of his life in this respect has a parallel but contrapuntal relation to Eduardo Plarr's: Charley is a son who finds that he has actually, in a sense, "become" his once-hated father; "I even imitate him" (143), he says, lifting his glass by way of illustration.

Variations on the oedipal theme recur throughout virtually every aspect of the novel's action. From Doctor Plarr's point of view, for instance, Charley Fortnum's house is a place haunted and dominated by a mysterious (and peculiarly remote) paternal English ghost. The Victorian sporting prints on the walls evoke the imagined homeland of Plarr's own father, especially a picture which features "a small stream lined by what he took to be willows" (84), and they become associated for him with a fabulous pastoral innocence. This quality in turn becomes definitive of the nature of Clara Fortnum's attraction for him: "The fragile body on Charley Fortnum's bed must have known hundreds [of men]. Her stomach was like the site of an old country battlefield where pale grass grew which had abolished the scars of war, and a small stream flowed peacefully between the willows: he was back in the passage, outside the bedroom, staring at the sporting prints and resisting the desire to return" (89). For Eduardo Plarr, Clara is in effect the embodiment of a fabulous or archetypal bride. In the context of the novel's oedipal pattern her attraction consists precisely in the fact that she is in every respect the reversed mirror image of Plarr's actual mother—the incarnation of a genuine life principle or ideal of perpetual renewal, as opposed to the death figure suggested by Senora Plarr—and in the fact of course that she is at the same time Charley's wife. But it is not until Plarr discovers the true identity of the man on the coffin in the kidnappers' hut that the honorary consul takes on "the appearance of a serious rival" (114): Charley Fortnum in this aspect suddenly presents something perilously close to the picture in the doctor's mind of his own father as someone at once imprisoned and buried.

Besides being a kind of usurped king, however, Henry Plarr also appears in the novel in a very different guise, one which in fact suggests the antithesis or mirror reversal of the role of prisoner: "Doctor Plarr remembered how at night his father in Paraguay would lock even the internal doors of his house, the bedrooms, the lavatories, the unused guest rooms, not against robbers but against the police, the military and official assassins, though they would certainly not have been deterred long by locked doors" (19). Although what the senior Plarr seems to have had in mind here was domestic safety—a faintly absurd effort at creating interior havens within the haven of the house itself—his son's most persistent image of him as a living man is of the figure of a kind of jailer. Lying in bed with Clara, the doctor dreams "as he hadn't dreamt for some years of the *estancia* in Paraguay": "He was lying in his child's bunk at the top of a ladder, he listened to the noise of keys which were turned and bolts which were pushed to—his father was making the house secure, but he was afraid all the same. Perhaps someone had been locked in who should have been locked out" (119). In the oedipal context, of course, the likeliest candidate for the part of concealed usurper is the dreamer himself. And the pattern becomes even clearer later when Eduardo Plarr, now as much a prisoner as Charley Fortnum, envisages his own and Clara's unborn child "as a boy . . . who resembled two early photographs of himself, one taken at four years and one at eight" (270). Plarr has by this stage become overtly jealous of the honorary consul, not simply because Charley is actually married to this putative boy's future mother but because the surrogate father has a capacity for love that seems to be absent in the real son. The doctor's jealousy is not so much paternal, in other words, as oedipal:

> Doctor Plarr suddenly saw the boy sitting up in his bunk, as he had done, listening to the distant locking of doors, to the low voices downstairs, the stealthy footsteps. There was one night he remembered when he had crept for reassurance to his father's room, and he was looking down now at the bearded face of his father stretched on the coffin—four days' stubble had begun to resemble a beard. . . . Doctor Plarr returned abruptly to the company of Charley Fortnum's future murderers. (271)

The honorary consul has by now taken on the appearance of a very serious rival indeed.

More than anything else, the novel's basic motif of incarceration suggests the figurative view of a ubiquitous process of repression that is as much personal and psychological as political. Life goes on in the world of *The Honorary Consul* inside various kinds of cages: in his concern for domestic security Henry Plarr locks love in; and this sense of human life as something to be circumscribed or confined for its own protection is one that pervades the whole texture of the narrative. For example, even the British ambassador to Argentina (very much a real rather than an honorary authority figure) is pointedly assimilated to the metaphorical terms of Aquino's "first poem." We are told that Sir Henry Belfrage

> was at home in his Embassy as he had been at home in his nursery. The chandeliers glittered like the glass fruit on a Christmas tree. In the nursery he could remember building neatly and quickly with his coloured bricks. "Master Henry is a clever boy," his nurse always said, but sometimes when he was let out on the vast green spaces of Kensington Gardens he strayed wildly. There were moments with strangers—just as there still were at his annual cocktail party—when he nearly panicked. (170)

But perhaps the preeminent image of confinement and constriction as the paradoxical expression of both love and the repression of love is the vision that emerges from Eduardo Plarr's final meditation on the birth of his child:

> He thought of the tangle of its ancestry, and for the first time in the complexity of that tangle the child became real to him—it was no longer just one more wet piece of flesh like any other torn out of the body with a cord which had to be cut. This cord could never be cut. It joined the child to two very different grandfathers—a cane-cutter in Tucumán and an old English liberal who had been shot dead in the yard of a police station in Paraguay. The cord joined it to a father who was a provincial doctor, to a mother from a brothel, to an uncle who had walked away one day from the cane-fields to disappear into the waste of a continent, to two grandmothers. . . . There was no end to the tangle which must constrict the tiny form like the swaddling bandages with which in old days they used to bind the limbs of a new-born child. (265–66)

What this amounts to in fact is a remarkably vivid allegory about the binding or imprisonment of Eros. But the figure of a caged Eros tends to signify something more, in political as well as in personal terms, than merely the idea of powerlessness.

To put the matter briefly: the energy of Eros bound or buried persists in ordinary human life, and the form that it takes there may be creative or destructive. Conventionally, sexual repression must inevitably result either in sublimation or in a kind of urge toward death, but in each case, and in both the political and the psychological contexts, the real imperative arising from repression becomes the need for escape. So Doctor Saavedra's real life, for example, becomes the life of creative fantasy: out of his weekly visits to Senora Sanchez's brothel, he devises the actors who people the austerely exotic settings of his fiction, and thus the cramped "bare" room in which he actually lives becomes the "womb" (202), as he tells Doctor Plarr with a certain heroic defiance, of those invariably crippled characters. In the political perspective the need for escape is usually less figurative: Aquino's life and the lives of the other Paraguayan guerrillas constitute a continuous desperate bid for a very basic sort of freedom, an effort to get out from behind the bars of real prison cells. But Eros repressed tends to become Thanatos. Doctor Saavedra's novels always end with the tragic demise of a strong, silent hero and Aquino's poems seem to be about nothing else than the subject of death. The inevitability of destructive violence is built into what might be termed the fundamental narrative rationale of *The Honorary Consul:* if the demands of the kidnappers are not met, then there must be a sacrificial victim—someone must die, even if it is the "wrong" man.

As the novel's protagonist, Eduardo Plarr is caught between the two possibilities of creative and destructive action. Plarr is a conscientious physician with a compassionate commitment to the poor and oppressed, but at the same time he has also unwillingly committed himself, in his desire to free his father, to the violent politics of the guerrillas. And in spite of his humane sympathies, the most striking thing about him is an inability or a refusal to love: in many ways, Doctor Plarr's vision of his world is not unlike the essentially petrified place inhabited by Querry throughout so much of *A Burnt-Out Case.* Living on a border, he exists in a state of limbo or constant suspension; because of the absence of his father, his identity remains an enigma, something not quite realized; like Querry's, his life seems to be conducted, so to speak, in the third rather than in the first person. His situation may be usefully considered as another possible response to the repression of love, one which lies somewhere between Doctor Saavedra's and Aquino's. This is the response, perhaps the most common of all, in which love becomes merely lust, in which genuine erotic energy congeals into what might be termed a physical "humor," a repetitive and essentially mechanical sexual urge. If Doctor Humphries, for instance, is characterized as a "humorous" character by his incessant irritability, Doctor Plarr is characterized in terms of the impersonal nature of his periodic sexual need, an occasional bodily function toward which he feels mostly contempt. He makes amorous conquests but has no use for his mistresses; and in this respect he is perhaps closer in spirit to the Latin code of machismo, itself a perversion of erotic tenderness, yet another mechanism of repression, than he likes to think.

Amused by Doctor Saavedra's absurdly taciturn heroes, he fails, however, to recognize something of himself in them. In short, he suffers from a more serious kind of impotence than Charley Fortnum's. It is a form of spiritual as opposed to physical powerlessness, a petrification of the soul. And it is in this context that his anxious dream about "someone" having been "locked in" acquires its real significance. Plarr feels not only that he has usurped his father's life but that his own capacity for life has somehow been usurped in the process as well.

If Eduardo Plarr glimpses one aspect of this significance when he first sees the honorary consul lying drugged on the coffin in the kidnappers' hut, another aspect begins to be clearer still as his obsessive relationship with Clara proceeds in Charley's absence. When he finds her unexpectedly in his own bed one evening, Plarr's suddenly impersonal and detached vision of the girl as "the body of Fortnum's wife" (207) is like a deliberate attempt to shift the incestuous implications of her presence to the distance of the third-person perspective, an effort to see her in strictly neutral or objective terms. Increasingly, too, he is haunted by the image of her husband as a man entombed, and all the quiet imagined appeals that he has ever attributed to his imprisoned father modulate to Charley's whispered repetitions of his name:

> The Honorary Consul lay stretched out on the coffin and whispered, "Ted." Doctor Plarr's father had called him Eduardo as though in compliment to his wife. When he tried to substitute Henry Plarr's face for Charley Fortnum's he found his father's features had been almost eliminated by the years. As with an ancient coin that has been buried a long time in the ground he could only distinguish a faint unevenness of surface which might once have been the outline of a cheek or a lip. It was Charley Fortnum's voice which appealed to him again, "Ted." (207)

All the fathers in the novel are in fact subsumed in the figure of Charley: even Father Rivas, with his constant pleas for Charley's "confession," consistently regards the honorary consul as *his* father confessor. León may be the leader of the guerrillas but, like Eduardo Plarr, he is also an estranged son. However, Doctor

Plarr's own role in this respect begins to change quite subtly but perceptibly once he is himself unable to leave the hut; he can no longer avoid the symbolic meaning of a state of affairs until then only half-consciously recognized—his sense of a kind of absolute identity with his father—and the oedipal theme modulates at this stage to the Christian one.

During the final long vigil in the hut, Plarr becomes increasingly obsessed with the idea that his role in the kidnapping drama—indeed, his life itself—differs radically from what it had been before. He says to Charley, "I'm as much a prisoner here as you are" (233), and to Aquino, "I'm in a bloody prison here" (257). At the same time he dreams that his mother, "in her usual vein of complaint" (229), tells him "how his father would not rest like a respectable man of property in the interior of his coffin. They had constantly to shuffle him back inside, and that was no way for a *caballero* to enjoy his eternal peace" (229). It is as if Henry Plarr had been freed at last by the fact of his son's having taken his place: it seems to Doctor Plarr now that "he was already his father's age, that he had spent as long in prison as his father had, and that it was his father who had escaped" (312). In Christian terms the son has become the agent of redemption for the father, has even, like Charley Fortnum, "become" the father; but the crucial metaphorical identification to be noted here is the one between the idea of revival and that of escape. Eduardo Plarr now begins to dream not only of the birth of his own son but of the need to escape from the real imprisonment which symbolizes his own form of death-in-life. And it begins to be clear at last that the genuine victim, the scapegoat whose sacrificial death will bring rain to the wasteland, is to be not the honorary consul but the "son" who is also his betrayer. Eduardo Plarr's deliberate capitulation to Aquino in their final game of chess has to do figuratively with the first glimmerings of a recognition that he has now become a "king" who must allow himself to be checkmated in order to be reborn. What the mystery of the identity of father and son ultimately means in the context of the Christian story is a mystery about a death and a resurrection. Eduardo Plarr can only "escape" his private prison—the condition of having been locked "in"—by what amounts to an act of suicide: offering himself up, in effect, in Charley Fortnum's place.

So, in its symbolically Christian aspect, the kidnappers' hut finally takes on the appearance of "some primitive above-ground tomb prepared for a whole family" (275); and so, within the framework of the wasteland symbolism, it becomes a kind of Chapel Perilous, the fearful place—like the watchtower in *The Quiet American* or Brown's empty hotel in *The Comedians*—in which the hero must endure the last long night of his quest. It is a place where the two worlds of the novel become one, a purely symbolic "domestic" territory that is at once both Argentina and Paraguay. We have seen that the doubling principle in Greene's work—as a technique having to do with characterization as well as setting—is based on a division of the action into two modes of "reality": an immediate and actual fictive environment and a mythic world of dream and death lying behind or beneath it, of which the actual world becomes the mirror image. This structural principle is what accounts not only for Plarr's peculiarly schizoid sense of himself, his notion of a personal identity divided between two nationalities, one real and the other legendary, but also for all the other forms of doubling in the novel, like Charley's habit of thinking of himself as both a redeemable "Fortnum" and an unworthy "Mason." The most striking manifestation of the principle in *The Honorary Consul* is of course the division of the characters into fathers and sons. But during the final vigil in the hut even the idea of the identity of God is translated into the terms of this duality. In his rather lengthy account of God the Father, León proposes a theological view which asserts that God is simultaneously good and evil and that his twofold nature is reflected in the nature of his creatures. Whatever sense this may or may not make as revolutionary theology, it is a view distinctly appropriate to the structure of this novel: God is both the tyrannical king, the figure of the jailer, and the true father who is as much imprisoned by the usurping king as Henry Plarr is by General Stroessner. Thus the Christian story about a savior who is also a Son takes on a special relevance in Father

Rivas's account: what the Son really redeems is not just the Father's divided world but the Father himself. And in Christian terms, an accursed duality becomes a mystical unity, the recovery of a single divine identity.

During the last night in the hut, then, Eduardo Plarr is almost overwhelmed by his perception that he is at once both son and prospective father, that he has been as it were taken over by an identity which somehow comprehends two hitherto different roles. The primitive above-ground tomb becomes the sepulcher from which, in both personae, he must escape. The novel is a romance, in other words, precisely because its ultimate focus is on "escape" as the fundamental condition of revival or rebirth. In Plarr's case, escape means death, but the tragedy of his death is assimilated to the wider context of the whole Christian myth—the story, which frames the story of the novel, whose ultimate principle of closure is comic and romantic: Charley's escape means not only that he survives and returns to his own world but that he will in a sense preside over the coming of a new life. So it is Eduardo Plarr, not Charley Fortnum, who ends up as the sacrificial victim and who thus finds himself transformed at the last into the true father and the true "king." After his final "confession" (which is really in effect León's confession), Charley Fortnum tells the priest, "I'm a lot luckier than you are. There's no one to give *you* absolution" (309); in the end, however, the last words that León hears are "*Ego te absolvo*" (316). The words are spoken, of course, by Eduardo Plarr.

The mythic or conspicuously fictive resonance of the central imagery of fathers and sons in *The Honorary Consul* is reflected in another pattern of imagery that has to do quite specifically with the theme of fictiveness itself. The notion of language or human speech as the inevitable narration of some kind of story becomes significantly reverberative in the context of the narration of the story about Charley Fortnum and Eduardo Plarr as fictive father and son. The pattern derives from a basic metaphorical dialectic, not unlike that in *The Quiet American*, of words and silences. Among other things, what the figure of a repressed Eros suggests is the suppression of speech. Near the beginning of the novel we are told that Father Rivas speaks to Charley "immoderately as a thirsty man drinks. Perhaps he had been unable to speak freely for a long time: perhaps this was the only way he could unburden himself" (143). He has just arrived of course from a country where an enforced silence is almost literally a condition of existence. But this kind of repression is not always due to political tyranny alone: near the end of the novel Charley Fortnum decides "to break the wall of silence which was growing up between" (331) himself and Clara, feeling as he begins to do so "as though he were relearning a language he hadn't spoken since a childhood in another country" (333). Language itself, that is to say, becomes an expression of love, a form of escape from a tyranny that seems profounder and more indeterminate in nature than General Stroessner's. Aquino composes poetry in prison because no other outlet of genuine human expression is available to him—"When death is on the tongue," as one of his favorite lines goes, "the live man speaks" (151)—but even Doctor Saavedra's machismo-obsessed novels seem to serve the same kind of function, attempting as they evidently do to comprehend and render intelligible the vastness and violence of a whole strange continent. Doctor Saavedra's loquaciousness and Senora Plarr's volubility are pointedly contrasted with Eduardo Plarr's taciturnity: Plarr is characterized, virtually from the outset, as "a good listener" (63), an isolated, silent man like Saavedra's tragic heroes. And his father lies buried in "the deepest silence of all" (220).

In this frame of reference any kind of human noise tends to acquire an unusually heightened significance, and speech in itself, as the most characteristically human noise, always tends toward the condition of metaphor: if language is to be regarded as a virtual code of life, then words become charged with a potency of meaning that is much denser than the merely referential. Ordinary speech is always liable, quite suddenly, to evoke something of the disinterested and self-contained authority of myth. So in particular terms, for example, Eduardo Plarr's fear of love is fre-

quently perceived as a fear of *words*. When Clara suggests rather
tentatively that she loves him, he is both horrified and terrified:

> "Love" was a claim which he wouldn't meet, a responsibility he
> would refuse to accept, a demand. . . . So many times his mother
> had used the word when he was a child. . . . Perhaps he had loved
> his father all the more because he had never used the word. . . . The
> English phrase "Old fellow" was the nearest which he ever came to
> an endearment. He remembered his mother, as she wept in the
> cabin while the ship pulled into the current, telling him, "I have
> only you to love me now"; she had reached at him from her bunk,
> repeating "Darling, my darling boy," as Margarita had reached at
> him years later from her bed . . . and he remembered how Mar-
> garita had called him "the love of my life" as his mother had some-
> times called him "My only boy." (212–13)

Plarr is specifically afraid of certain locutions: the word "love" is
like an indecency, affecting him as obscenities might affect someone else. All this has to do of course with oedipal guilt, but his
preoccupation with verbal formulas is given a particular and
pointed stress. During his own imprisonment in the hut he is
haunted by a "question" (223) that Clara had asked him: it is not
so much that he has forgotten its general import as that he is
afraid to remember her actual words—"Eduardo, will you always be angry if I love you?" (213). "It was no use," he tells
himself, "trying to remember now what it was she had asked
him" (234), and his ambivalence about her continues to be expressed by an inability to find "the right word" (246): "It certainly wasn't 'passion'. What was the question she had asked him
just before he left her?" (246). Later he says to Father Rivas,
"That word love has such a slick sound. We take credit for loving
as though we had passed an examination with more than the
average marks" (272)—an echo of an earlier remark made to
Doctor Saavedra: "Love, love, I wish I knew what you and all the
others mean by the word" (206).

Against the imagery of the word is set the imagery of silence.
When Plarr finally learns of his father's death "the small patch of
marble floor on which he stood seemed like the edge of an

abyss. . . . He stood and listened to the silence—in the flat where Clara lay, in the midnight street outside . . . in the *barrio popular* where something must have happened among the huts of mud and tin. Silence, like a thin rain, blew across the great river into the world-abandoned republic where his father was lying dead in the deepest silence of all" (220). When the radio news broadcasts in the hut do not even mention Doctor Saavedra's offer to take Charley Fortnum's place as the kidnappers' hostage, Plarr wonders if the novelist is "listening . . . in that little room near the prison, listening to a silence which must seem to him more humiliating than a rejection" (235). And the hut itself, of course, becomes increasingly silent as the last night sets in: "The evening seemed interminably drawn out. It was as though, sitting there for hours in silence, they formed part of a universal silence all around them, the silence of the radio, the silence of the authorities, even the silence of nature. No dogs barked. The birds had ceased to sing, and when rain began to fall it was in heavy spaced drops, as infrequent as their words—the silence seemed all the deeper between the drops" (245).

In the context of an emptiness like this, "love" tends to seem legendary, a fabulous word pertaining to a strictly fictive world. Yet the silence here is ultimately broken by the telling of a story about love that bears unmistakably on the direction in which the actual events of the novel are clearly moving. Father Rivas is persuaded by his wife to say a mass, the verbal celebration, that is to say, of the redemption offered by the archetypal sacrifice of God the Son; and while the symbolic relevance of this "story" to the situation in the hut is clear enough, it is Plarr and not the designated victim, Charley Fortnum, who recognizes that the idiom of the ritual also offers the possibility of what might be termed "a sense of reality": "The priest lifted up the maté gourd and spoke the only phrases of the Mass which Doctor Plarr had for some reason never forgotten. 'As often as you do these things you shall do them in memory of Me.' How many acts in a lifetime had he done in memory of something forgotten or almost forgotten?" (305). Although he cannot remember the formulation of Clara's "question," Plarr listens to "phrases" retained in his memory since childhood. His own final question here looks rhetorical, but in the context of the imagery of words and silence, what he has "forgotten or almost forgotten" would seem to be the meaning of "love." He recognizes, it is being suggested, that the "acts" in which he has been able to feel nothing but transient lust have at least the emotive significance derived from the dim memory of "something" which is in fact an incarnate Word.

There is a good deal of play altogether with the idea of conventional verbal structures as potentially magical formulas of redemption in the face of a universal silence. In León's presence, Charley "interjected 'Father' as often as he could: it was somehow reassuring" (145); and in the same context he recalls the story of a biblical patriarch: "A father didn't usually kill his son, although of course it had been a near miss in the case of Abraham" (145). To the extent that the celebration of the mass is somehow reassuring as well, it offers a degree of comfort to the participants as listeners: it has an almost domestic familiarity for them by virtue of being a commonly understood verbal ritual, another old incanted story. Charley's efforts to write his letter to Clara reflect a similar but rather more desperate kind of faith in the redemptive or healing power of words in themselves. In the framework of this novel, though, stories are inherently absurd because inherently "escapist": structures of words have a *designed* quality which, when set against the apparent absence of any principle of *telos* in reality, makes them look more than anything else like forms of wishful thinking.

The English detective story that León reads during the last night in the hut becomes a conspicuous symbol of the absurd gap between fictive and real experience. From the point of view of the South American guerrilla-priest, this story would seem to be the sheerest artifice, even a form of literary pastoral: the representation of an imaginary but wholly intelligible world which evidently bears no relation whatever to the suffering and struggles of life as he actually knows it. And yet the fact remains that he becomes unexpectedly absorbed by the story, so much so that Plarr has the impression as he watches León reading that "he might have been praying" (264). Underlying the comic business here, in

which the story is as it were deconstructed by the two of them—
"the Edinburgh express is steaming into a station called King's
Cross. King's Cross. Would that be symbolic?" (266)—is the
theme of the inherent tendency of almost any given fictive world
to reverberate with the power of myth. Imaginative energy is also
the creative energy of Eros, a designing power that does not in
fact merely reflect reality but transforms it by interpreting or
shaping it. The detective story is as much a verbal ritual as the
mass, and its central archetype of the uncovering of a mystery
informs the story of the events which "frame" it just as much as
the more overtly mythic drama about a divine sacrifice does. The
conventional principle of closure in detective fiction is the kind of
surprise that is also, paradoxically, a sense of the inevitability of
the outcome. "The end was exactly what I thought," León an-
nounces with a certain satisfaction: "You can always tell. The
murderer went and committed suicide on the Edinburgh express.
That was why it was half an hour late and why the man Brad-
shaw was wrong" (271). It is not that this outcome is somehow
thematically prophetic of Plarr's own death (although the phrase
"King's Cross" does indeed have a certain symbolic aptness) but
that this exact combination of surprise and ritual inevitability
becomes the very quality that characterizes the actual climax of a
sequence of events which seems on the face of it to be as far
removed from any principle of creative design as South American
politics are from detective stories in general.

Fictive reverberativeness—the principle of narrative structure
which lies behind León's "You can always tell"—is exemplified
by the element of formal verbal remembrance embodied in the
idiom of the mass. But this dimension of ritual inevitability really
pertains to the novel as a whole, in that it is a function not just of
its general tone but of the narrative perspective as well. While the
mass is being prepared a curious and apparently irrelevant memory surfaces in Eduardo Plarr's mind:

> The last day had begun. He remembered an occasion years ago
> when he sat with his mother at a *son-et-lumière* performance out-
> side Buenos Aires. The searchlights came and went like a pro-
> fessor's white chalk, picking out a tree, under which someone—

San Martín was it?—had sat—an old stable where another figure
of history had tethered his horse, the windows of a room where a
treaty or a constitution—he couldn't remember what—had been
signed. A voice explained the story in a prose touched with the
dignity of the unrecallable past. He was tired from his medical
studies and he fell asleep. When he woke for the third time it was to
see Marta busy at the table laying a cloth, while daylight seeped
through the interstices of window and door. There were two unlit
candles on the table stuck in saucers. (299–300)

The mass itself, so the implication here goes, is also a kind of
"performance," a story told "in a prose touched with the dignity
of the unrecallable past." And so too is the novel. The narrative
perspective is provided by just such a disembodied voice. Greene's
choice of third-person narration in *The Honorary Consul* has to
do with the opportunity it affords not so much for omniscience as
for the type of incantatory formality appropriate to a story which
echoes a verbal ritual celebrating the archetypal feast of redemptive sacrifice.

It is this kind of narrative formality which accounts, for example, for the rather self-consciously distanced view of the characters: when the narrator's voice is not actually presenting events
from Eduardo Plarr's or Charley Fortnum's perspective, the tone
that it takes is deliberately impersonal. Characters are invariably
identified by professional or public titles rather than by names:
Doctor Plarr, Doctor Humphries, Doctor Saavedra (one has the
impression sometimes that the world of the novel is populated by
physicians), Colonel Perez, Senora Plarr, and so on; although the
guerrilla-priest is known as León to his friends, he is always "Father Rivas" to the narrator. At the same time, because Eduardo
Plarr is the central character, this narrative impersonality tends to
merge with his own distant nature, to become an aspect of his
own persona, in much the same way as the character of Querry
becomes virtually identified with the persona of the narrating
voice in *A Burnt-Out Case*. In other words, the third-person
technique represents a formal distancing device in the conventional sense but also constitutes a signal that the protagonist is a
man distanced, so to speak, from himself. The narrative point of

view is itself a way of dramatizing Plarr's self-alienation and self-division; the only other individual perspective assimilated to it is Charley Fortnum's, so that the sense of a fundamentally schizoid identity in the novel, the division of all roles into fathers and sons, becomes an aspect of technique as well as of theme.[7] If *Travels with My Aunt* is Henry Pulling's own Tennysonian monodrama (and it is arguable that all Greene's first-person novels can be read as monodramas), then *The Honorary Consul* amounts to what might be called a third-person version of that genre. It "argues," in effect, that a fictional structure of words is not only a form of ritual but a form from which, in this case, its central figure finds himself estranged or excluded. The protagonist is central to the ritual in the sense that he becomes its scapegoat. Until the final moments of his life, it is as if Eduardo Plarr never gets beyond a sense of language as a "performance" enacted by other people. His (and the novel's) sense of reality, in other words, seems in Greene's terms to be even more peculiarly fictive than usual.

Thus Charley's final reconciliation with Clara is perceived both as a verbal process and by means of a specifically verbal metaphor—his feeling, in discussing the impending birth of the child, that he is relearning a forgotten language. He is pleading on Plarr's behalf, arguing with Clara that her lover did actually love her, and when she demurs he goes on, extending the linguistic figure, to suggest that Plarr's emotional shortcomings really represented a kind of illiteracy: " 'Perhaps he'd begun, Clara. Some of us . . . we are a bit slow . . . it's not so easy to love . . . we make a lot of mistakes.' He went on for the sake of saying something, 'I hated my father . . . I did not much like my wife. . . . But they were not really bad people . . . that was only one of my mistakes. Some of us learn to read quicker than others. . . . Ted and I were both bad at the alphabet' " (333–34). Charley's words of comfort move haltingly toward one of the central revelations of the novel: that words in themselves are ultimately an expression of love and a guarantee in themselves of the perpetual renewal of life. As he "ramble[s] on, making a little human noise in the darkness in the hope that it might reassure her" (334), the sound of his own voice

validates his argument. This "noise" is perhaps the novel's definitive normative value and at the same time its assertion of it—a
vision of something restored to life by means of language alone. In
the novel's conclusion, words themselves become almost everything: "There seemed at last to be a sort of communication between them and he tried hard to keep the thin thread intact. 'What
shall we call the child, Clara?'" (334). When the girl weeps and
says that she never did in fact love Eduardo Plarr, Charley is quite
conscious that their conversation has moved at last into the realm
of sheer fictiveness. He remains, significantly, undisturbed:

> Her lie meant nothing to him now at all. It was contradicted too
> plainly by her tears. In an affair of this kind it was the right thing to
> lie. He felt a sense of immense relief. It was as though, after what
> seemed an interminable time of anxious waiting in the ante-room
> of death, someone came to him with the good news that he had
> never expected to hear. Someone he loved would survive. He real-
> ized that never before had she been so close to him as she was now.
> (334–35)

If there has been a reconciliation of fathers and sons in this novel,
there has also been a process of rescue: not only will Clara "survive" but a new life will be brought to birth. Survival becomes,
literally as well as figuratively, revival. And the symbolic agent of
this process is the figure known in Christian terminology as "the
word," an "alphabet" in terms of which the tragedy of death may
be read not as an "ending" but as a phase in a different kind of
story.

Survival rather than death is the theme of *The Honorary Consul,* just as it was of Greene's first full-length romances, *The Third
Man* and *The End of the Affair,* written almost twenty-five years
earlier. Harry Lime dies, but Rollo Martins walks out at the end
of the story from the cemetery that he entered at the beginning;
Sarah Miles dies, but Maurice Bendrix walks away across the
common from the private prison cell constructed by his own narcissism. The descent into death becomes the prelude to an emergence out of it. Eduardo Plarr's and Charley Fortnum's journey,
like those of Martins and Bendrix, takes them into a place of

imprisonment that is also an underworld, so that what is perceived as the need for escape becomes a quest for some way into a different *kind* of world, a quest in effect for birth. Plarr's death means Charley's survival, and the novel actually concludes with the imminent emergence of a new human identity.

Greene's later protagonists tend to be escapists, then, not merely because they are irresponsible romantics but because they need to recover a sense of identity that has somehow been lost. Paradoxically, the process of recovery usually involves a process of getting even more profoundly lost, as it does most obviously in the cases of Thomas Fowler and Querry. Escape begins as descent and burial but ends as imaginative revival: Thomas Fowler's "cage," for example, is also a tower of vision, a place of renewal where what is awakened is a figurative rather than a literal sense of sight, where what is reborn is a dead soul. Escape increasingly becomes a distinctly fictive business, a heroic literary pilgrimage into the archetypal underground territory of the imagination itself. And despite all Greene's protestations that he represents the world as it "is," this territory *is* the real Greeneland.

His later novels ultimately celebrate fictiveness. For, outside the context of religious belief, the idea of a genuine escape from death becomes fictional "escapism." Survival in the ultimate sense of resurrection can be nothing other than fictive. But this is not to say that the possibility of survival therefore becomes merely an illusion. In an important sense, the real Greeneland is also the real world, because whatever else it may be, the world as it "is" looks very much like Charley Fortnum's empty "anteroom of death." We begin to escape from it only by "making a little human noise in the darkness." We begin, in other words, by making the place mean something. Querry's last words after he has been shot, like an adulterer by a jealous husband in a bad play, are, "this is absurd, or else . . .": the implication of the final phrase is that it is what we call "reality" and not what we think of as dramatic artifice that is truly absurd. Fictions are made out of words, and the word becomes primary, indeed archetypal, in Greene's later fiction because language has the power to make Charley's "anteroom of death" into what Doctor Saavedra calls a "womb." The idiom of Doctor Saavedra's own fictions may also be absurd, but its absurdity is creative and not of the order of meaninglessness. In *Ways of Escape*, Greene focuses on his career as a writer by writing about his life as a wanderer; in *Travels with My Aunt*, wandering becomes a metaphor for storytelling. The ultimate way of escape in the last phase of Greene's fiction is the making of fiction itself.

Notes

ONE
The Third Man and *The End of the Affair*

1. Graham Greene, *Ways of Escape* (London: Bodley Head, 1980), pp. 134–35.

2. Graham Greene, *The Third Man,* in *The Third Man and The Fallen Idol* (London: William Heinemann, 1950), p. 21. All subsequent references to *The Third Man* will be to this edition, with the relevant page numbers incorporated within parentheses in the text.

3. In his preface to the first English edition, Greene actually describes the foreground setting of the novel as that of "a fairy tale." *The Third Man and The Fallen Idol,* p. 6.

4. See, for example, A. F. Cassis, "The Dream as Literary Device in Graham Greene's Novels," *Literature and Psychology,* 24 (1974), 99–108.

5. There is a lucid discussion of the parrot as a symbol of narcissism in Northrop Frye, *The Secular Scripture: A Study of the Structure of Romance* (Cambridge, Mass.: Harvard Univ. Press, 1976), pp. 106–9.

6. Northrop Frye, "Dickens and the Comedy of Humours," in *The Stubborn Structure: Essays on Criticism and Society* (London: Methuen and Co., 1970), pp. 218–40. See especially pp. 236–40.

7. Frye, "Dickens and the Comedy of Humours," p. 236.

8. Frye, *The Secular Scripture,* pp. 114–15.

9. Frye, *The Secular Scripture,* pp. 97–157.

10. *Ways of Escape,* p. 135.

11. *Ways of Escape,* p. 136.

12. Graham Greene, *The End of the Affair* (London: William Heinemann, 1951), p. 38. All subsequent references to *The End of the Affair* will be to this edition, with the relevant page numbers incorporated within parentheses in the text.

13. *Ways of Escape,* p. 136.

14. *Ways of Escape,* pp. 134–35.

Notes

TWO
The Quiet American

1. Diana Trilling, "America and *The Quiet American*," *Commentary*, 22 (July 1956), 66–71; Dorothy Van Ghent, "New Books in Review," *Yale Review*, Summer 1956, pp. 629–30; John Lehmann, "The Blundering, Ineffectual American," *New Republic*, 134 (12 March 1956), 26–27; A. J. Liebling, "A Talkative Something-or-Other," *New Yorker*, 7 April 1956, pp. 136–42; Orville Prescott, "Books of the Times," *New York Times*, 9 March 1956, p. 21; Granville Hicks, "In a Novel It's the Life, Not the Politics, That Counts," *New York Times Book Review*, 12 August 1956, p. 5; Philip Rahv, "Wicked American Innocence," *Commentary*, 21 (May 1956), 488–90.

2. Northrop Frye, *The Secular Scripture: A Study of the Structure of Romance* (Cambridge, Mass.: Harvard Univ. Press, 1976), p. 115.

3. Graham Greene, *The Quiet American* (London: William Heinemann, 1955), p. 237. All subsequent references to *The Quiet American* will be to this edition, with the relevant page numbers incorporated within parentheses in the text.

4. Graham Greene, *Ways of Escape* (London: Bodley Head, 1980), pp. 164–65.

5. *Ways of Escape*, p. 140.

6. *Ways of Escape*, pp. 139–40.

7. The jargon of "existentialism" seems unavoidable in any discussion of the novel. On this general subject, see, for instance, Robert O. Evans, "Existentialism in Graham Greene's *The Quiet American*," *Modern Fiction Studies*, 3 (Autumn 1957), 241–48, and Hilda Graef, "Existentialist Attitudes and Christian Faith: Graham Greene," in *Modern Gloom and Christian Hope* (Chicago: Henry Regnery Co., 1959), pp. 84–97.

THREE
A Burnt-Out Case

1. Graham Greene, *Ways of Escape* (London: Bodley Head, 1980), p. 139.

2. *Ways of Escape*, pp. 139–40.

3. *Ways of Escape*, p. 134.

4. Graham Greene, *A Sort of Life* (London: Bodley Head, 1971), p. 169.

5. *Ways of Escape*, pp. 238–40.

Notes

6. Graham Greene, *Our Man in Havana* (London: Heinemann, 1958), p. [v], "Disclaimer."

7. This view is lucidly summarized by David Lodge in his *Graham Greene*, Columbia Essays on Modern Writers, No. 17 (New York and London: Columbia Univ. Press, 1966), pp. 42–44.

8. *Ways of Escape*, p. 259.

9. See, for example, R. W. B. Lewis, "The 'Trilogy' of Graham Greene," in *The Picaresque Saint: Representative Figures in Contemporary Fiction* (Philadelphia: J. B. Lippincott, 1959), p. 239.

10. Graham Greene, *The Potting Shed* (London: Heinemann, 1958), p. [vi], "Author's Note." All subsequent references to *The Potting Shed* will be to this edition, with the relevant page numbers incorporated within parentheses in the text.

11. The differences between the two productions seem to reflect a slightly different conception of the tone of the play just prior to its conclusion. In the English version, James Callifer's family is trying to decide whether he should be locked up in an insane asylum; in the American one, they are ostensibly worried that he might commit suicide. The point in either case is that they would prefer to believe that he is mad and should be restrained rather than that he has been miraculously resurrected. There is some internal evidence suggesting that, in fact, the American, and not the English, version constitutes the original conception here. This suggestion is supported by some bibliographical evidence as well: see Robert H. Miller, "Graham Greene: *The Potting Shed*, Act III," *Papers of the Bibliographical Society of America*, 71 (January 1977), 105–7. But the issue is much less important than it might appear, and since Greene's note about the priority of the English text has not been conclusively controverted, I have decided to take him at his word: all references are to the English edition of the play.

12. He describes the play as "unsatisfactory" in *A Sort of Life*, p. 169, and elaborates on his dissatisfaction in *Ways of Escape*, p. 235.

13. *Prometheus Unbound*, Act I, lines 192–99, in *Shelley: Poetical Works*, ed. Thomas Hutchinson, rev. G. M. Matthews (Oxford: Oxford Univ. Press, 1970), p. 212.

14. Northrop Frye points out that the amnesia and identical-twins themes are two of the most basic structural archetypes in romance. See *The Secular Scripture: A Study of the Structure of Romance* (Cambridge, Mass.: Harvard Univ. Press, 1976), pp. 102–4 and 110–11.

15. Frye is helpful on the subject of the ubiquity of the dog or animal companion in romance. See *The Secular Scripture*, pp. 115–16.

16. See *The Waste Land*, lines 69–76, in T. S. Eliot, *Collected Poems, 1909–1935* (London: Faber and Faber, 1936), p. 63.

17. *The Waste Land*, lines 382–83, in Eliot, *Collected Poems, 1909–1935*, p. 76.

18. Graham Greene, *Brighton Rock* (London: William Heinemann, 1938), p. 142.

19. Graham Greene, *Journey without Maps* (London: William Heinemann, 1936), p. 264.

20. Northrop Frye, *Anatomy of Criticism: Four Essays* (Princeton: Princeton Univ. Press, 1957), p. 140.

21. *Ways of Escape*, p. 235.

22. *Ways of Escape*, p. 259.

23. Marie-Françoise Allain, *The Other Man: Conversations with Graham Greene*, trans. Guido Waldman (New York: Simon and Schuster, 1983), p. 62.

24. Frank Kermode, "Mr Greene's Eggs and Crosses," *Encounter*, 16 (April 1961), pp. 69–75.

25. Kermode, p. 75.

26. Graham Greene, *In Search of a Character: Two African Journals* (London: Bodley Head, 1961), p. 13.

27. *In Search of a Character*, p. 13.

28. Graham Greene, *A Burnt-Out Case* (London: Heinemann, 1961), p. 3. All subsequent references to *A Burnt-Out Case* will be to this edition, with the relevant page numbers incorporated within parentheses in the text.

29. Patricia A. Parker, *Inescapable Romance: Studies in the Poetics of a Mode* (Princeton: Princeton Univ. Press, 1979), p. 173.

30. Parker, p. 177.

31. In his "Congo Journal," Greene records "a recurring dream" which seems intriguingly relevant here: "that my mouth is full of vegetation, which I drag out in great handfuls and there is always more to come." *In Search of a Character*, p. 53.

32. "Warning to Children," in Robert Graves, *Collected Poems, 1975* (London: Cassell, 1975), p. 30.

FOUR
A Sense of Reality

1. Marie-Françoise Allain, *The Other Man: Conversations with Graham Greene*, trans. Guido Waldman (New York: Simon and Schuster, 1983), p. 135.

Notes

2. Philip Stratford, *Faith and Fiction: Creative Process in Greene and Mauriac* (Notre Dame, Ind.: Univ. of Notre Dame Press, 1964), p. 323.

3. Graham Greene, "Under the Garden," in *A Sense of Reality* (London: Bodley Head, 1963), pp. 18–19. All subsequent references to the stories in *A Sense of Reality* will be to this edition, with the relevant page numbers incorporated within parentheses in the text.

4. "A Visit to Morin" was first published in a limited edition of 250 copies in 1960. The story can obviously be read both as a private joke and as the rather tortuous version of an authorial statement of faith, a provisional ironic credo.

5. Northrop Frye, "Dickens and the Comedy of Humours," in *The Stubborn Structure: Essays on Criticism and Society* (London: Methuen and Co., 1970), p. 222.

6. In this connection, Greene remarks: "When *A Sense of Reality* came out, the title, which was meant to be ironical, was taken at face value. It seemed to me rather amusing to apply the word 'reality' to a book which was so remote from it. I served up quite a new dish—but nobody noticed." Allain, *The Other Man*, p. 135.

7. "A Young Man's Exhortation," in *The Collected Poems of Thomas Hardy* (London: Macmillan, 1930), p. 569.

8. "The Emperor of Ice-Cream," in *The Collected Poems of Wallace Stevens* (New York: Alfred A. Knopf, 1955), p. 64.

FIVE

The Comedians

1. Graham Greene, *Ways of Escape* (London: Bodley Head, 1980), pp. 265–69.

2. Marie-Françoise Allain, *The Other Man: Conversations with Graham Greene*, trans. Guido Waldman (New York: Simon and Schuster, 1983), p. 78.

3. Greene, *Ways of Escape*, p. 270.

4. Graham Greene, *The Comedians* (London: Bodley Head, 1966), p. 24. All subsequent references to *The Comedians* will be to this edition, with the relevant page numbers incorporated within parentheses in the text.

5. "The Great Good Place," in *The Complete Tales of Henry James*, XI, *1900–1903*, ed. Leon Edel (London: Rupert Hart-Davis, 1964), pp. 13–42.

6. Northrop Frye, *The Secular Scripture: A Study of the Structure of Romance* (Cambridge, Mass.: Harvard Univ. Press, 1976), p. 109.

7. Frye, *The Secular Scripture*, p. 109.

Notes

SIX
Travels with My Aunt and *The Honorary Consul*

1. Walter Kendrick, "Taking What You Get," *London Review of Books*, 6–19 December 1984, p. 22.

2. Marie-Françoise Allain, *The Other Man: Conversations with Graham Greene*, trans. Guido Waldman (New York: Simon and Schuster, 1983), p. 135.

3. Graham Greene, *Travels with My Aunt* (London: Bodley Head, 1969), p. 15. All subsequent references to *Travels with My Aunt* will be to this edition, with the relevant page numbers incorporated within parentheses in the text.

4. "Maud," in *The Poems of Tennyson*, ed. Christopher Ricks (London: Longmans Green and Co., 1969), pp. 1086–90.

5. "Ode: Intimations of Immortality from Recollections of Early Childhood," in *The Poetical Works of William Wordsworth*, IV, ed. E. de Selincourt and Helen Darbishire (Oxford: Clarendon Press, 1947), p. 279.

6. Graham Greene, *The Honorary Consul* (London: Bodley Head, 1973), p. 144. All subsequent references to *The Honorary Consul* will be to this edition, with the relevant page numbers incorporated within parentheses in the text.

7. The perspective of the British ambassador is also, very briefly, represented (see *The Honorary Consul*, pp. 163–73). In the present context Sir Henry Belfrage embodies the genuine paternal authority which is parodied in Charley, but the ironic point here is that the short exploration of *his* mental processes reveals much the same well-meaning helplessness.

Selected Bibliography

Primary Sources

Greene, Graham. *Brighton Rock*. London: William Heinemann, 1938.

———. *A Burnt-Out Case*. London: Heinemann, 1961.

———. *Carving a Statue*. London: Bodley Head, 1964.

———. *The Comedians*. London: Bodley Head, 1966.

———. *The Complaisant Lover*. London: Heinemann, 1959.

———. *The Confidential Agent*. London: William Heinemann, 1939.

———. *Doctor Fischer of Geneva or The Bomb Factory*. London: Bodley Head, 1980.

———. *The End of the Affair*. London: William Heinemann, 1951.

———. *England Made Me*. London: William Heinemann, 1935.

———. *A Gun for Sale*. London: William Heinemann, 1936.

———. *The Heart of the Matter*. London: William Heinemann, 1948.

———. *The Honorary Consul*. London: Bodley Head, 1973.

———. *The Human Factor*. London: Bodley Head, 1978.

———. *In Search of a Character: Two African Journals*. London: Bodley Head, 1961.

———. *It's a Battlefield*. London: William Heinemann, 1934.

———. *Journey without Maps*. London: William Heinemann, 1936.

———. *The Lawless Roads: A Mexican Journey*. London: William Heinemann, 1939.

———. *The Living Room*. London: William Heinemann, 1953.

———. *Loser Takes All*. London: William Heinemann, 1955.

———. *The Man Within*. London: William Heinemann, 1929.

———. *The Ministry of Fear*. London: William Heinemann, 1943.

———. *Our Man in Havana*. London: Heinemann, 1958.

———. *Monsignor Quixote*. London: Bodley Head, 1982.

———. *The Name of Action*. London: William Heinemann, 1930.

———. *The Potting Shed*. London: Heinemann, 1958; New York: Viking Press, 1957.

———. *The Power and the Glory*. London: William Heinemann, 1940.

———. *The Quiet American*. London: William Heinemann, 1955.

Selected Bibliography

. *The Return of A. J. Raffles.* London: Bodley Head, 1975.
———. *Rumour at Nightfall.* London: William Heinemann, 1931.
———. *A Sense of Reality.* London: Bodley Head, 1963.
———. *A Sort of Life.* London: Bodley Head, 1971.
———. *Stamboul Train.* London: William Heinemann, 1932.
———. *The Tenth Man.* London: Bodley Head, 1985.
———. *The Third Man and The Fallen Idol.* London: William Heinemann, 1950.
———. *Travels with My Aunt.* London: Bodley Head, 1969.
———. *Ways of Escape.* London: Bodley Head, 1980.

Secondary Sources

Adamson, Judith. *Graham Greene and Cinema.* Norman, Okla.: Pilgrim Books, 1984.
———, and Philip Stratford. "Looking for *The Third Man*: On the Trail in Texas, New York, Hollywood." *Encounter,* 50 (June 1978), 39–46.
Adinarayana, L. "Greene's *Our Man in Havana*: A Study of Its Narrative Structure." *Literary Endeavour,* 4, No. 3–4 (1984), 22–29.
Adler, Jacob H. "Graham Greene's Plays: Technique versus Value." In *Graham Greene: Some Critical Considerations.* Ed. Robert O. Evans. Lexington: Univ. of Kentucky Press, 1963, pp. 219–31.
Allain, Marie-Françoise. *The Other Man: Conversations with Graham Greene.* Trans. Guido Waldman. New York: Simon and Schuster, 1983.
Allen, Walter. "Awareness of Evil: Graham Greene." *Nation,* 182 (21 April 1956), 344–46.
———. "*The Comedians.*" *London Magazine,* 5 (March 1966), 73–80.
———. "Graham Greene." In *Contemporary Novelists.* Ed. James Vinson. London: St. James Press, 1972, pp. 530–34.
———. "New Novels." *New Statesman,* 56 (11 October 1958), 499–500.
———. *Tradition and Dream: The English and American Novel from the Twenties to Our Time.* London: Phoenix House, 1964.
Allott, Kenneth, and Miriam Farris. *The Art of Graham Greene.* London: Hamish Hamilton, 1951.
Allott, Miriam. "Graham Greene and the Way We Live Now." *Critical Quarterly,* 20 (Autumn 1978), 9–20.
———. "The Moral Situation in *The Quiet American*." In *Graham*

Selected Bibliography

Greene: Some Critical Considerations. Ed. Robert O. Evans. Lexington: Univ. of Kentucky Press, 1963, pp. 188–207.

———. "Surviving the Course, or a Novelist for All Seasons: Graham Greene's *The Honorary Consul.*" In *The Uses of Fiction: Essays on the Modern Novel in Honour of Arnold Kettle.* Ed. Douglas Jefferson. Milton Keynes: Open Univ. Press, 1982, pp. 237–48.

Alloway, Lawrence. "Symbolism in *The Third Man.*" *World Review,* NS 13 (March 1950), 57–60.

Amis, Kingsley. "Slow Boat to Haiti." *Observer,* 30 January 1966, p. 27.

A[rnold], G. L. "Adam's Tree." *Twentieth Century* (London), 154 (October 1951), 337–42.

Atkins, John. *Graham Greene: A Biographical and Literary Study.* London: J. Calder, 1957; New York: Roy Publishers, 1958. New rev. ed. London: Calder and Boyars, 1966.

———. "Two Views of Life: William Golding and Graham Greene." *Studies in the Literary Imagination,* 13, No. 1 (1980), 81–96.

Atkinson, Brooks. "Theatre: Greene's *The Potting Shed.*" *New York Times,* 30 January 1957, p. 32.

Atkinson, F. G. "*Floreat Augusta*—Or, On First Looking into *Travels with My Aunt.*" In *Gleanings from Greeneland.* Ed. J. S. Ryan. Armidale, New South Wales: Univ. of New England, 1972, pp. 81–90.

Auden, W. H. "The Heresy of Our Time." *Renascence,* 1 (Spring 1949), 23–24.

Barker, Paul. "The Masks of Graham Greene: *The Comedians.*" *New Society,* 27 January 1966, p. 29.

Barlow, G. "L'Art de Graham Greene." *Esprit,* 27 (March 1959), 517–25.

Barratt, Harold. "Adultery as Betrayal in Graham Greene." *Dalhousie Review,* 45 (1965), 324–32.

Barthelme, Donald. "The Tired Terror of Graham Greene." *Holiday,* 39 (April 1966), 146, 148–49.

Beirnaert, Louis. " 'La Fin d'une liaison,' par Graham Greene." *Etudes,* 272 (March 1951), 369–78.

Bellow, Saul. "The Writer as Moralist." *Atlantic Monthly,* 211 (March 1963), 58–62.

Bergonzi, Bernard. "A Conspicuous Absentee: The Decline and Fall of the Catholic Novel." *Encounter,* 55 (August–September 1980), 44–56.

———. "Graham Greene Supplied the Lyrics: A Footnote to the Thirties." *Encounter,* 47 (December 1976), 67–71.

———. "Greeneland Revisited." *New Society,* 20 November 1969, pp. 824–25.

Bertram, Anthony. "Books of the Week: Another Part of the Wood." *Tablet,* 198 (8 September 1951), 156.

Boardman, Gwenn R. *Graham Greene: The Aesthetics of Exploration.* Gainesville: Univ. of Florida Press, 1971.

———. "Greene's 'Under the Garden': Aesthetic Explorations." *Renascence,* 17, No. 4 (Summer 1965), 180–90, 194.

Bogan, Louise. "Good beyond Evil." *New Republic,* 125 (10 December 1951), 29–30.

Bowen, Elizabeth. "Story, Theme, and Situation." *Listener,* 56 (25 October 1956), 651–52.

Boyd, John D. "Earth Imagery in Graham Greene's *The Potting Shed.*" *Modern Drama* (Toronto), 16, No. 1 (June 1973), 69–80.

Boyle, Alexander. "The Symbolism of Graham Greene." *Irish Monthly,* 80 (March 1952), 98–102.

Bradbury, Malcolm. "New Novels." *Punch,* 244 (26 June 1963), 937–38.

Braybrooke, Neville. "An End to Anguish?" *Commonweal,* 63 (20 January 1956), 406–07.

———. "Graham Greene." *Envoy,* 3 (September 1950), 10–23.

———. "Graham Greene and the Double Man: An Approach to *The End of the Affair.*" *Dublin Review,* 226 (First Quarter 1952), 61–73.

———. "Graham Greene as Critic." *Commonweal,* 54 (6 July 1951), 512–14.

Brennan, Neil. "Coney Island Rock." *Accent,* 16 (Spring 1956), 140–42.

Brion, Marcel. "Les Romans de Graham Greene." *Revue des Deux Mondes,* 6 (15 March 1950), 367–75.

Brooke, Jocelyn. "New Fiction." *Listener,* 69 (20 June 1963), 1049.

Bryden, Ronald. "Graham Greene, Alas." *Spectator,* 209 (28 September 1962), 441–42.

Burgess, Anthony. *The Novel Now: A Student's Guide to Contemporary Fiction.* London: Faber and Faber. Rev. ed., 1971, pp. 61–72.

———. "Graham Greene as Monsieur Vert." *Tablet,* 229 (15 March 1975), 259–60.

———. "New Fiction." *Listener,* 75 (3 February 1966), 181.

———. *The Novel Today.* British Council Series. London: Longmans Green, 1963.

———. "Politics in the Novels of Graham Greene." *Journal of Contemporary History,* 2 (April 1967), 92–99.

_____. "Religion and the Arts: 1. The Manicheans." *Times Literary Supplement,* 3 March 1966, pp. 153–54.

Burns, Wayne. "The Novelist as Revolutionary." *Arizona Quarterly,* 7 (1951), 13–27.

Burstall, Christopher. "Graham Greene Takes the Orient Express." *Listener,* 80 (21 November 1968), 672–74, 676–77.

Byatt, A. S. "Evil as Commonplace." *Encounter,* 26 (June 1966), 66, 68–70.

Cain, Alex Matheson. "A Modern Lazarus." *Tablet,* 211 (15 February 1958), 152–53.

Cargas, Harry J., ed. *Graham Greene.* St. Louis: B. Herder, 1969.

Cassidy, John. "America and Innocence: Henry James and Graham Greene." *Blackfriars,* 38 (June 1957), 261–67.

Cassis, A. F. "The Dream as Literary Device in Graham Greene's Novels." *Literature and Psychology,* 24 (1974), 99–108.

_____. "A Note on Point-of-View and Self-Revelation in Graham Greene's Novels." *Dublin Magazine,* 10, No. 3 (Autumn/Winter 1973), 69–73.

Casson, Allan. "Greene's Comedians and Amis' Anti-Death League." *Massachusetts Review,* 8 (Spring 1967), 392–96.

Chapman, Raymond. "The Vision of Graham Greene." In *Forms of Extremity in the Modern Novel.* Ed. N. A. Scott, Jr. Richmond, Va.: John Knox Press, 1965, pp. 75–94.

Church, Richard. "Graham Greene." In his *British Authors.* London: Longmans Green, 1948, pp. 137–40.

Clancy, L. J. "Graham Greene's Battlefield." *Melbourne Critical Review,* 10 (1967), 99–108.

Clancy, W. "The Moral Burden of Mr. Greene's Parable." *Commonweal,* 63 (16 March 1956), 622.

Clarke, D. Waldo. "Graham Greene." In his *Writers of Today.* Essential English Library Series. London and New York: Longmans Green, 1956, pp. 59–68.

Clurman, Harold. "Theatre." *Nation,* 184 (16 February 1957), 146–47.

Clurman, Robert. "In and Out of Books: The Quiet Englishman." *New York Times Book Review,* 26 August 1956, p. 8.

Cockshut, A. O. J. "Sentimentality in Fiction." *Twentieth Century* (London), 161 (April 1957), 354–61.

Connolly, Francis. *The Types of Literature.* New York: Harcourt, Brace, 1955.

Consolo, Dominick P. "Graham Greene: Style and Stylistics in Five Novels." In *Graham Greene: Some Critical Considerations.* Ed.

Robert O. Evans. Lexington: Univ. of Kentucky Press, 1963, pp. 61–96.

Corke, Hilary. "Matters of Opinion." *Encounter*, 6 (January 1956), 88–89.

———. "A Strong Smell of Fish." *New Republic*, 149 (31 August 1963), 31–33.

Cosman, Max. "An Early Chapter in Graham Greene." *Arizona Quarterly*, 11 (Summer 1955), 143–47.

Cottrell, Beckman W. "Second Time Charm: The Theatre of Graham Greene." *Modern Fiction Studies*, 3 (Autumn 1957), 249–55.

Cournos, John. "*The Third Man*." *Commonweal*, 52 (26 May 1950), 182.

Cranston, Maurice. "New Novels." *Listener*, 54 (22 December 1955), 1097.

Crubellier, Maurice. "Graham Greene: La Tragédie de la pitié." *Vie Intellectuele*, 12 (December 1951), 57–78.

Daiches, David. "The Possibilities of Heroism." *American Scholar*, 25 (Winter 1956), 94–106.

Davenport, John. "The Last Albigensian." *Spectator*, 216 (28 January 1966), 110–11.

Davidson, Arnold C. "Graham Greene's Spiritual Lepers." *Iowa English Bulletin Yearbook*, 15 (Fall 1970), 50–55.

Davis, Elizabeth. *Graham Greene: The Artist as Critic*. Fredericton, N. B.: York Press, 1984.

Derrick, Christopher. "Grammar of Assent." *Tablet*, 225 (21 January 1961), 58.

De Vitis, A. A. "The Catholic as Novelist: Graham Greene and François Mauriac." In *Graham Greene: Some Critical Considerations*. Ed. Robert O. Evans. Lexington: Univ. of Kentucky Press, 1963, pp. 112–27.

———. "The Entertaining Mr. Greene." *Renascence*, 14 (Autumn 1961), 8–24.

———. *Graham Greene*. Twayne's English Authors Series. New York: Twayne, 1964.

———. "Greene's *The Comedians*: Hollower Men." *Renascence*, 18 (Spring 1966), 129–36, 146.

———. "Religious Aspects in the Novels of Graham Greene." In *The Shapeless God: Essays on Modern Fiction*. Ed. Harry J. Mooney, Jr., and Thomas F. Staley. Pittsburgh: Univ. of Pittsburgh Press, 1968, pp. 41–67.

Selected Bibliography

Didion, J. "Marks of Identity." *National Review,* 10 (25 March 1961), 190–91.

Dinkins, Paul. "Graham Greene: The Incomplete Version." *Catholic World,* 176 (November 1952), 96–102.

Dinnage, Paul. "Two Entertainments." *Spectator,* 6371 (4 August 1950), 158.

Dombrowski, Theo. Q. "Graham Greene: Techniques of Intensity." *Ariel,* 6, No. 4 (1975), 29–38.

Donaghy, Henry J. "Graham Greene's 'Virtue of Disloyalty.'" *Christianity and Literature,* 32, No. 3 (Spring 1983), 31–37.

Donnelly, Tom. "A Detective Story for Grown-Ups." *New York World Telegram,* 30 January 1957, p. 18.

Donoghue, Denis. "A Visit to Greeneland." *Commonweal,* 99 (30 November 1973), 241–42.

Dooley, D. J. "*A Burnt-Out Case* Reconsidered." *Wiseman Review,* 237 (Summer 1963), 168–78.

_____. "The Suspension of Disbelief: Greene's *Burnt-Out Case.*" *Dalhousie Review,* 43 (Autumn 1963), 343–52.

_____. "Greeneland Explored." *Canadian Forum,* 44 (August 1964), 115–16.

Downing, Francis. "The Art of Fiction." *Commonweal,* 55 (28 December 1951), 297–98.

_____. "Graham Greene and the Case for Disloyalty." *Commonweal,* 55 (14 March 1952), 564–66.

Duesberg, Jacques. "Chronique des lettres anglo-saxonnes: un épigone du 'Miserabilisme': Graham Greene." *Synthèse,* 69 (February 1952), 348–53.

Dworkin, Martin S. "The Writing on the Screen." *Trivium,* 12 (May 1977), 17–25.

Eagleton, Terence. "Reluctant Heroes: The Novels of Graham Greene." In his *Exiles and Emigrès: Studies in Modern Literature.* London: Chatto and Windus, 1970, pp. 108–37.

Evans, Robert O. "Existentialism in Graham Greene's *The Quiet American.*" *Modern Fiction Studies,* 3 (Autumn 1957), 241–48.

_____, ed. *Graham Greene: Some Critical Considerations.* Lexington: Univ. of Kentucky Press, 1963.

Fagin, Steven. "Narrative Design in *Travels with My Aunt.*" *Literature/Film Quarterly,* 2 (Fall 1974), 379–83.

Falk, Quentin. *Travels in Greeneland: The Cinema of Graham Greene.* London: Quartet Books, 1984.

Selected Bibliography

Faulkner, Peter. "Recent Religious Novelists: Waugh, Greene, Golding." In his *Humanism in the English Novel*. London: Elek Books, 1976, pp. 156–78.

Fielding, Gabriel. "Graham Greene: The Religious Englishman." *Listener*, 72 (24 September 1964), 465–66.

Fleming, Peter. "The Quest for Querry." *Listener*, 66 (26 October 1961), 673.

Flood, Ethelbert, OFM. "Christian Language in Modern Literature." *Culture*, 12 (March 1961), 28–42.

Foster, Joseph R. "Graham Greene." In his *Modern Christian Literature*. London: Burns and Oates, 1963, pp. 47–55.

Fowler, Alistair. "Novelist of Damnation." *Theology*, 56 (July 1953), 259–64.

Fraser, George Sutherland. "The 'Serious' 1930s." In his *The Modern Writer and His World*. London: D. Verschoyle, 1953. Rev. ed. London: Andre Deutsch, 1964, pp. 131–47.

Freedman, Ralph. "Novel of Contention: *The Quiet American*." *Western Review*, 21 (Autumn 1956), 76–81.

Fremantle, Anne. "In Pursuit of Peace." *Saturday Review*, 27 October 1951, pp. 11–12.

French, Philip. "Man of Mystery: The Enigma of Graham Greene." *Listener*, 102 (4 October 1979), 441–43.

————. "On the Frontier." *New Statesman*, 86 (14 September 1973), 353–54.

Friedman, Melvin J., ed. *The Vision Obscured: Perceptions of Some Twentieth-Century Catholic Novelists*. New York: Fordham Univ. Press, 1970.

Frye, Northrop. *Anatomy of Criticism: Four Essays*. Princeton, N.J.: Princeton Univ. Press, 1957.

————. "Dickens and the Comedy of Humours." In his *The Stubborn Structure: Essays on Criticism and Society*. London: Methuen and Co., 1970, pp. 218–40.

————. *The Secular Scripture: A Study of the Structure of Romance*. Cambridge, Mass.: Harvard Univ. Press, 1976.

Furbank, P. N. "New Novels?" *Encounter*, 21 (October 1963), 82–83.

Gale, George. "From a View to a Death." *Spectator*, 230 (5 May 1973), 555–56.

Gamble, R. M. "The Lonely Battle." *Irish Times*, 14 January 1961, p. 6.

Gardiner, Harold C., SJ. "Mr. Greene Does It Again." *America*, 86 (27 October 1951), 100–101.

————. *Norms for the Novel.* New York: America Press. Rev. ed. New York: Hanover House, 1960.

————. "Seekers, Finders in the Congo." *America,* 104 (18 February 1961), 671–72.

Gassner, John. "Religion and Graham Greene's *The Potting Shed.*" In his *Theatre at the Crossroads.* New York: Holt, Rinehart and Winston, 1960, pp. 155–57.

Gaston, Georg M. A. *The Pursuit of Salvation: A Critical Guide to the Novels of Graham Greene.* Troy, N.Y.: Whitston Publishing Co., 1984.

————. "The Structure of Salvation in *The Quiet American.*" *Renascence,* 31 (Winter 1979), 93–106.

Ghent, Dorothy Van. "New Books in Review." *Yale Review,* Summer 1956, pp. 629–30.

Gillie, Christopher. "The Critical Decade 1930–1940." In his *Movements in English Literature, 1900–1940.* London: Cambridge Univ. Press, 1975, pp. 122–50.

Gilman, Richard. "Up from Hell with Graham Greene." *New Republic,* 154 (29 January 1966), 25–28.

Glicksberg, Charles I. "Graham Greene: Catholicism in Fiction." *Criticism,* 1 (Fall 1959), 339–53.

Gomez, Joseph A. "The Theme of the Double in *The Third Man.*" *Film Heritage,* 6, No. 4 (Summer 1971), 7–12, 24.

————. "*The Third Man:* Capturing the Visual Essence of Literary Conception." *Literature/Film Quarterly,* 2 (Fall 1974), 332–40.

Graef, Hilda. "Existentialist Attitudes and Christian Faith: Graham Greene." In her *Modern Gloom and Christian Hope.* Chicago: Henry Regnery Co., 1959, pp. 84–97.

Gransden, K. W. "Graham Greene's Rhetoric." *Essays in Criticism,* 31 (January 1981), 41–60.

Gregor, Ian. "Dead Centre." *Guardian,* 20 January 1961, p. 7.

————. "*The End of the Affair.*" In *Graham Greene: A Collection of Critical Essays.* Ed. Samuel Hynes. Englewood Cliffs, N.J.: Prentice-Hall, 1973, pp. 110–26.

————. "The Green Baize Door." *Blackfriars,* 36 (September 1955), 327–33.

————. "*A Sense of Reality.*" *Blackfriars,* 44 (October 1963), 439–41.

————, and Brian Nichols. "Grace and Morality." In their *The Moral and the Glory.* London: Faber and Faber, 1962, pp. 185–216.

Selected Bibliography

Grob, Alan. "*The Power and the Glory:* Graham Greene's Argument from Design." *Criticism,* 11 (Winter 1969), 1–30.

Haber, Herbert R. "The End of the Catholic Cycle: The Writer versus the Saint." In *Graham Greene: Some Critical Considerations.* Ed. Robert O. Evans. Lexington: Univ. of Kentucky Press, 1963, pp. 127–51.

Hackett, Francis. "The Quiet Englishman." *New Republic,* 135 (30 April 1956), 27–28.

Hall, James. "Efficient Saints and Civilians: Graham Greene." In his *The Lunatic Giant in the Drawing Room: The British and American Novel since 1930.* Bloomington: Indiana Univ. Press, 1968, pp. 111–23.

Hanlon, Robert M., SJ. "The Ascent to Belief in Graham Greene's *A Burnt-Out Case.*" *Christianity and Literature,* 26, No. 4 (Summer 1977), 20–26.

Harris, Wendell V. "Molly's 'Yes': The Transvaluation of Sex in Modern Fiction." *Texas Studies in Literature and Language,* 10 (1968), 107–18.

Hartt, Julian N. *The Lost Image of Man.* Baton Rouge: Louisiana State Univ. Press, 1963.

Hawton, Hector, and Roger Manvell. "A Sort of Roman." *Humanist,* 86 (October 1971), 303–35.

Hays, H. R. "A Defense of the Thriller." *Partisan Review,* 12 (Winter 1945), 135–37.

Hebblethwaite, Peter. "How Catholic Is the Catholic Novel?" *Times Literary Supplement,* 27 July 1967, pp. 678–79.

Hesla, David H. "Theological Ambiguity in the 'Catholic Novels.'" In *Graham Greene: Some Critical Considerations.* Ed. Robert O. Evans. Lexington: Univ. of Kentucky Press, 1963, pp. 96–112.

Hewes, Henry. "Resurrection Will Out." *Saturday Review,* 16 February 1957, pp. 26–27.

Hicks, Granville. "Gestation of a Brain Child." *Saturday Review,* 6 January 1962, p. 62.

———. "In a Novel It's the Life, Not the Politics, That Counts." *New York Times Book Review,* 12 August 1956, p. 5.

———. "An Inner Climate of Emptiness." *Saturday Review,* 18 February 1961, p. 16.

———. "Strangers in Paradox." *Saturday Review,* 22 June 1963, pp. 35–36.

_____. "Trials of the Uncommitted." *Saturday Review,* 29 January 1966, pp. 29–30.

Higdon, David Leon. "Saint Catherine, Von Hugel 28714 and Graham Greene's *The End of the Affair.*" *English Studies,* 62, No. 1 (January 1981), 46–52.

Highet, Gilbert. "Our Man in Purgatory." *Horizon,* 3, No. 5 (May 1961), 116–17.

Hoggart, Richard. "The Force of Caricature: Aspects of the Art of Graham Greene, with Particular Reference to *The Power and the Glory.*" *Essays in Criticism,* 3 (October 1953), 447–62.

Hollis, Christopher. "The Quest for Querry." *Tablet,* 225 (28 October 1961), 1028, 1030.

Hortmann, Wilhelm. "Graham Greene: The Burnt-Out Catholic." *Twentieth-Century Literature,* 10 (1964), 64–76.

Hoskins, Robert. "Through a Glass Darkly: Mirrors in *The End of the Affair.*" *Notes on Contemporary Literature,* 9, No. 3 (1979), 3–5.

Hughes, Catherine. "Innocence Revisited." *Renascence,* 12 (Autumn 1959), 29–34.

Hughes, R. E. "*The Quiet American:* The Case Reopened." *Renascence,* 12 (Autumn 1959), 41–42, 49.

_____. "New Novels: *The End of the Affair.*" *Catholic World,* 174 (January 1952), 312.

Hynes, Samuel. "Religion in the West End." *Commonweal,* 59 (12 February 1954), 475–78.

_____, ed. *Graham Greene: A Collection of Critical Essays.* Englewood Cliffs, N.J.: Prentice-Hall, 1973.

Isaacs, Rita. "Three Levels of Allegory in Graham Greene's *The End of the Affair.*" *Linguistics in Literature,* 1, No. 1 (1975), 29–52.

Jarrett-Kerr, Martin. *Studies in Literature and Belief.* London: Rockcliff Publishing House, 1954.

Jones, James Land. "Graham Greene and the Structure of the Moral Imagination." *Phoenix,* 2 (1966), 34–56.

Joselyn, Sister M., OSB. "Graham Greene's Novels: The Conscience in the World." In *Literature and Society: A Selection of Papers Delivered at the Joint Meeting of the Midwest Modern Language Association and the Central Renaissance Conference, 1963.* Ed. Bernice Slote. Lincoln: Univ. of Nebraska Press, 1963, pp. 153–72.

Karl, Frederick R. "Graham Greene's Demoniacal Heroes." In his *A Reader's Guide to the Contemporary English Novel.* New York: Noonday Press, 1959, pp. 85–107.

Selected Bibliography

Karnath, David. "Bernanos, Greene, and the Novel Convention." *Contemporary Literature,* 19 (1978), 429–45.

Kazin, Alfred. "Graham Greene and the Age of Absurdity." In his *Contemporaries.* Boston, Mass.: Little, Brown, 1962, pp. 158–61.

Kellogg, Gene. "The Catholic Novel in Convergence." *Thought,* 45 (1970), 265–96.

Kelly, Edward E. "Absurdity but Faith with Suffering in Greene's *A Burnt-Out Case.*" *Greyfriar,* 21 (May 1980), 29–34.

Kelly, Richard. *Graham Greene.* New York: Frederick Ungar, 1984.

Kendrick, Walter. "Taking What You Get." *London Review of Books,* 6–19 December 1984, pp. 22–23.

Kennedy, Alan. "Inconsistencies of Narrative in Graham Greene." In his *The Protean Self: Dramatic Action in Contemporary Fiction.* London: Macmillan, 1974, pp. 231–49.

Kermode, Frank. "Havana Rock." *Spectator,* 201 (10 October 1958), 496.

————. "The House of Fiction: Interviews with Seven English Novelists." *Partisan Review,* 30 (Spring 1963), 61–83.

————. "Mr Greene's Eggs and Crosses." *Encounter,* 16 (April 1961), 69–75.

————. "Myth, Reality and Fiction." *Listener,* 68 (30 August 1962), 311–13.

Kiely, Robert. "The Craft of Despondency—The Traditional Novelists." *Daedalus,* 92 (1963), 220–37.

Kohn, Lynette. *Graham Greene: The Major Novels.* Stanford Honors Essays in Humanities, No. 4. Palo Alto, Calif.: Stanford Junior Univ., 1961.

Kort, Wesley. "The Obsession of Graham Greene." *Thought,* 45 (1970), 20–44.

Kulshrestha, J. P. *Graham Greene: The Novelist.* New Delhi: Macmillan Co. of India, 1977.

Kunkel, Francis L. "Greeneland Improved." *Renascence,* 18 (Summer 1966), 219–21.

————. "The Hollow Man." *Renascence,* 13 (Autumn 1961), 48–49.

————. *The Labyrinthine Ways of Graham Greene.* New York: Sheed and Ward, 1959. Rev. and expanded ed. Mamaroneck, N.Y.: Paul P. Appel, 1973.

————. "The Sexy Cross." In his *Passion and the Passion: Sex and Religion in Modern Literature.* Philadelphia: Westminster Press, 1975, pp. 157–69.

_____. "The Theme of Sin and Grace in Graham Greene." In *Graham Greene: Some Critical Considerations*. Ed. Robert O. Evans. Lexington: Univ. of Kentucky Press, 1963, pp. 49–61.

Kurismmootil, K. C. Joseph, SJ. *Heaven and Hell on Earth: An Appreciation of Five Novels of Graham Greene*. Chicago: Loyala Univ. Press, 1982.

Lambert, Gavin. "The Double Agent." In his *The Dangerous Edge*. London: Barrie and Jenkins, 1975.

_____. "Story into Film." *New Statesman*, 40 (16 September 1950), 280, 282.

Lardner, John. "A Strong Greene, A Weak James." *New Yorker*, 9 February 1957, pp. 66, 68, 70–72.

Larsen, Eric. "*The Quiet American*." *New Republic*, 175 (7–14 August 1976), 40–42.

Lees, F. N. "Graham Greene: A Comment." *Scrutiny*, 19 (October 1952), 31–42.

Lehmann, John. "The Blundering, Ineffectual American." *New Republic*, 134 (12 March 1956), 26–27.

Lerner, Laurence. "Graham Greene." *Critical Quarterly*, 5 (Autumn 1963), 217–31.

_____. "Love and Gossip: Or, How Moral Is Literature?" *Essays in Criticism*, 14 (April 1964), 126–47.

Levine, Norman. "Mr. Greene, Mellowed." *Atlantic Advocate*, 56 (February 1966), 72.

Lewis, R. W. B. "The Fiction of Graham Greene: Between the Horror and the Glory." *Kenyon Review*, 19 (Winter 1957), 56–75.

_____. "The 'Trilogy' of Graham Greene." *Modern Fiction Studies*, 3 (Autumn 1957), 195–215. Rpt. with minor changes as a section of Ch. vi in his *The Picaresque Saint: Representative Figures in Contemporary Fiction*. Philadelphia: J. B. Lippincott, 1959, pp. 220–74.

Liebling, A. J. "A Talkative Something-or-Other." *New Yorker*, 7 April 1956, pp. 136–42.

Lodge, David. "Books for the Week: Black Comedy." *Tablet*, 220 (29 January 1966), 128.

_____. *Graham Greene*. Columbia Essays on Modern Writers, No. 17. New York and London: Columbia Univ. Press, 1966.

_____. "Graham Greene's Comedians." *Commonweal*, 83 (25 February 1966), 604–06.

_____. "Greeneland Revisited." *Tablet*, 226 (21 October 1972), 1002–3.

————. "The Liberty of Fantasy: Graham Greene's New Departure." *Tablet,* 217 (22 June 1963), 679–80.

————. "Romantic Realist." *Tablet,* 227 (15 September 1973), 873–74.

————. "Use of Key Words in the Novels of Graham Greene: Love, Hate and *The End of the Affair." Blackfriars,* 42 (November 1961), 468–74.

Lohf, Kenneth A. "Graham Greene and the Problem of Evil." *Catholic World,* 173 (June 1951), 196–99.

Lumley, Frederick. "Britain: Graham Greene." In his *New Trends in 20th Century Drama: A Survey since Ibsen and Shaw.* London: Oxford Univ. Press, 1967, pp. 289–92.

McCaffrey, Bertrand, O. P. "Graham Greene: A Catholic Writer?" *Dominicana,* 48 (1963), 120–27.

McCarthy, Mary. "Graham Greene and the Intelligentsia." *Partisan Review,* 11 (Spring 1944), 228–30.

————. "Theatre Chronicle: Sheep in Wolves Clothing." *Partisan Review,* 24 (Spring 1957), 270–74.

McConnell, F. "Reconsideration: *The End of the Affair." New Republic,* 178 (11 March 1978), 35–37.

McCormick, John O. "The Rough and Lurid Vision: Henry James, Graham Greene and the International Theme." *Jahrbuch für Amerikastudien,* 2 (1957), 158–67.

McDonald, James L. "Graham Greene: A Reconsideration." *Arizona Quarterly,* 27 (1971), 197–210.

McDougal, Stuart J. "Visual Tropes: An analysis of *The Fallen Idol." Style,* 9, No. 4 (Fall 1975), 502–13.

McInery, Ralph. "The Greene-ing of America." *Commonweal,* 95 (15 October 1971), 59–61.

McLaughlin, John J. "*The Potting Shed* and the Potter's Wheel." *America,* 97 (4 May 1957), 168–70.

Macleod, Norman. "'This Strange, Rather Sad Story': The Reflexive Design of Graham Greene's *The Third Man." Dalhousie Review,* 63 (Summer 1983), 217–41.

Maddocks, Melvin. "Greene's New Novel: *A Burnt-Out Case." Christian Science Monitor,* 23 February 1961, p. 7.

Mahood, M. M. "The Possessed: Greene's *The Comedians.*" In his *The Colonial Encounter: A Reading of Six Novels.* London: Rex Collings, 1977, pp. 115–41.

"The Man Within." *Times Literary Supplement,* 17 September 1971, pp. 1101–2.

Marian, Sister, IHM. "Graham Greene's People: Being and Becoming." *Renascence*, 18 (Autumn 1965), 16–22.

Markovic, Vida E. "Graham Greene in Search of God." *Texas Studies in Literature and Language*, 5 (Summer 1963), 271–82.

Marshall, Bruce. "Graham Greene and Evelyn Waugh." *Commonweal*, 51 (3 March 1950), 551–53.

Mass, Roslyn. "The Presentation of the Character of Sarah Miles in the Film Version of *The End of the Affair*." *Literature/Film Quarterly*, 2 (Fall 1974), 347–51.

Mauriac, François. "Graham Greene." In *Graham Greene: A Collection of Critical Essays*. Ed. Samuel Hynes. Englewood Cliffs, N.J.: Prentice-Hall, 1973, pp. 75–78.

Maxwell, J. C. "'The Dry Salvages': A Possible Echo of Graham Greene." *Notes and Queries*, 11 (October 1964), 387.

Mayhew, Alice. "The Comedians." In *Graham Greene*. Ed. Harry J. Cargas. St. Louis: B. Herder, 1969, pp. 134–41.

Mayne, Richard. "Where God Makes the Scenery." *New Statesman*, 66 (2 August 1963), 144.

Merry, Bruce. *Anatomy of the Spy Thriller*. London: Macmillan, 1977.

Mesnet, Marie-Beatrice. *Graham Greene and the Heart of the Matter: An Essay*. London: Cresset Press, 1954.

_____. "Le 'Potting Shed' de Graham Greene." *Etudes*, 296 (September 1958), 238–47.

_____. "La Vision Politique de Graham Greene." *Etudes*, 333 (December 1970), 686–705.

Meyers, Jeffrey. "Graham Greene: The Decline of the Colonial Novel." In his *Fiction and the Colonial Experience*. Totowa, N.J.: Rowman and Littlefield, 1973, pp. 97–115.

Miller, Robert H. "Graham Greene: *The Potting Shed*, Act III." *Papers of the Bibliographical Society of America*, 71 (January 1977), 105–7.

Mitchell, Julian. "Grim Grin in the Gloom." *New Statesman*, 78 (21 November 1969), 733.

Monroe, N. Elizabeth. "The New Man in Fiction." *Renascence*, 6 (Autumn 1953), 9–17.

Muir, Edwin. "Love and Hate." *Observer*, 2 September 1951, p. 7.

Murphy, John P. "On Graham Greene." *Wiseman Review*, 225 (Spring 1961), 85–89.

_____. "*The Potting Shed*: Dogmatic and Dramatic Effects." *Renascence*, 12 (Autumn 1959), 43–49.

Murray, Edward. "Graham Greene and the Silver Screen." In his *The Cinematic Imagination: Writers and the Motion Pictures*. New York: Frederick Ungar, 1972, pp. 244–60.

Newby, P. H. *The Novel, 1945–1950*. The British Council Series. London: Longmans Green, 1951.

Nott, Kathleen. "Augustinian Novelists." In her *The Emperor's Clothes*. London: Heinemann, 1953, pp. 299–311.

Noxon, James. "Kierkegaard's Stages and *A Burnt-Out Case*." *Review of English Literature*, 3, No. 1 (January 1962), 90–101.

Nye, Robert. "How to Read Graham Greene without Kneeling." *Books and Bookmen*, 19 (October 1973), 18–21.

O'Brien, Conor Cruise. "A Funny Sort of God." *New York Review of Books*, 18 October 1973, pp. 56–58.

———. "Old Black Magic Has Him in Its Spell." *Bookweek*, 6 February 1966, p. 5.

O'Donnell, Donat [Conor Cruise O'Brien]. "Mr. Greene's Battlefield." *New Statesman*, 50 (10 December 1955), 804.

———. "Our Men in Africa." *Spectator*, 6917 (20 January 1961), 80.

O'Faolain, Sean. "Graham Greene: I Suffer; Therefore, I Am." In his *The Vanishing Hero: Studies in Novelists of the Twenties*. London: Eyre and Spottiswoode, 1956, pp. 73–97.

Pake, Lucy S. "Courtly Love in Our Own Time: Graham Greene's *The End of the Affair*." *Lamar Journal of the Humanities*, 8, No. 2 (Fall 1982), 36–43.

Palmer, James W., and Michael M. Riley. "The Lone Rider in Vienna: Myth and Meaning in *The Third Man*." *Literature/Film Quarterly*, 8 (1980), 14–21.

Parker, Patricia A. *Inescapable Romance: Studies in the Poetics of a Mode*. Princeton: Princeton Univ. Press, 1979.

Peters, W. "The Concern of Graham Greene." *Month*, 10 (November 1953), 281–90.

Phillips, Gene D., SJ. *Graham Greene: The Films of His Fiction*. New York: Teachers' College Press, Columbia Univ., 1974.

Poole, Roger. "Graham Greene's Indirection." *Blackfriars*, 45 (June 1964), 257–68.

———. "'Those Sad Arguments': Two Novels of Graham Greene." *Renaissance and Modern Studies*, 13 (1969), 148–60.

Prescott, Orville. "Books of the Times." *New York Times*, 9 March 1956, p. 21.

Pritchett, V. S. "Brown's Hotel: Haiti." *New Statesman*, 71 (28 January 1966), 129.

_____. "The Congo of the Mind." *New Statesman*, 61 (20 January 1961), 102–4.

_____. "The World of Graham Greene." *New Statesman*, 55 (4 January 1958), 17–18.

Pryce-Jones, David. *Graham Greene*. Writers and Critics Series. Edinburgh: Oliver and Boyd, 1963.

_____. "Graham Greene's Human Comedy." *Adam*, Nos. 301–3 (1966), pp. 19–38.

Quennell, Peter. *The Sign of the Fish*. London: Collins, 1960.

Raban, Jonathan. "Bad Language: New Novels." *Encounter*, 41 (December 1973), 76–80.

Rahv, Philip. "Wicked American Innocence." *Commentary*, 21 (May 1956), 488–90.

Raine, Kathleen. *The Land Unknown*. London: Hamish Hamilton, 1975.

Reed, Henry. *The Novel since 1939*. British Council Series. London: Longmans Green, 1946.

Reed, John R. *Old School Ties: The Public Schools in British Literature*. Syracuse, N.Y.: Syracuse Univ. Press, 1964.

Reinhardt, Kurt F. "Graham Greene: Victory in Failure." In his *The Theological Novel of Modern Europe: An Analysis of Masterpieces by Eight Authors*. New York: Frederick Ungar, 1969, pp. 170–203.

Rewak, William J., SJ. "*The Potting Shed*: Maturation of Graham Greene's Vision." *Catholic World*, 186 (December 1957), 210–13.

Robson, W. W. "Graham Greene." In his *Modern English Literature*. London: Oxford Univ. Press, 1970, pp. 138–41.

Routh, Michael. "Greene's Parody of Farce and Comedy in *The Comedians*." *Renascence*, 26 (Spring 1974), 139–51.

Rudman, Harry W. "Clough and Graham Greene's *The Quiet American*." *Victorian Newsletter*, 19 (1961), 14–15.

Ryan, J. S., ed. *Gleanings from Greeneland*. Armidale, New South Wales: Univ. of New England, 1972.

Sale, Roger. "High Mass and Low Requiem." *Hudson Review*, 19 (Spring 1966), 123–34.

Savage, D. S. "Graham Greene and Belief." *Dalhousie Review*, 58 (Summer 1978), 205–29.

Schwab, Gweneth. "Graham Greene's Pursuit of God." *Bucknell Review*, 26, No. 2 (1982), 45–57.

Scott, Carolyn D. "The Urban Romance: A Study of Graham Greene's Thrillers." In *Graham Greene*. Ed. Harry J. Cargas. St. Louis: B. Herder, 1969, pp. 1–29.

Selected Bibliography

————. "The Witch at the Corner: Notes on Graham Greene's Mythology." In *Graham Greene: Some Critical Considerations*. Ed. Robert O. Evans. Lexington: Univ. of Kentucky Press, 1963, pp. 231–44.

Scott, J. D. "Polished Answer." *New Statesman*, 42 (8 September 1951), 258.

Scott, Nathan A., Jr. "Catholic Novelist's Dilemma." *Christian Century*, 73, No. 31 (1 August 1956), 901–2.

————. "Graham Greene: Christian Tragedian." *Volusia Review*, 1 (Spring 1954), 29–42.

Scott-James, R. A. "Novelists—Recent and Contemporary." In his *Fifty Years of English Literature, 1900–1950*. London and New York: Longmans Green, 1956, pp. 163–88.

Sewell, Elizabeth. "Graham Greene." *Dublin Review*, 108 (First Quarter 1954), 12–21. Co-published as "The Imagination of Graham Greene." *Thought*, 29 (March 1954), 51–60.

Sharrock, Roger. "Graham Greene: The Tragic Comedian." *Tablet*, 203 (4 January 1969), 8.

————. *Saints, Sinners and Comedians: The Novels of Graham Greene*. Tunbridge Wells, Kent: Burns and Oates, 1984.

Sheed, Wilfred. "Enemies of Catholic Promise." *Commonweal*, 77 (22 February 1963), 560–63.

Sheridan, John D. "Graham Greene and the Irish." *Irish Monthly*, 81 (1953), 211–16.

Shor, Ira Neil. "Greene's Later Humanism: *A Burnt-Out Case*." *Literary Review*, 16 (Summer 1973), 397–411.

Shuttleworth, Martin, and Simon Raven. "The Art of Fiction. III: Graham Greene." *Paris Review*, 1 (Autumn 1953), 25–41.

Simon, John K. "Off the Voie Royale: The Failure of Greene's *A Burnt-Out Case*." *Symposium*, 18 (1964), 163–70.

Smith, A. J. M. "Graham Greene's Theological Thrillers." *Queens' Quarterly*, 68 (Spring 1961), 15–33.

Smith, Francis J., SJ. "The Anatomy of *A Burnt-Out Case*." *America*, 105 (9 September 1961), 711–12.

Snape, Ray. "Plaster Saints, Flesh and Blood Sinners: Graham Greene's *The End of the Affair*." *Durham University Journal*, 74, No. 2 (June 1982), 241–50.

————. "The Political Novels of Graham Greene." *Durham University Journal*, 75, No. 1 (December 1982), 73–81.

Sonnenfeld, Albert. "The Catholic Novelist and the Supernatural." *French Studies* (Cambridge), 22 (October 1968), 307–19.

Selected Bibliography

_____. "Children's Faces: Graham Greene." In *The Vision Obscured: Perceptions of Some Twentieth Century Catholic Novelists.* Ed. Melvin J. Friedman. New York: Fordham Univ. Press, 1970, pp. 109–28.

Sordet, Etienne. "Signification de Graham Greene." *Cahiers Protestants,* 38 (1953), 239–50.

Spier, Ursula. "Melodrama in Graham Greene's *The End of the Affair.*" *Modern Fiction Studies,* 3 (Autumn 1957), 235–40.

Spurling, John. *Graham Greene.* London: Methuen, 1983.

Stanford, Derek. "The Potting Shed." *Contemporary Review,* 1110 (June 1958), 301–3.

Sternlicht, Sanford. "Prologue to the Sad Comedies: Graham Greene's Major Early Novels." *Midwest Quarterly,* 12 (1971), 427–35.

_____. "The Sad Comedies: Graham Greene's Later Novels." *Florida Quarterly,* 1, No. 4 (October 1968), 65–77.

Stewart, Douglas. "Graham Greene—Catholicism." In his *The Ark of God: Studies in Five Modern Novelists.* London: Carey Kingsgate Press, 1961, pp. 71–99.

Stratford, Philip. "Chalk and Cheese: A Comparative Study of *A Kiss for the Leper* and *A Burnt-Out Case.*" *University of Toronto Quarterly,* 33, No. 2 (January 1964), 200–218.

_____. *Faith and Fiction: Creative Process in Greene and Mauriac.* Notre Dame, Ind.: Univ. of Notre Dame Press, 1964.

_____. "Graham Greene: Master of Melodrama." *Tamarack Review,* 19 (Spring 1961), 67–86.

_____. "Greene's Hall of Mirrors." *Kenyon Review,* 23 (Summer 1961), 527–31.

_____. "The Uncomplacent Dramatist: Some Aspects of Graham Greene's Theatre." *Wisconsin Studies in Contemporary Literature,* 2, No. 3 (Fall 1961), 5–19.

_____. "Unlocking *The Potting Shed.*" *Kenyon Review,* 24 (Winter 1962), 129–43.

_____. "What Seems Is." *Kenyon Review,* 25 (Autumn 1963), 757–60.

Symons, Julian. "The Strength of Uncertainty: Graham Greene." *Literary Half-Yearly,* 24, No. 1 (January 1983), 1–12.

Thale, Jerome, and Rose Marie Thale. "Greene's 'Literary Pilgrimage': Allusions in *Travels with My Aunt.*" *Papers on Language and Literature* (Edwardsville, Ill.), 13 (1977), 207–12.

Theroux, Paul. "Graham Greene's *The Honorary Consul* and *Collected Stories.*" *Book World,* 7 (30 September 1973), 1–3, 10.

Selected Bibliography

"The Third Man and The Fallen Idol." *Times Literary Supplement,* 4 August 1950, p. 481.

Thomas, D. P. "Mr. Tench and Secondary Allegory in *The Power and the Glory.*" *English Language Notes,* 7, No. 2 (December 1969), 129–33.

Toynbee, Philip. "Graham Greene at His Best." *Observer,* 15 January 1961, p. 29.

———. "The Heart of the Matter." *Observer,* 4 December 1955, p. 11.

———. "Log-Books of the Creative Process." *Observer,* 5 November 1961, p. 29.

Traversi, Derek. "Graham Greene: I. The Earlier Novels." *Twentieth Century* (London), 149 (March 1951), 231–40.

———. "Graham Greene: II. The Later Novels." *Twentieth Century* (London), 149 (April 1951), 318–28.

Trilling, Diana. "America and *The Quiet American.*" *Commentary,* 22 (July 1956), 66–71.

Tucker, Martin. *Africa in Modern Literature: A Survey of Contemporary Writing in English.* New York: Frederick Ungar, 1967.

Turnell, Martin. *Graham Greene: A Critical Essay.* Contemporary Writers in Christian Perspective. Grand Rapids, Mich.: Eerdmans, 1967.

———. "Graham Greene: The Man Within." *Ramparts,* June 1965, pp. 54–64.

Tynan, Kenneth. "Whiskey Galore." *Observer,* 9 February 1958, p. 13.

Van Wert, William F. "Narrative Structure in *The Third Man.*" *Literature/Film Quarterly,* 2, No. 4 (Fall 1974), 341–46.

Vargo, Lisa. "*The Quiet American* and 'A Mr. Liebermann?' " *English Language Notes,* 21, No. 4 (June 1984), 63–70.

Vinson, James, ed. *Contemporary Novelists.* London: St. James Press, 1972.

Voorhees, Richard J. "Recent Greene." *South Atlantic Quarterly,* 62 (Spring 1963), 244–55.

Wain, John. "Graham Greene Takes a Liberty." *Observer,* 23 June 1963, p. 25.

Walker, Peregrine. "*A Burnt-Out Case.*" *Blackfriars,* 42 (March 1961), 138–39.

Walker, Ronald G. "World without End: An Approach to Narrative Structure in Greene's *The End of the Affair.*" *Texas Studies in Literature and Language,* 26 (Summer 1984), 218–41.

Wall, Stephen. "Aspects of the Novel, 1930–1960." In *The Twentieth Century: The Sphere History of Literature in the English Language.*

Vol. VII. Ed. Bernard Bergonzi. London: Cresset Press, 1970, pp. 222–76.

Wansborough, John. "Graham Greene: The Detective in the Wasteland." *Harvard Advocate*, 136 (December 1952), 11–13, 29–31.

Ward, J. A. "Henry James and Graham Greene." *Henry James Review*, 1 (1979), 10–23.

Watts, Richard, Jr. "Graham Greene's Absorbing Drama." *New York Post*, 30 January 1957, p. 64.

Waugh, Evelyn. "The Heart's Own Reasons." *Commonweal*, 54 (17 August 1951), 458–59.

———. "Last Steps in Africa." *Spectator*, 208 (27 October 1961), 594–95.

Weaver, Robert. "*The Honorary Consul*." *Tamarack Review*, 61 (November 1973), 73.

Webster, Harvey Curtis. "The World of Graham Greene." In *Graham Greene: Some Critical Considerations*. Ed. Robert O. Evans. Lexington: Univ. of Kentucky Press, 1963, pp. 97–124.

West, Anthony. "Saint's Progress." *New Yorker*, 10 November 1951, pp. 141–42, 144.

West, Paul. "Graham Greene." In his *The Wine of Absurdity: Essays on Literature and Consolation*. University Park: Pennsylvania State Univ. Press, 1966, pp. 174–85.

Wilkie, Brian. "Stories by Greene." *Commonweal*, 78 (12 July 1963), 432, 434.

Wilshere, A. D. "Conflict and Conciliation in Graham Greene." In *Essays and Studies, 1966*. Ed. R. M. Wilson. New York: Humanities Press, 1966, pp. 122–37.

Wolfe, Peter. *Graham Greene: The Entertainer*. Carbondale and Edwardsville: Southern Illinois Univ. Press, 1972.

———. "Graham Greene and the Art of Entertainment." *Studies in the Twentieth Century*, 6 (Fall 1970), 35–61.

———. "*The Honorary Consul*." *Studies in the Twentieth Century*, 14 (Fall 1974), 117–20.

———. "*Travels with My Aunt*." *Studies in the Twentieth Century*, 6 (Fall 1970), 119–23.

Wood, F. T. "Current Literature: *Our Man in Havana*." *English Studies* (Belgium), 41 (1960), 50.

Woodcock, George. "Graham Greene." In his *The Writer and Politics*. London: Porcupine Press, 1948, pp. 125–53.

"The Workaday World That The Novelist Never Enters." *Times Literary*

Supplement, 9 September 1960, p. vii. Special Number on "The British Imagination."

Wyatt, Euphemia van Rensselaer. "God in a Garden." *Drama Critique,* 1 (February 1958), 45–48.

Wyndham, Francis. "*A Burnt-Out Case.*" *London Magazine,* 8 (March 1961), 62–63.

―――. *Graham Greene.* British Book News on Writers and Their Work, No. 67, British Council Series. London: Longmans Green, 1955; rpt. 1962.

Zabel, Morton Dauwen. "Graham Greene." *Nation,* 157 (3 July 1943), 18–20. Enlarged and rev. in his *Craft and Character: Texts, Method, and Vocation in Modern Fiction.* London: Gollancz, 1957, pp. 276–96.

Index

Index

Index